For Sky, Grace,
Henry and Mabel Candy

Could I *be* more embarrassing? . . . No, seriously, could I?

'Mum, What's Wrong With You?'

101 Things Only Mothers of Teenage Girls Know

LORRAINE CANDY

4th ESTATE • London

4th Estate
An imprint of HarperCollins*Publishers*
1 London Bridge Street
London SE1 9GF

www.4thEstate.co.uk

HarperCollins*Publishers*
1st Floor, Watermarque Building, Ringsend Road
Dublin 4, Ireland

First published in Great Britain in 2021 by 4th Estate
This 4th Estate paperback edition published in 2022

1

Typeset in Granjon by Palimpsest Book Production Limited, Falkirk, Stirlingshire

Printed and bound in the UK using 100% Renewable Electricity at CPI Group (UK) Ltd

MIX
Paper from
responsible sources
FSC
www.fsc.org
FSC™ C007454

This book is produced from independently certified FSC™ paper
to ensure responsible forest management.

For more information visit: www.harpercollins.co.uk/green

Contents

Preface

Dear mum of teenage girls,

Feeling a bit lonely? Confused, even? Maybe you are wondering what you have done wrong and are fearful of what is going to happen next on this parenting journey? Perhaps, like I was, you're in maternal shock, jolted from one stage of mothering into the next without warning. Or perhaps you are just overwhelmed and perplexed by the wonderful fizzy giddiness of it all, this new, raw 'aliveness' of the special human you've nurtured ricocheting round the house, setting off little fires everywhere.

Wherever you are on the road to parenting a teenage girl, I am here from your future to reassure and comfort you with empathy and humour. To let you know what to expect.

This book is a collection of friendly suggestions to guide and relax you. I hope it helps you feel less alone, especially if you've reached that part of the maternal experience that is as tense as those electric moments before a thunderstorm (probably any age after eleven years).

I suspect that before now it was all going fairly well. You may be a bit exhausted, made a few predictable mistakes, celebrated a few triumphs, come to the end of your occasional trips to A & E, but you've survived the heart-stopping anguish of keeping a newborn alive, said goodbye to toddler tantrums, cried a little at the first day of school. Hallelujah and well done. A sigh of relief perhaps? Feet up with a cup of tea and a Hobnob?

Not quite. Lurking on the horizon is something different: female adolescence, a world full of weird and wonderful surprises, which I wish someone had told me about in advance. So here I am telling you. As a mum of four children now aged nine to eighteen (three girls and a boy), I was knocked sideways by the teenage years. Nothing spectacularly dramatic happened, I just felt it was lonelier landscape, a place where I feared one wrong mothering move would result in the detonation of emotional time bombs. At times I felt like a parenting hero and other times I felt rubbish – a rubbish mum, a rubbish human (mostly I felt like this because my girls would tell me I was, bless them). It was all so confusing.

I could be both proud and ashamed of my teen daughters simultaneously. Moments when I loved them so much I couldn't bear to leave a room they were in. Other moments I hoped they'd get eaten alive by a passing T-Rex. Some days felt completely out of control and others were flooded with the melancholy sadness of the eventual parting lurking ahead of us.

Often I just didn't know what to do, what to think, how to smooth the edges and not feel quite so rejected, panicked or overwhelmed with self-doubt. And on many occasions, I was just absolutely furious. This rainbow of feelings hitting me during the challenging midlife years was hard to deal with calmly. I noticed that the biology, psychology and fury of female midlife happening at exactly the same time as female adolescence was the perfect storm for domestic unrest. It explained a lot. No one really talks about this aspect of mothering, though. There are no NCT-like support groups for the mums of teen girls; because there are so many private situations and conversations that you cannot share. So I wanted to help women through those more baffling moments. Especially mums who had been telling me that their daughters had suddenly rejected them. One woman summed it up perfectly in a Facebook post I read:

> I feel like a stranger, I find myself wistfully hoping for some kind of relationship with my daughter. But over the past months she has changed completely. I see tiny glimmers of who she was, but it is as if someone took my daughter and swapped her. I feel heartbroken, I miss her. Anyone else feeling this way?

I know many of you do, so I thought I would take my personal experience and all the advice I have been given during my years of writing a parenting column in one national newspaper or another and compile it all into one helpful book.

I've been writing about my family for over a decade, and apart from documenting the humorous minutiae of our daily life, I have also explored parenting dos and don'ts with many experts. I've interviewed neuroscientists, family therapists, bestselling parenting gurus, professionals working on the front line of teenage mental health, tech professionals in the digital world, plus I've quizzed all the young female staff I've managed during my time editing women's magazines about their relationships with their mums, I've read parenting books new and classic, and all the weighty newspaper think pieces on adolescence. And of course, I have experienced some of it personally as a mum working full time living in a busy city. I hope my humour comes through in all the information I've put here in preparation for what is to come, because humour is your secret weapon in the teenage years.

This book is not a mum's to-do list and it's not about adhering to a set of specific rules. Your child is unique and your childhood is unique (and we all bring our own childhood into the room when we parent). The combination of all this and many other variable factors, not least environment, school, friendship groups and genetics, means I cannot offer a foolproof 'how to' for your daughter. No one can, in my opinion. So this book invites you to try out what could be useful to you, and encourages you to rely on your instinct. I hope it will allow you to take a step back, and to relax more around your brilliant daughter, so that she may blossom in her own way. After all, parenting a teenager is not about fixing a problem, or completing a project.

Maybe my words will save you time and tears, because you could be gazing at your eleven-year-old now, wondering what the hell I am talking about. She is, after all, adorable. You may be looking forward to the Spotify playlists you'll create together, and happy days shopping, with breaks for ridiculously named coffees. Oh, the fun you'll have. Except it won't always be fun: there may be dark days, perilous moments when you think you've obviously done something terribly wrong as a parent to create such an impolite young woman. One you should not let loose on the world without informing the Guardians of the Galaxy that everyone's safety is at risk. This switch from adorable to unpredictable can feel harsh and the rejection brutal, but once you know what is coming you can experiment with a few strategies that will hopefully make life more harmonious for you both.

And this book is for those who are ready to support their girls in these modern times. For curious mums who want to trust their teens to become independent and resilient themselves rather than snowplough them forcefully into it. For those prepared to let go of some of their parental expectations. And it is for mums who don't want to play into the traditional, old-fashioned and unhelpful narrative that teenage girls are deliberately grumpy, lazy and hormonal.

I hope this book also reads as a light-hearted memoir that could help you spot the signs of a lost connection with your daughter and keep you informed of the small ways in which life could be improved for everyone, even if your teen is the best-behaved girl in the world (how unusual, lucky you). I want this book to feel like a comforting pep talk to remind you that you're not alone.

However, it is not for those families in crisis, battling the more desperate challenges adolescence may bring, especially around mental health. There are more specific books by clinically trained and experienced professionals for that (there's a list of suggestions in the back for you).

Being a teenage girl is tough: all that rapid change, swooshing in just as you've settled into a lovely family routine can be overwhelming. Building your new identity, new sexuality, new morality, new body to take out into the world alone for the first time may feel terrifying; you might mess up and need your mum alongside you rather than striding out in front or pushing you hard from behind or panicking around you.

I hope my perspective, based on everything I have absorbed and witnessed, will help you mother this amazing new woman with enthusiasm and patient understanding and allow you to recognise that no one gets it right all the time. Small changes may make all the difference when it comes to tackling big problems. I also want the book to remind you to take care of yourself as well as you want to take care of your daughter.

There are, of course, way more than 101 things that only the mums of teenage girls know, but I haven't numbered them because, well, you've got a lot on your plate already.

Love,
A mum of teenage girls

Angel of the morning

Where have my babies gone?

The day my eldest was born, on an August Sunday at 8.26 a.m., after thirty-six hours in labour, the heartbreakingly beautiful song 'Angel of the Morning' was playing on the telly. It was the soundtrack to a car advert and the only external thing to seep into my morphine-addled consciousness as I gazed at my 6 lb 3 oz miracle in her plastic hospital crib.

I couldn't bear to put her down for even a moment, couldn't bear anyone else touching her or moving her more than millimetres from my side. The nurse had to unfurl my fingers subconsciously gripping the edge of the plastic crib when the time came for me to go to the loo after my emergency C-section. How could you love something this much? She was so tiny, so quiet. Bright-red hair, intense blue eyes wide open. All velvety, milky cuddles and tiny breaths. Here she was, my real-life Angel of the Morning. I didn't need anyone else that sunny August bank-holiday weekend. It was as if the world kept turning but for us everything stopped moving. She would be my everything, always and forever.

Sadly, that precious little baby girl is no longer with us. She has gone, possibly temporarily, but certainly for the foreseeable future. She is now pretty shouty, actually. Inexplicably impolite, sarcastic and a bit self-righteous. I barely recognised her at first, what with the fierce eyebrows, multiple ear-piercings and the flashes of garish pink in her once natural strawberry-blonde hair. She flounced off into the street coatless (teenage girls never wear coats), deliberate holes in her tights, school skirt rolled over at the waistband, AirPod earbuds in.

Would I step in front of a runaway lorry for her still? Of course I would (it is a love like no other), but maybe there would be a millisecond of doubt just before the relief of being knocked over and possibly spending some time alone, asleep in hospital, without the constant commentary on TikTok or YouTube stars as a backdrop to my life. Without someone asking: 'What is wrong with you?' every five minutes.

As my eldest teenager and her sister, who is seventeen months younger, often tell me, it really does 'suck to be me' (mum) right now.

The thing is, I can still faintly feel the shadow of her tiny toddler hand in mine and there is still glitter between the floorboards in our kitchen, poignant reminders of the early mornings we spent doing art at the table in our PJs, dunking our digestives into warm, milky tea. But that girl isn't here right now. In her place is an adolescent. She was a pre-teen, then a tween and now a teenager.

And I just never expected it to be like this when I had her, aged thirty-three. Adolescence is all a bit of a shock, frankly. The glorious parenting highs, the occasional desperate maternal lows. The working-mum guilt I personally had of not being there enough for toddlers replaced by the mum shame of the times you discovered one of your teens had done something so unacceptable you couldn't say it out loud. *How could I raise a person who behaves like that?* you think in the dead of the night, when you're kept awake with worry and recriminations.

People compare most feelings to a roller coaster, but parenting a teenager really is the closest it gets, physically and emotionally. It can be exhausting. Each morning I am looking over the top, waiting for my stomach to fall through my pants or speeding upwards filled with the wondrous joy of being around a new adult-in-the-making whose optimistic and enthusiastic take on life is addictive. Days of darkness, then moments of blinding sunshine and some disturbing and confusing shadows of grey in between.

One minute you're secretly sniffing the top of their delicate heads as you slip their ladybird wellies on and the next you are the mother of dragons, quite literally putting out fires everywhere. It's like there is one (or more) of them skulking round your kitchen making SCOTs (selfish cups of tea) and setting your hair ablaze if you dare ask her to take the cup to the bin before she removes the teabag and trails it dripping all over the floor.

This stage of mothering can sometimes feel like living with the worst boyfriend you ever had but with whom you are still crazy in love. He's rude to you, criticises your appearance and absentmindedly pokes holes in your deteriorating self-esteem just as you hit midlife, BUT you can't leave him and you won't hear a bad word about him from anyone else because in the sunlight of his rare approval there lies the deepest love of all.

When I had my second baby, she came into the world on a January morning yelling her head off and grew into the most adorable, funny little girl. Gracie filled our days with laughter. 'See my mum,' she once told a lady on the checkout at Sainsbury's, 'she has no belly button.' We used to sing 'You are my sunshine, my only sunshine' together at the tops of our voices and run around the garden at sunset as she declared 'my feet are magic'. She was a beautiful ball of positivity. Indeed, she still is on some days, but back then she truly was 'my only sunshine'. Now there are some school mornings when she is like a black storm cloud following me round the kitchen, making fun of my sparse, greying eyebrows. I miss the little her of then so much it's physically painful. The blonde bob has gone in favour of beautiful hip-length blonde or pink or green locks that swing around with menace, often making the dog bark. Much of her is pierced.

I wasn't ready for this newly forming Grace (no longer Gracie – too childish a name, apparently) because I missed the first version so much; I missed the cuddles and the giggles. She was so incredibly tactile as a little girl and yet so awfully resistant to touch as a teen. Like so many mums around me all this was a surprise. Of course I knew about the traditional narrative of adolescent hormones, the huffy door-slamming, the mess that's so awful you need a full biohazard suit to clear it, love bites, poor decisions on alcohol volumes . . . yada yada yada. I knew all the usual commentary, often unfairly mocking teens, making them caricatures and offering parents a prediction of stereotypes, but I had not foreseen the loneliness and shame that can come with parenting at this stage, because it is rarely acknowledged, rarely voiced. But it is visceral and unpleasant, so even the smallest recognition of what may be on the horizon for you may perhaps lessen the blow when you reach it, soften the shock as you soldier on, mothering.

Another parenting surprise for you is how much more time-consuming teenagers are than toddlers. When my girls were little, I couldn't believe how long everything took; leaving the house took hours and the children's physical needs were all-consuming. All those wriggly tantrums, putting of large plastic things up their noses and a worryingly relaxed attitude to bowel movements in public. Surely I would get more time once they grew up and became more independent, I used to muse. Spoiler: you don't. Teens don't go to bed until later, so you lose your evenings. If you don't see them immediately after school, they are on the phone to you constantly, wherever you are. They take up your Saturdays driving them everywhere and then collecting them in the early hours. There are no naps providing scheduled times off for mums, like when they were toddlers. And teens sometimes need to talk to you just as you are drifting off to sleep . . . for *hours*. You may think your toddlers are tiny time-thieves but they have got nothing on teens. Brace yourself.

I was brainwashed into traditional thinking: that we were 'taming toddlers' relentlessly like badly behaved puppies and that as soon as they can understand what you are saying and sleep through the night, you're on the home stretch as a mum. *It will get easier,* I thought through the sleep-deprived years, mostly because everyone said it would. But it isn't easier at all.

Teens are much more illogical than toddlers. It's more complicated because the stakes are higher. Anything they do as teens could affect the rest of their lives; generally, anything they do as toddlers might ruin your day, make you late or perhaps require a quick trip to A & E to get yet more of those dissolvable stitches, but it won't usually change the course of their lives. It doesn't usually put others in potential danger or make you question your moral stance on things or make you contemplate running away forever. Or ruin your self-esteem as a woman. I often wished I had saved my maternity leaves until my two eldest were teenagers.

I cannot believe I am going to say this out loud, given my first baby didn't sleep through the night until she was four, but parenting newborns and toddlers can feel easier than parenting adolescents. The teen years require superhuman effort and vigilance from everyone involved.

Casting that invisible safety net over your sometimes unpredictable, vulnerable, insecure and rapidly changing teenage daughter can feel more stressful than you could ever envisage during the days when you're wiping pureed peas off the kitchen wall and wondering exactly how long colic, teething or toilet training will last. You cannot delegate any of the teenage mothering: they mostly need you and only you. It's the time to step up, be the responsible adult and nurture a selfless mindset.

There is much research to show that it's after the age of twelve that children most need their parents to be present, both physically and emotionally. Which is ironic, because it is around this time that they appear to want you the least (to quote Nanny McPhee).

However, don't panic if you have a pre-teen right now because the upside is that, according to all the experts I have interviewed, family harmony can come from your simply being in the room. Being present is often enough to keep everyone happy, you don't have to solve all their problems. Admittedly, I have found it is sometimes like being in the room with a wasp: they are constantly buzzing around you, drawn to you like wasps to sugar, potentially about to sting at any moment. This, you just have to endure.

I certainly had no idea how much listening would be involved, how time-consuming a teenage girl's monologues are on a daily basis. Half the time they don't want to talk to you and half the time they just won't *stop* talking to you.

I had also assumed they would be independent. After all, by this age they can wipe their own bottoms, cross the road alone and even cook their own breakfast. Yet they may find they cannot handle all their new feelings without your help. They can be easily overwhelmed by the choices facing them, by the way they are changing and growing, physically and mentally. The majority of the time no other adult apart from you will do, even if they often do their utmost to push you away. And by god it is damned hard to keep that all-important connection with them.

My final baby, Mabel, aged nine as I write, serves as a reminder of how it used to be with my two eldest. She still includes me in all her plans, from loo breaks, choice of snack to underwear. She even parrots back my parenting, often questioning me on the speed of my showers: 'That was quick,' she will say. 'Have you really washed everything?' mimicking the way I mother her.

Our teens, meanwhile, purposefully and deliberately exclude their dad and me from everything. And this can make it much trickier to parent well during the moments they do suddenly call on you for support, because you must try to be on constant alert. It's also harder to be responsible for them when they need to become more responsible for themselves; you have to become a ninja decision-maker with the patience of the Dalai Lama, judging when to step in and when to step back.

I remember I briefly tried to put our first baby into a daft Gina Ford-type routine (the parenting book of the moment back then) to get her sleeping longer than two hours at a time. I would fret about it constantly when she was a newborn and it would drive me to distraction, yet now I wish I had preserved my energy and just sat on the sofa with her, resting a Rich Tea biscuit on her head while I dunked it in my tea, watching *Cash in the Attic*. I should have saved my crying for the blazing rows of adolescent dependence, the days when you shut yourself in the loo alone to think about what you've done, for often it is not just your teen who lets herself down with her behaviour.

These moments, coming as they do in between the joys of seeing your beloved growing up and becoming her own person, can feel cataclysmically awful, possibly irredeemable.

I inhaled the parenting books about how to make a baby sleep but I didn't know where to turn to tackle the thorny issue of one of the people you love most in the world occasionally being so repulsed by you she cannot bear the sound of you breathing. I didn't foresee these raw, tear-filled moments when I was just as ashamed of my behaviour as hers (which had usually caused the row in the first place!). We had no idea, did we, as we wrestled those toddlers into ridiculously hard-to-fasten babygros that we'd feel like this.

The vanishing

I can remember exactly when we lost our eldest to the lure of new teenagerdom. Or 'the vanishing', as we call it. It was the summer of 2014. I could see her aged eleven, looking across a sea of endless hope and optimism, teetering on the horizon of a new, more exciting and independent life. The questions had started earlier in the year: 'When I am twelve, will I be able to stay up later?' she would ask incessantly.

'Yes,' I would reply, though why anyone would want to stay up to witness two ancient adults asleep on the sofa in front of the ten o'clock news each night, god knows.

She also informed us nicknames were no longer allowed, and I did not have a free pass to her room any more without getting permission to enter first. I wasn't welcome.

She stopped spending her pocket money in Lush or the Body Shop and started to buy eyeliner from Topshop. Showers replaced baths.

And the summer of 2014 was the last summer our children were a foursome. Then aged two, seven, ten and eleven, they would happily eat, watch TV and play together, but my eldest was gradually drifting away. I tried to capture it in my mind, and I have an enduring memory of the four of them in their PJs one evening, sorting shells they had collected on the beach in Cornwall, where we always go on holiday and where I grew up.

I recall the toddler refusing to hand over the big shells and being cajoled into it by the others. A united posse of four small children.

Frozen was their favourite movie that summer, and if any one of them got upset they were still easily cheered up by watching a baby panda sneezing on YouTube. By September it was over. Pandas weren't funny, *Frozen* was for babies and a boy's name kept cropping up in conversations. The eldest had turned twelve in August.

She started to stay out with friends after school on Friday afternoons; she headed off to see them again as soon as she got up on Saturday, the hour of her waking getting later. We started driving her all over the place at weekends.

Even if she was at home, she stayed in her room alone for greater periods of time. These are the signs of the vanishing to look out for with a tween: it is a precursor to the teenage years. She also started to take longer and longer showers and wanted to leave the table as soon as she put her fork down after family roast on a Sunday. She was just there a lot less and I had the creeping realisation that the girl who had once followed me round everywhere, asking to bake cupcakes or play Monopoly, simply wasn't present, even if she was in the house. Then I started to relish the moments when she was in the room with me more and more and to heed the advice I read in all the books of actively including her where I could, given her default setting was to actively exclude herself.

In these moments I reached out to her with the lightest of inquisitions: Did she want a cup of tea? elicited the best response. And then we really began this journey into full-on teenage; for a moment it was calm but different, and then all hell sort of broke loose . . .

'Mum, What's Wrong With You?'
Conversations with Teens

'You'll never guess what I learned to do today,' I say with jolly cheer in my voice, just trying to make conversation over the kettle boiling as the teens potter around the kitchen after school.

'To be nice to your children,' one replies, without looking up.

'To get a life,' the other says. They high-five each other and wander off. They don't care what I learned to do today.

The surprise signs you suddenly have a teenager

1. Endless bedtimes. It gets later and later. Then you lose control of it at weekends around the age of eleven. Suddenly it's bye-bye formal bedtime. You can't watch what you want on telly any more and soon you start to go to bed first. So unnerving.

2. School parents' evening gets weird. They come with you. It's awkward, more awkward even than those small junior-school seats you used to sit on. They have also started to set rules about what you wear to the school, how you speak, who to speak to, who not to wave at. There is so much glaring and so many unsaid admonishments during parents' evening that you start to feel as if you are in trouble and don't know what you've done. This is extremely stressful. And 'for godssakes, woman,' as my then fifteen-year-old would utter, do not say '*Bonjour*' to the French teacher. Also there is some form of normcore uniform for parents that teens favour but none of us know about, until you

discover that everything you wear is wrong. And do not mention what position you once played in netball either to the PE teacher. No one cares. Don't ask too many questions; don't smile too enthusiastically; do not chat too long to other parents on the imaginary 'not approved' list either. If possible, try and pretend you are not related to your own daughter. This is of course impossible but probably the only thing that would be approved on parents' evening.

3. Piercings. These come overnight. Usually in pairs. They are either talking about them or getting them done. They all have strange names. Tragus, conch, helix. You pay through the nose for a bottle of salty water they don't bother to use or spill on your bathroom floor, leaving you wondering for ages what the hell has happened in there. Then you end up going on at least one emergency medical appointment to sort it out. You will be amazed they can endure the hideous pain of a cartilage piercing but have to lie down on the floor writhing in agony if a sibling bumps into them by accident. And you were WRONG about how much it would hurt, because the one you may have yourself was obviously done by a caveman in an actual cave in 'olden times' and now it is all far more modern and doesn't hurt at all, OK? Also 'all' their friends have one. This is probably the only sentence that begins 'but all my friends', which is actually true in teenage. Resistance is futile, this is not the battle to have. Let them do it.

4. Swearing in music. Absolutely mandatory after the age of thirteen. Do not google what WAP means.

5. Love bites. Now you know what your parents meant. Shocking to the core. Especially over breakfast, not to mention embarrassing at parents' evening. Also the hypocrisy of the love bite, because if your partner shows any

outward sign of affection to you, they mimic vomiting noises or mutter 'disgusting' as they leave the room in haste.

6. G-strings and massive ugly shoes. Either are left all over the place. Most trainers are second-hand as well (#savetheplanet), which means they smell particularly vibrant. Some teen girls have scant regard to personal hygiene despite them being outraged by any infringement of hygiene rules yourself. They cannot, for example, eat an apple if you touched it.

7. They start saying 'Can we go now?' every time they appear in the kitchen. Which means they want you to take them somewhere at forty-five seconds' notice, but they have to believe they told you about this arrangement in advance because they cannot possibly ask for permission or admit they forgot to tell you. It's so confusing, because this sudden need to make a swift exit has not been mentioned until that moment. I often stand there wondering what is going on and where I agreed to be when I was obviously in a coma at some point earlier in the day.

8. Hair dye as a way of killing time. They dye it all the time to kill time. Bored? Dye your hair pink. What to do before lunch? Dye your hair. Mum asks you to wash up. Can't – dyeing my hair. Hamster needs cleaning out. Dyeing my hair.

9. Masks. Hair masks, face masks, all masks all the time. Sticky, messy packets-left-all-over-the-floor, carpet, beside-the-bin masks.

10. 'My friend was . . .' This phrase enters the room at about thirteen. Up until then they name everyone they know, and you know everyone they know. Then they meet new friends from other places, not just school, and won't share their names. It is an unexpected secrecy, which seems to

be secret for no other reason than pretending it is a secret. Or it is a boy. Or it is 'the' bad friend with whom any association ends badly (in your opinion).

11. Bum eyes. Bear with me. This is when they open a drawer, the fridge, your handbag, the cupboard, the tumble dryer and ask where something is after you have told them specifically, with detailed instructions, exactly where it is. When they are little, they see everything, like mini spies, but when they hit teenage a weird, learned helplessness makes them blind. I will say such-and-such is in the door of the fridge on the left by the ketchup. They will say: Where? And even though you are in the middle of threading some elastic back through a school PE skirt, you have to drop it (and will have to start this tedious task again later) and come over to point to the thing they cannot see. Exactly where you said it was five minutes of huffing ago. In our house we shout, 'Bum eyes!' when this happens: as in, 'Are you looking with the eyes in your bum? Oh, you don't have eyes in your bum, so maybe that is why you can't see the thing, which is RIGHT IN FRONT OF YOU.' Dads do this too.

12. The 4 p.m. phone call. It happens with annoying regularity when they hit teenage. This is the after-school request for something: food, money, an extension of previously agreed coming-home times, being able to go to a party 400 miles away with ten minutes' warning.

13. They start to call you by your first name around the age of fifteen. Of all the things I didn't expect, this is the oddest one. It's the cruellest separation tool they use, a sort of ironic flex of teenage power. At first I thought it was just me, but this is common according to mums and dads in the unofficial focus group. 'Lorraine!' my eldest will bellow

over her three siblings. 'What have you done with my dark chocolate?' I don't like it. As my nine-year-old, who still calls me Mummy, says, 'I do not agree with this disrespectful malarkey.' I tried to put a stop to it as soon as it started – I mean, imagine calling your parents by their names. Mine would probably send me to my room, and I am fifty-two. My fourteen-year-old son does still mumble 'Mum', but the sixteen-year-old, who considers herself something of a wit, will also refer to me by my Instagram handle, @lorrainecandy. There was a time when the relentless demands that accompanied the call of 'Mum!' echoing through the house made my nerves jangle, but now I cherish it as a title, a definition of who I am. But our eldest explains that she has grown out of 'Mum' and also expresses annoyance at the fact that our WhatsApp group, which is mostly me issuing instructions at 8 a.m., has the word 'family' in it. It is embarrassing when an alert pops up on her phone. She asks if I can offer an alternative to the word Mum that doesn't make her sound so young – but there isn't one. I am suspicious of the motives behind this name change too, given that I overheard another teen in our house explain that they used their parents' first names in a passive aggressive way to undermine their parents' authority. It does remove the hierarchy of the household if we all use first names, which makes me uncomfortable. They are discovering their new identity while playing fast and loose with the happiest part of my identity: my motherhood.

14. Mystery ailments (a sore eyeball, anyone?) and chronic, dramatic, impressive, over-the-top, Oscar-winning hypochondria. You will not have enough plasters for this (Boots does not sell enough plasters for this), enough painkillers or enough TCP.

15. 'What is wrong with you?' This goes on the end of every sentence. Even if you had said, 'I discovered the cure to cancer just now,' they would still look at you with fury and disbelief, and answer 'What is wrong with you?' as if you had done something so inexplicably bad you should hang your head in shame.

So, these are the surprising (well, they were surprising to me) new-mum rules. They may make you feel like you are living in a particularly complicated Agatha Christie murder mystery. You know all the clues are there, but you're not quick enough to work them out. It can all be explained, however. You thought it was their hormones: well, some of it is, but mostly it is neurology. Basically, it is not entirely their fault, so bear with them.

4

It's not me, Mum, it's you

(Actually, it's their brains)

Teenage girls can be so illogical, can't they? I find that much of their behaviour makes no rational sense. Sometimes it is remarkably funny or loveable, other times it most certainly is not. I can often catalogue about twenty different extreme emotions before 8 a.m. on a school morning. Living this way looks exhausting from an adult standpoint and seems to bring a turmoil into their lives that could easily have been avoided. Plus, all this 'feeling' and all this irrational chaos can cause arguments and disharmony at home. On such occasions it is me that is usually saying 'what's wrong with you' after yet another set of keys has been lost; another debit card misplaced; another ridiculously organised escapade's descent into farce; another loud argument. Too frequently I unfairly mistake their behaviour as wilful or deliberate when usually it isn't at all.

So, what exactly is going on? The experts say much of it is down to their developing brains. For years we had been led to believe their hormones were always the culprit, but that is not entirely true; mostly it's their brains. The science around the teenage brain is in its infancy right now; until around twenty years ago it was thought that our brains were physically sorted by the end of childhood, just before the tween years (ages nine to twelve), but now new research tells us that this is not true.

Around the age of ten, teenage brains become construction sites: everything is changing and being updated from a neural point of view alongside the hormonal and biological changes of growing up. So when you put your gorgeous little girl to bed one night, hair neatly brushed and unicorn nightie on, and she comes down to breakfast the next day transformed into a sarky she-devil wearing oversized second-hand trainers who loses her travel pass every five minutes and can argue with inanimate objects, it isn't always her fault. Please bear with her.

The scene that starts to play out in front of you as your child goes from pre-tween or tween to actual teenager is at its roots a physiological miracle. I think puberty is a miracle. Really you should be howling 'hallelujah' at the human enormity of it instead of yelling, 'How can you find anything in this mess?'

So my advice is to try to avoid demonising girls at this tricky stage, or judging them, or comparing them to grown-ups; perhaps just observe them instead? It will take some extra patience on your part but may make your life easier if you do this and it may support them better. They are not like adults, they think differently from the way you think, so bear that in mind when you try to use grown-up logic during disagreements.

Girls in particular can seem consumed by emotions. One minute they are mid-sulk, the next they are happy as Larry. This will partly be because their brains are flooding them with new feelings, provoking reactions that may seem extreme to you but feel normal for your daughters.

This is the making of an adult in full Technicolor glory, a proper person finally coming into focus. It's a mammoth task, a huge amount of rapid change. Teenagers are a work in progress each day, so don't underestimate how sensitive that can make them to everything going on around them at home or school.

The brain's prefrontal cortex, which controls the ability to reason, make decisions, forward plan or stop inappropriate behaviour, is undergoing massive change.

For example, maybe you're expecting your teenager to understand that if you don't bring your PE kit home it won't get washed and therefore it will be filthy the next time you wear it. Their developing brain doesn't know this; it's just thinking, *PE kit? What is PE kit? Oh look, a cat singing 'Nine to Five' on TikTok*. This brain may not think more than a few moments ahead of time. It may struggle to be logical because the wrong cable is plugged into the wrong socket and the wiring is all over the place. This is how I see it in layman's terms, but if you'd like specific details of what is going on here, see the back of the book for suggested reading.

According to the US neuroscientist Frances Jensen, the connectivity of the brain is changing constantly (which makes it 'plastic'), with the back of the brain (which controls emotions) maturing faster than the front (which is responsible for reasoning and therefore decisions around risk taking). So no, teenagers aren't necessarily being 'lazy' or making daft decisions deliberately; they are not acting hysterically or, indeed, overreacting; they just have a different brain from yours and their biology is not as advanced as yours, so go easy on them when you get frustrated. I am of course generalising here as it is different for each teen but in my experience it won't matter how many times you tell them the same thing – often they may not be able to remember it, let alone understand it.

I once spent thirty minutes explaining to one of my daughters, whose teachers deemed gifted at maths, why a dirty duvet cover must be removed before being replaced by a clean one. For ages I'd been wondering why our duvet covers were disappearing until I found some of the dirty ones still on her bed under clean covers. About seven minutes into the conversation I could see she had no idea what I was talking about; her brain had not yet caught up with my adult logic. She was also doing that thing where they say yes, pretending they get what you're talking about just to hasten your move from their line of vision.

It's the same with mess. Most of the time they just don't see it. Rational thinking may not come into action until the early twenties. Now if you know that, then you can perhaps accept the chaos that comes with their changing mind and body more easily?

When I tell parents about the brain changes, they often have a light-bulb moment and begin to relax, realising that they don't have to set such hard-and-fast rules or get quite so frustrated every time something unpredictable or downright foolish happens. I remember one mum thanking me, with a huge sigh of relief, after an Instagram Live I had done with a psychologist explaining all this brain malarkey. She thought she had done something terribly wrong and caused her teen's dire 'crabbiness' and chaotic behaviour. We need to remember adolescence can be a complex and extremely sensitive time neurologically.

The 2017 *TIME* report *The Science of Childhood* states that 70 per cent of mental illnesses begin in adolescence, and other statistics confirm that three quarters of mental illness starts before the age of twenty-four, when the brain is believed to be almost fully developed. Teenagers tend, therefore, to be more vulnerable mentally at this stage than they were in childhood, and it is part of your job to help them protect their mental health.

Remember not to take the mistakes teenagers make due to the immaturity of their brains personally or view their misadventures as a failure of your parenting or their personalities. They should learn from these mistakes and failures as they mature. I think we expect far too much from teenagers because we don't take into account how much their brains and bodies are changing. Much of this happens between the ages of twelve and seventeen. If you think back to how you were five years ago, you were probably much the same as you are now but a twelve-year-old is a different species from a seventeen-year-old. Perhaps the compassionate thing to do is understand this and adjust your behaviour and responses accordingly. The benefit for you is that if you know it is coming, you can devise strategies to deal with it so that it won't affect the whole family adversely. Curious calmness is a good strategy, yet hard to enforce I agree, but is perhaps something to aim for.

Then there is puberty, which can be a minefield for girls: they suddenly sprout hair everywhere, their periods start, their skin changes and they grow breasts and hips. And many are at the mercy of PMS (Pre-Menstrual Syndrome), their hormones fluctuating over a monthly cycle, affecting their moods and causing extreme physical discomfort for some.

A loving and compassionate environment with reasonable, consistent boundaries and a reliable routine alongside nutritious food and sleep will undoubtedly help a developing body and brain. Sleep in particular helps set up healthy neural pathways.

Talking to them about why they do what they do when they make mistakes and it all goes wrong may be helpful too, but try to do this with empathy, rather than criticism or judgement or by labelling them as specific personality types. Your teens will also benefit from working some things out for themselves; it is helpful for them if they learn to recognise and acknowledge the risks they may have taken with certain decisions or behaviour. Active listening on your part as they sort this out themselves is crucial, as is setting consequences for behaviour you consider too dangerous, or ill advised. For my husband and me, consequences are usually the removal of cash or limiting phone access, a sort of grounding if the boundaries we set are ignored.

Consequences help teach them where the edges of any poor decision making lie and this is important because teens are thought to be more susceptible to risks such as addiction. Due to the plasticity of their developing brains, the positive reward system is particularly sensitive for them, so some may seek higher highs. This may lead to all sorts of poor decisions. But if you are constantly angry, in parental punishment mode or on at them to think more smartly, they may not begin to understand what has gone wrong. Your furious feelings will be too much to process alongside their feelings. What they may appreciate instead is your support in explaining the dangers after the event and your calmly setting boundaries, and consequences if broken, for the future. This they can lean against safely as their neurology changes. I know it is stressful to discipline a teenager, to set consequences that cause all manner of domestic disharmony, but if you don't they may assume it is therefore OK to try all the things their immature brains are inclined to test, because you haven't told them specifically it is dangerous to do so. This is why they can sometimes end up in situations they will regret. Sticking to your boundaries with steadfast determination is comforting for them even if they keep trying to test those boundaries and make a huge fuss about what they may deem unreasonable consequences. You may just have to grin and bear it.

The immaturity of their brains also helps explain why some teenagers may have little or no empathy for others: you haven't accidentally made potentially bad adults (this is what I worried about occasionally). It may be that they really cannot help it.

Personally, I found this strange lack of empathy in teenage girls the hardest pill to swallow during my midlife years. This element of change was the biggest surprise to me, especially coming at a time when many parents may feel exhausted after over a decade of mothering and wondering if they themselves have enough empathy left to take everyone's feelings into account all of the time. Midlife mums can be an angry tribe, and I sometimes wonder if our empathy levels decline at the same rate as our oestrogen levels. But many teenage girls seem to have no empathy for mums whatsoever. It's a little heartbreaking, and a shock if you don't know it is coming your way. I used to hear other women's teens talk to them like servants and swear to god mine would never be like that, but as everyone begins to separate from each other, it isn't uncommon.

The 'I couldn't care less' attitude is taken up by many teens, according to the mums I have quizzed, not just yours, so don't take it personally. I often suspect that if I got knocked over on the way to Starbucks on the Saturday-morning trip to get one of mine her frappalatteobeso coffee (or whatever daft drink she wants), she would step over my broken body, queue for the coffee, take time to moan they have spelled her name wrong on the cup and *then* call the ambulance to save my life.

The neuroscientist Sarah-Jayne Blakemore was of great comfort to me during such confusing times. I snuggle up to her logic around brain development because it makes me feel better as a mother. Her book, *Inventing Ourselves: The Secret Life of the Teenage Brain*, and her TED Talk on the adolescent brain gave me the catch-all catchphrase, 'It's OK, it's just their synapses.' In our house, the general ungrateful attitude or rudeness that may sometimes creep into conversations with adolescents is batted away with this phrase. I can cope with chats that begin 'Could you just talk and breathe a lot more quietly' by understanding it probably comes from a neurological place.

Blakemore tells the story of a dad taking his two small daughters to the shop, where they mess about. He says, 'If you behave, I will sing your favourite song in a minute.' Overjoyed, they instantly do their best. When they get older, he says the same thing, except him singing their favourite song is now a threat, because the brain has flipped the rules on how they interact socially. We've all been there on the singing front. It's the same with hugs: once a delicious treat, suddenly an embarrassing punishment. I unthinkingly tried to hold my eldest's hand when we crossed the road at her uni Open Day and I thought she would probably kill me in my sleep later that night. She wouldn't sit with me on the bus back to the station from the campus, she was so cross.

This brain change may also be one of the reasons they cannot get up early. No amount of hoovering right outside their bedroom door will work, believe me. Anyway, of all the things to worry about with teenagers, I think their Olympian ability to stay in bed until the afternoon should actually be the least of your worries. Please don't punish them for this. Most experts in sleep, neurology and teenage development will agree they aren't physically equipped to rise as early as school requires them to and, frankly, all our lives would be easier if they could start school each day at 10 a.m., not 9 a.m. Late rising is also to do with melatonin levels and while this so-called 'darkness hormone' is produced in greater quantities around 11 p.m. for adults, studies have found that for teens it doesn't kick in until around 1 a.m. This is the hormone that can help you get to sleep, so it makes sense your teens stay up later playing Fortnite. But they also need more hours of sleep than anyone over about twenty-five, so letting them lie in is not a crime against productivity. It may be a physical need. Indeed, in some US schools they delay the start time for teenagers. You don't want them to switch their sleep schedules completely so that they verge on nocturnal but you could perhaps let them lie in at weekends. Teens usually need around nine hours proper sleep to function well so helping them achieve that alongside their later bedtimes may be a help.

As everything is undergoing such enormous change neurologically this is the point at which you should perhaps become more a coach than a parent (certainly not a best friend). The thought of no longer being needed as much may be hard to rationalise for some mothers, I certainly found it so, and your loss of maternal influence can be especially confusing when younger siblings are around, over whom you continue to have so much power to love and help. Cuddles still work for my nine-year-old. But it is not always about you and how you feel. Your adolescent daughters are changing day by day as their brain develops and nothing is set in stone for teens: their interests, their relationships, their likes and dislikes.

I know many mums who threw themselves into their daughters' childhood hobbies, taking them to matches, gymnastics and the like only to find that in teenage their girls had little or no interest in the hobbies that had once consumed them. The withdrawal was sudden for many and confusing for the mums whose future expectations were dashed almost overnight as their teens' brains changed so be prepared for this. They may come back to what they once loved, they may not. And this stage of development may be the time to let go of your urge to problem solve or future proof them with your expectations of them. It's maybe easier and healthier to simply live more in the moment alongside them, like a coach.

And for many families disagreements may become more common during adolescence as the brain develops, and as long as conflict isn't continuous (you may need professional help if it is), then you will have to learn to ignore much of it, or walk away. However, try your best not to alienate her, especially if your family is going through challenging circumstances. And of course, each teen is different; the ebb and flow of each personality will affect you all in different ways, so stay attuned to the differences and the needs rather than expecting the worst. Never expect the worst.

Leaving childhood and entering the teenage years is, after all, the beginning of a never-ending story: the search for their own identity. As their body changes, their sexuality comes into view and their insecurities potentially exaggerated for the whole of the outside world to see, they must work out who they are. A lot of this is happening inside their brains, all those neural pathways suddenly working in a different way and reacting to different things. It's a lot to take on board, for them and you.

I remember asking my seven-year-old son why his then thirteen-year-old sister was suddenly ignoring me all the time, not replying to calls, shutting herself away to chat to friends on the phone and suddenly leaving a room if I entered it.

'Maybe she was just pretending to love you all along,' he replied, which is exactly how it may feel in the madness of some of these moments and this is not unusual, you are not alone if you feel this. They do, of course, love you; they just don't want you in the same way as they did before. And as their brains develop with differing responses you don't recognise, as they begin to physically separate too; they begin to disappear into independence. Like the moments on wildlife documentaries when they release animals back into the wild. They come back less and less as the curious dance of parting ways finally gets started. Much patience from everyone is required as their brain rebuilds itself. At least if you know what is going on, you can cut them some slack. And that is exactly what you have to do, for their peace of mind and yours.

'Mum, What's Wrong With You?'
Conversations with Teens

Her: I will come with you and help if you don't do anything weird.
[Reply to my request for her company on the weekly food shop.]

Me: What do you mean weird? I don't do weird stuff. Be specific.

Her: Yes, you do – you hug me. In public. It's weird.

5

Don't touch my stuff

(Or, what's yours is yours and mine too)

One morning I had had enough. Unless a plastic-plug-eating giant hungry caterpillar had taken up residence in our house, there was only one reasonable explanation for the continuing disappearance of mobile-phone chargers. The teenagers had had them (and no doubt distributed them haphazardly across London). I know everyone is innocent until proven guilty, but I had to go full metal jacket with this dilemma. I am not proud. But it was one victory under my belt that sent a clear message over enemy lines.

I Sellotaped a picture of a bare bottom on my charger plug. I told the girls it was my bare bottom. It was just a random bum pic. But the thought of touching my bare bottom revolted them so much they left the charger plugged in by my bed alone.

Listen, I wasn't just being selfish about my charger, or petty, you understand, because the knock-on effect of my phone running out of battery is more stressful for me than worrying about what they are posting on Snapchat, frankly. Being on call to the teenage girls in your life requires 100 per cent battery. The shopping list is on the phone, the passwords – crucial day-to-day stuff that affects us all if I can't get to it quickly (for example, being able to transfer money). This is a higher need than just being able to talk to my friend Vic on WhatsApp about whether or not we're drinking too much wine on weeknights. So the bare bottom was an experiment.

The picture didn't have to stay there too long – it was more of a Pavlov's dog experiment than a proper solution. It worked (for a moment) but was obviously a little embarrassing and hard to explain to visitors when my charger was occasionally plugged in in more-visible rooms in the house. The point had been made and a visual reference stamped into their changing brains. Many of these quick-thinking maternal shenanigans are about preventing the behaviour in the first place, to avoid the endless illogical rows later, which give you a headache over one eye and tempt you to bury your head in a tin of Hobnobs.

It's no use just hiding things around the house to prevent the theft of your stuff, because by the time you hit midlife your days are a chorus of 'Where did I put my keys/coat/cash?': you don't need anything else to hunt for with fury. It is a waste of energy.

They don't teach this kind of malarkey at parenting school or in episodes of *SAS: Who Dares Wins*, which is how parenting sometimes feels to me. But it's this kind of sneaky mindset that gets you through living with these dragons. This is what you'll thank me for later if you're calmly playing the shopping-list game with your five-year-old right now, promising there will be 'no shouting in this house', as I once did.

So if you have daughters you will lose the following the moment they hit thirteen: nail scissors, white trainer socks, tweezers, cream jumpers without stains on, expensive gym leggings, box-fresh trainers, fancy chocolates, small mirrors that enlarge things, eyelash curlers, did I say tweezers?, moisturiser, even if it says anti-ageing on the front, your good hairbrush, tiny earrings, hoop earrings, eighties-band t-shirts, luxury conditioner. That's it off the top of my head, but much more will come to me.

A friend of mine bought a small digital safe from Amazon to hide the things her teens kept taking without asking. 'If it is precious, I hide it,' she whispered to me, looking over her shoulder like Inspector Clouseau.

Our girls were outraged by Bottomgate and called me disgusting for coming up with such an idea. They said I was childish and immature, but sarcastic survival skills are crucial on the domestic front line, because sometimes the girls make me feel as if they are metaphorically wearing a t-shirt that says 'I'm with stupid'. You have to lighten the mood every now and again.

And if you can't charge your phone, you can't pick up when they start calling or texting you after 4 p.m. each day. See what I mean? It is all about preventing trouble further down the line. Bottom pictures, hiding things: this is the path of least resistance. It's an avoidance tactic; you are avoiding the possibility of an argument that is always brewing somewhere with an adolescent. And you're bringing humour into the room. Farce is underrated as a parenting tool. These are all stories to tell over family dinner. Though your teens will, of course, say, 'well, that never happened,' about anything that embarrasses them.

Being forward thinking means you are also preventing the murderous overreaction if you dare ask for something of yours back that they have 'borrowed'. That's like poking a sleeping scorpion with a sharp stick.

I must say it is perplexing that one minute everything you have is to be ridiculed and mocked (from what you wear to the colour you chose to buy it in) and the next minute it has been 'borrowed'. After lengthy chats with many mums of teenage girls, I have come to the conclusion this is a mildly entertaining form of gaslighting, if such a thing can be entertaining in any way at all. Of course it happens with boys too, but I can only relay my experience with girls because boys don't usually want the expensive mascara you have only used once. Or the one pair of scissors that are sharp enough to cut your smaller kid's toenails.

I could fill several books with the tall tales of teen girls emphatically denying they have nabbed something so vehemently you'll wonder if you ever had such an item in the first place. You'll teeter between the fantasy and reality of it all. Every day becomes an episode of *Lost* or *The Twilight Zone*. 'Did I get some new headphones or did I imagine getting some new headphones?' you'll ask, rooting through the chaotic kitchen drawers looking for them. They're just messing with your head in a *One Flew Over the Cuckoo's Nest* fashion. 'Are you sure you haven't left them at work, Mum?' one teen will say sympathetically as she helps you look in an uncharacteristic show of interest. 'I don't think you did get those new ones, you know. Maybe you just looked at them online and didn't press "checkout",' they'll conclude with a fake smile. Like a medicated patient in an old persons' home (for this is where it will end, and which one puts you there is still up for grabs), you nod happily, a little bit grateful for the show of affection you've just received.

She's all right, really, you think, even though you know that if she ever has to fill in a form on your behalf, she'll put 'gullible nincompoop' in the occupation box.

But though it is a small transgression, it is an infuriating one, which can change the fabric of the day and set the mood to 'poor' from the outset. Little things. If they take your only good mascara for example, as a working mum it means you lose time looking for it, which makes you late. Or they pinch the cotton wool you need for other child-related activities. It delays your day and has a knock-on effect, which feels small but eventually ripples into something much more stressful. Often, with four children to get out of the door on a school day I had seven minutes logged in to do make-up – so no mascara meant leaving the house looking like I had no eyelashes for that important work presentation first thing. Seems minor, but it really isn't, so it is worth avoiding it by hiding a spare. This is when motherhood is like an Olympic sport: think of yourself like one of those swimmers who always has spare goggles for when theirs snap just before they enter the pool for a race.

I have another version of the bum picture. My knicker drawer. It's where I put covetable belongings. For smaller items your underwear drawer is perfect because nothing will tempt them into it. 'Uh, gross, bruh,' as my sixteen-year-old often says. This is your safe stash place. It's my version of licking something so no one else wants to eat it. I did once lock some things in the car boot overnight, but that is a huge faff and you forget what is there, and then your husband takes it to the recycling. Sometimes I put high-end luxury biscuits I like in my underwear drawer, but I have to stop doing that because it makes me look like that unbalanced elderly relative who comes to stay. I did enjoy those bourbons, though.

On those tougher days when you have been blamed for everything from Brexit, A levels being cancelled and the super blood moon causing sleeplessness (true story), it is the little treats that keep you going. You could threaten to turn off the wi-fi after such thieving misdemeanours or, indeed, to thrash them all with a birch, as the baby-boomer generation were in favour of ('a good hiding', as my dad calls it), but in the interests of family harmony it is just easier to hide stuff. Pick your battles, as they say wisely.

Then there's their brains. When they take something, they may at first have every intention of putting it back, but their jumbled-up neurology prevents this occurring. And their inability to see the mess on the bedroom floor means they just forget. Which is damned annoying for you, but often it is not their fault.

Meanwhile, if you are over forty you may be entering perimenopause, which means your hormone levels drop and your brain undergoes changes due to the lack of testosterone. They call it brain fog. It's a dire combination; your teens cannot recall losing the items they have swiped and you cannot be sure you had it in the first place!

Occasionally I wonder if there might be a hidden message underneath all the borrowing, especially when it tips into borrowing more expensive items. If all behaviour is communication, as the experts sometimes say, perhaps it could be about needing attention? Or it might just be their 'see it, take it' magpie behaviour: they have little ability to weigh up the outcome of risk at this age and they are living in the moment. Obviously, when it comes to stealing, that is different from run-of-the-mill borrowing. Stealing requires you to set boundaries and constantly reinforce what is right and wrong in your home. But, again, what is going on underneath the stealing?

Communication is key: a calm conversation about your daughter's thoughts and feelings might be a good place to start rather than immediately accusing her of stealing. This may need to be done in stages but you need to be firm about what will happen, what privileges will be withdrawn, if stealing occurs: pocket money cut, phone access reduced, that kind of thing, and you should stick to these consequences no matter how difficult it is and how it affects the atmosphere at home.

Steel yourself to get over the irony that you cannot set foot in their room even though they appear to have granted themselves permission to come and go as they please in yours.

Buy a jewellery box with a key or a bathroom door you can lock from the outside. Just be prepared for it; being prepared will prevent the rows. After all, information is power: the power to dissolve the extremities of your response to things, power to give you more patience, power for you to overlook this kind of thing and save your energy for the more serious stuff. And also the power to still be you, because being a parent is not your only job in life, remember that.

6

Meanagers

(Or, 'why don't you just go to your zumba class now')

Bad weather, lost homework, late-running buses, pens with no ink in them, broken pencil sharpeners, unacceptable exam results, Pritt Sticks with no lids, nail varnish that has dried up, past-its-sell-by-date sliced bread, toast that is toasted too much, missing Twix, teabags that burst in cups, oversubscribed festivals, mysterious stains on new duvets, the cold weather, Wetherspoon's questioning fake ID, the traffic jams . . . it's all your fault. Everything. Is. Your. Fault. For this moment you become the most unpopular girl in class in your own home, courtesy of your own offspring. Your teenager begins to view you as the biggest nitwit anyone could ever meet. This is not her rejecting you forever, it's her separating herself from you. The little girl who once worshipped you to the moon and back now has to untether herself from you, and it seems to me that she sometimes uses a surprisingly mean, self-righteous moral superiority to do that. It's her adolescent weapon of choice. She begins to talk to you in the patronising voice reserved for admonishing toddlers who are wearing their clothes upside down and eating jelly with a fork. Or very deaf elderly people.

I was once so viciously reprimanded in the street on a cycle trip with my sixteen-year-old because I took a left instead of a right turn that a passer-by stopped to commiserate with me as my teen sped off up a hill shouting, 'Get a move on.' The wonderful mature lady walking along the path said, 'I feel your pain, I've been there,' and she blew a raspberry at my daughter on my behalf (because I was too scared to). It's like being a freemason: only those in the know, know. That's all mothers of girls. You may unwittingly become a new superhero – Moron Mum.

I didn't see this attitude coming, but I'm giving you advance warning, so suit up like a medieval knight, flip the faceguard down and allow the illogical insults to your intelligence to bounce off you in a cartoon fashion. (Of course, I am generalising here, they aren't like this all the time and indeed some teenage girls may never be like this. Lucky you, if that is the case . . .)

The jibes aren't meant in a malicious way; it's just that mums are often seen as rubbish at this stage of the parenting journey, otherwise it doesn't make sense to separate from us. And when you recall some of this cruel behaviour with humour, they will look at you blankly and say, 'Well, that never happened.' Their brains have allegedly erased most of it, even though later on, in their twenties, they will feel guilty. I have worked with a lot of young women and they *all* tell me they feel guilty about being mean to their mums as teenagers. At this point in parenting they need to believe that you just aren't important enough to them to remember specifics about you, though they can remember what everyone in the TikTok Hype House had for breakfast three days ago.

I can only describe it this way: imagine your teenage daughter had to write a 2,000-word essay on any subject. She may not be able to manage it on something she is actually studying at school, but she could easily pen one entitled 'An idiot's guide to Mum, the idiot that lives with me'. There would be an epilogue and a prologue too, because you are such a dimwitted fool who has achieved nothing in life that your crimes are endless. She can only write this of course because she has been closely monitoring your every move since the day she was born. She is inextricably tied to you (with love, for that is what you must remember in these testing times, love is the bond).

My eldest once said to me when she was fourteen and I was demanding some minor details of her next escapade, 'Oh my god, Mum, what is the point of you?' It was a blow to my self-esteem because I often find myself sitting quietly on the bottom of our stairs on my way up with the clean washing, questioning the point of me anyway – midlife will do that to you. The decline in oestrogen and testosterone whips away some of your memory and offers you brain fog and little dollops of despair instead. So much questioning is going on that it's doubly hard to deal with a bright young thing dismissing your life away as she swishes out of the room. All ponytail and hi-top trainers. But deal with it you must. And you can at least love her new-found assertive confidence to say what she means, if you are looking for positives and let's face it, we're always looking for them in the teenage years.

If you are the mum of a pre-teen right now you may not believe this will happen to you but it will. I was once asked to come and give a talk at my daughter's school about fashion, having worked in the magazine industry for thirty years. I have won awards for the glossy publications I have edited. I've been on lists entitled 'Fashion's 100 Most Powerful'. I have given speeches in front of fashion's most iconic names. Goddammit, I once had lunch with Donatella Versace and Vivienne Westwood *at the same time*. Yet the eldest looked at me with a genuinely perplexed expression on hearing of my school-assembly debut and said: 'But what would you know about fashion?'

She dismissed a whole career in one sentence. When we were both interviewed by broadcaster Anne Robinson for a BBC show about parenting my daughter, then thirteen, made the same remark again for the benefit of thousands of viewers concluding, 'Well, she doesn't actually do fashion.'

Those 'bring your kids to work' days were wasted on her, clearly, though of course other people's mums do exist outside of the bubble of dismissal, I find. Issey's mum, for example, is 'an artist', my daughter tells me with pride, and Siobhan's mum, don't you know, is 'a beauty entrepreneur'. When I lightly questioned the meaning of this job title (again, as someone who has worked in the beauty industry for decades myself, on magazines) both the teens looked at me with savage fury. 'Why do you always criticise people for being good at things you know nothing about?' they said, with no irony.

For mums of daughters, parenting is not a popularity contest. You are not their best friend: please don't try and be one, because they benefit from boundaries. A teen without proper boundaries is a scared young woman, in my opinion.

At this age they often seem to go right off you – as they are separating from you – while still recognising the balance of power is in their favour because they know you love them so much you'll do anything for them.

I watch mine come into the kitchen some days and the pain of not being able to hold them close like I did when they were little is unbearable. No gently putting their hair behind their ears for them any more or smoothing Gracie's little fringe down.

The absolute proof they are going to leave me is inevitable as I observe them in these moments. Imagine a romantic affair where you are desperately and deliriously in love beyond your wildest dreams but you know with absolute certainty that the object of your affections will one day leave you, that really, every minute is a step towards that parting. You don't see this when they are little, it feels as though childhood will go on forever, but it comes into focus as they hit adolescence. Yet it is all normal adolescent development, a stage they will pass through and out the other side.

This teenage untethering alongside your midlife unravelling touches every part of your soul, because at times it can feel brutally personal. We don't often talk about this, do we, as women? We just get on with life, taking each day as it comes, but the effect of this uncoupling must surely shake us; it is a subtle form of grief and it troubled me greatly at a time of life when I was questioning the point of everything anyway. Doing the 'death maths' on the years left and what could be achieved during them. We must talk about it, because if you know it is coming, the path to parting and eventually regrouping as mum and adult daughter could be much less bumpy.

My eldest seemed to be standing in the room in front of me both as the woman she is becoming and the baby she had been, like layers of tracing paper softly resting against each other until it is too hard to see the picture beneath the first one, just a shadow of her beginning visible.

Mothering them at this point is all about being the most responsible you have ever been, and you may have to move up a level in patience and emotional maturity. This is Jedi parenting, which requires so much inner calm. A virtue of mine patience is not.

So I wasn't prepared for this abrupt dismissal of me, a supposedly intelligent woman, as a parental buffoon. Another mum once sadly told me that her daughter, aged thirteen, waves her away with the line, 'Leave me alone and just go to your zumba class.' I cannot think of a more cruelly dismissive phrase for a middle-aged woman grappling with the loss of life's drama and all her vital hormones than that.

All those hours of love lavished for this to be the end result? It is so hard to remind yourself this is just a developmental phase. Hang on in there, because this is the real test of unconditional love, isn't it? These five years or so are a complex time for mums, because you have to be firm and permissive at the same time, learn to judge when a boundary is needed and when setting one is a waste of time and energy now that your daughter views you differently.

To explore exactly what is going on from a psychological point of view, in 2020 I interviewed Alicia Drummond, a psychotherapist who works with teenagers and parents, and trains teachers to help teenagers at school. She has two grown-up daughters and runs Teen Tips, a website and coaching business. She has worked with hundreds of teens in trauma and many parents traumatised by their teen's behaviour.

She smiles with recognition at all the stories I recount of women perplexed by the savage and brutal teenage-girl monstering mums may get and begins to explain by pointing out that you are their main female role model, the most influential of them all. They watch you and take from you the bits they want, Drummond says and then they file this away for use later, often away from home. (I find mine, for example, are never rude to anyone else but me and their dad.) At the same time they have to prove they are different from you, so they may behave in the opposite way to you. Their identity is tied to yours, but as they need a new, separate identity from you, they may push you away. So, while they could be nicer to you, and they certainly know how to because they have watched you do it, if they are, it makes it much harder for them to separate away. And that's the conundrum.

Think about that while you are being made to feel a fool or as my nine-year-old calls it, a 'bidiot' – big idiot. You are their Number One Woman at this stage, however insignificant you feel. They look to you, albeit unconsciously, and they take a pick-and-mix approach to adopting the parts of you they want to be like and jettisoning the parts they are less comfortable with. Alicia puts it beautifully, and this phrase has helped me in the depths of my confusion around this maternal rejection.

Commenting on all the rebuffs and poor behaviour she says you have to 'hold it lightly' not take it personally as it all comes towards you. And most importantly not to bear a grudge – quite a skill to learn as an adult, I have found, and one you may need to practise.

'It can feel vicious,' Alicia acknowledges. 'They still need you but they don't want you any more.

'In therapy I often find older girls in their twenties feel extremely guilty about how they treated their mums and, ironically, we then have to deal with that emotion after resolving all the other stuff. They know they are testing you and pushing boundaries, but you may be one of the few people they are sure loves them unconditionally, so they can only try it out on you.

'It is the theory of the street angel but home devil, isn't it? If they are behaving properly externally, they are often trying out all the other stuff at home, which feels safer. They know how to behave well – they have learned that from watching you – but they want to find out what happens when they don't sometimes. They are learning about being a grown-up.'

As they are always watching you, be mindful of displaying the unhelpful bits of you, as they won't just copy the good bits. This, of course, requires you to be much more self-aware and to question if her bad behaviour could be in any way influenced by the way you behave.

However, we don't have to soak up all the impoliteness like a sponge; feel your power now and again (you are the Number One Woman, remember). Alicia points out that setting boundaries is part of your Mum job now; it is why you cannot be a best friend; be friendly but not a friend.

'They do want you to say enough is enough, to teach them

where the edges of their bad behaviour lie. This is the age of disrespect, but you should be firm and say what you can cope with and what is unacceptable, no matter how hard that is for you.

'And this is the time you work out what to pick a fight about and what not to. I often ask mums I am working with to write down one hundred things that annoy them about their teenagers, and then we have a specific hierarchy of what causes the most trouble for you as a mum. We start solving what is top of the list and agree the rest can wait – we won't let that cause a problem for now. If you think about it like that, then you do not go off on one every time you feel they are being disrespectful. That is exhausting and no way to live. Don't sweat all the small stuff is my advice.'

It is obvious really, but according to Alicia, as they start to develop their own identity, teenagers have to reject being part of yours; they cannot be seen as an extension of you either, which is why they hate it if their friends see them with you in the street or, worse still, you talk to their friends at home.

She adds, 'They may reject the bigger differences between the two of you, the parts they no longer want to connect with. They may also subconsciously accept parts of you too, characteristics they may adopt from your personality as they evolve.'

And occasionally your success in a role – maybe as a high-flier at work or being a high achiever generally – could be putting them off. Perhaps some girls feel overwhelmed by that and may have to tear it down to relieve themselves of the pressure to be as good as you at something?

I suspect that even Nobel Prize-winning nuclear scientists are made to feel like grade-A simpletons by their teenage daughters. An eminent professor of engineering once relayed to me the story of how she was told the only question she could ask when accompanying her daughter to a uni engineering Open Day was: Where is the toilet?

Basically, why it may feel like you can't win with a meanager is because you are so entwined as mum and daughter. They cannot like what you like as it stops them separating from you. So they may belittle anything you like or have achieved. On the flipside, they cannot stand anything that you do which may be different from how they envisage themselves: the stuff you wear, perhaps, or music you listen to. They simply won't tolerate any of it. It can feel like it is a lose-lose situation for you – and it's certainly confusing – but what you have to remember is that this is a developmental phase. They will move through and out of it; they won't be like this forever.

When we first hit the tweens period I was glad I hadn't succumbed to the most popular parent trend when my eldest was born, which was attachment parenting, a movement that gained an almost religious following from the mid-2000s onwards. Imagine if you'd Velcroed your child to you, as was advocated by the kind of experts who encouraged breastfeeding until the age of five, only to find perhaps that your children wanted very little to do with you as soon as they hit thirteen. That they won't be grateful forever and will rarely thank you (not that that is what you should expect, anyway). Often mine can't bear to be in the same room as me, and I sometimes lurk on the edges, fearful of embarrassing them in my own home. It's a cataclysmic shock, this parental fall from grace. The US family therapist Lisa Damour also makes the point that the more horrible your children are to you, the better their childhood relationship with you may have been. They are secure in their faith that you care, confident you won't reject them. If they are, however, struggling with everyone else, not just their parents, or perhaps in constant conflict situations then perhaps they will need some form of expert counselling to work out what is going on.

Damour's theory prompted a huge sigh of relief in our house, because that merry-go-round of 'she loves me, she loves me not' is hard to endure and can feel all-consuming for the whole household. It certainly helped when I stopped taking any of my teen daughters' behaviour personally and tried not to be in a confrontational mindset around them. I have now learned to pick my battles but I still set boundaries: you should feel able to give your teens guidance on what is acceptable and what is not. You're still the boss at home.

They are always going to test the boundaries, so politely and calmly hold firm on to those that matter most to you, even if is uncomfortable. This is not tough love; it is simply you keeping a promise. Don't confuse the two. If you do give in, you risk subconsciously telling them you don't care about their safety or well-being enough, that to have an easier life is more important to you, and that may frighten them. If you abandon boundaries and the consequences for breaking them then you are also perhaps subconsciously signalling that you cannot keep your word and you might give up on other things. It is unnerving for them. Unfortunately, you may also need to reassess these boundaries frequently. So, for example, you say no phones in your room after 9 p.m., then find they keep smuggling their phones into their rooms: you will need to keep reaffirming your rule, rather than giving in simply 'because they are going to do it anyway'.

I am also a fan of pressing the 'reset' button with meanagers. Sometimes when mine are being rude to me, I will say I don't want to talk about it now and will instead discuss it tomorrow, when they have reset the rudeness levels to zero. This can plant a seed in their minds that tomorrow is another day and gives them time to grapple with their feelings so that they can then present a better version of who they are to me the next day. It also reminds them of how the world works: poor behaviour shouldn't get you what you want. Friends of mine with much older teens reassure me that the seeds of good behaviour you plant do come to fruition later in life. *Your work gets through.*

Change can be stressful for everyone and cause us to be fractious. It is hard to be reasonable in the midst of it but try to remember that teenagers are usually doing the best they can. As are you, so try not to be too self-critical.

However, we should try to be mindful of what younger siblings are witnessing while we're dealing with flashpoints with our teenage girls. One of my parental regrets is my tendency to shout, especially as our two younger children will be witnessing it. I feel it is my greatest maternal weakness and while my anger is probably an expression of fear, I feel guilty about it. Therapists I have interviewed and asked about my shouting during arguments advise explaining to my girls in advance of the flashpoint situations, i.e. where I will usually lose it, what the consequences will be of their poor behaviour. Sort of to anticipate my blow-ups. So, for example, I tell one of my daughters her refusal to take her key with her when she stays out late drives me crazy and may lead to my losing my temper and yelling at her. She now understands that of all the things, this is the one that enrages me most. Warned of the possibility of a row in advance, she therefore knows how her future behaviour could help us to avoid it (some of the time).

You have to try to keep communicating where the boundary is, how poor behaviour makes you feel and what the consequences for it may be. I try to keep negotiations simple, as at this stage, long discussions on logic and reason will not always work. I am reminded of when they were little and would become furious if their favourite toy was in the wash. There was no point explaining why they couldn't have it back: best just to let them know it wasn't possible, empathise with how furious that made them feel and sit next to them as they threw themselves to the floor in a ball of snot and tears. Now they are teens I say no to things and they rage all around the house in a noisier version of the toddler meltdown, dealing with the disappointment themselves, deep breaths all round.

Important sidenote: don't ever add 'because I said so': that is 'hashtag bad parenting', as my teens often say. State your boundaries clearly, stick to your reasons and while they may not agree with them, they know you have thought them through and therefore care.

I have also learned to say things like 'perhaps you should walk away now, you're being rude,' when the arguing gets too much. And of course, if you know what to expect at this stage of parenting you can perhaps modify your behaviour in advance. It is useful to be able to say things like 'I would never talk to you like that' to a rude teen but that will only work if you *have* never talked to them like that!

My husband is much calmer than me, so I often deploy him in situations that make me yell, because the yelling doesn't work. They don't remember it and it isn't a deterrent, more a stressful irritant, which is unhelpful all round, particularly for those of us who have more sensitive daughters. It floods everyone with cortisol, the stress hormone, and little can be agreed or achieved.

If your teenager is a 'screamer' or shouts at you, then you should try never to shout back. A screamer could be a teen who feels insecure or scared, and is in emotional pain, which is the opposite of what she is projecting. Let her yell it out safely; don't react in that moment. More than anything, it is important they feel heard, because they have got themselves into an extreme place if they are screaming. They may feel powerless when they lose their way like this, and you can try and support them by listening. Calmly tell them you don't want to be a verbal punchbag or that you don't want them to speak to you that way, but that the cause of the problem is something you should tackle when everyone has calmed down.

I know it is hard not to get angry about the huge lack of respect you may begin to experience, but this sort of behaviour is acknowledged as a developmental stage. And don't forget teenage girls are, to borrow a phrase I read somewhere, 'exquisitely attuned to you' as a mother, and while it can be ever so painful to listen to the insults, try to make sure you stay available or present for your girls. There are times when you feel like withdrawing, rather than sticking your face into the furnace of their reprimands, but if you do that, they may feel they have no safe place to go. They may worry you are avoiding them, or that you are not strong enough to continue to love them.

Mostly I maintain an air of magnificent indifference and wear the coat of maternal stupidity, for this is what mothers seem to do at this stage: suck it up. Hold your head high and find your validation elsewhere, your sense of achievement in other things.

If you are a mum who cannot handle feeling rejection, you could perhaps need a psychological expert to help you with that, because you may have to put up with those feelings on a daily, sometimes hourly, basis. It may not be a reflection of who you are. They can give and then they can take away: avoiding them so they don't keep taking it away will not be the best thing to do. They are separating from you, but you must not separate from them.

A fellow mum once told me that her daughter was often so cruel to her they had all but stopped communicating. Her seventeen-year-old would occasionally bound excitedly in and lean in close as though for a friendly chat and the mum would feel the warm glow of their relationship from days gone by, but then her teen would tell her that her hair looked dreadful or ask her something awful like, 'Have you cleaned your teeth yet?' and a row would quickly escalate. After a series of these moments, the mum told me she just kept out of her daughter's way to protect herself from the on-off love affair. It's hard not to back off but if you do, you may be doing so at the moment your daughter needs you most. We're not all as emotionally robust as we'd like to be all the time but do try not to lose your connection for long because it gets harder to repair as time goes on. And as I have said before, while their occasional cruel behaviour may make you feel unwanted, in fact the opposite is true.

The days when I lose it, or I am just not strong enough for the meanage battering I get my love elsewhere. The dog comes in handy at this point. Or friends. Anyone who is pleased to see you. Or I wander off and have a bath with the door locked. Sometimes I use their shampoo as a small revenge.

Perhaps have a strong coffee, take a deep, rejuvenating breath, and focus on the blossoming of their confident, assertive new voice as a wonderful thing to behold, then you can possibly persuade yourself you should take some credit for that if that makes you feel any better! I try to see them as the little girls they once were; visualising that can take the heat out of their new-found certified genius persona in the crueller moments. And now and again I will look at old videos or pictures and set a memory in my mind so that when they talk to me as though I'm a nuisance caller then I have that childhood showreel to play in my head. It's why I keep the pictures of them as teeny ones up all round the house (against their wishes, it must be said). My heart breaks for all the mums swapping notes on this on Facebook. One posted sadly that her seventeen-year-old daughter had started to hug her again after avoiding her like the plague. It wasn't a newsflash post; it was a serious question. 'I am worried. Is this normal?' she asked forlornly. It is shocking how quickly you can go from being hugged all the time to being worried a hug is abnormal.

Some girls may not reject mums in this way and instead simply give you the cold shoulder. Maybe this is tougher to handle, because the silent treatment is ominous. A friend whose teenage daughter has withdrawn says she longs to be shouted at or told what an idiot she is. Anything other than this festering glow of unsaid disapproval.

But unless your daughter is locking herself away from the world entirely, the only thing you can do is make as much effort to be alongside her rather than in front of her as possible. There is no magic wand to relieve you of your emotional pain here. No to-do list or parenting strategy guaranteed to work, it's back to that exhausting strategy of unconditional love, of keeping her company, of just being in the room.

Seeking ways to be where she is or pottering around while she goes about her day ignoring will remind her you are still there for her even in the face of this occasionally upsetting but unfortunately not unusual behaviour. Your mantra is: don't give up.

Note to the wise: dads generally escape the more dire personal attacks and patronising. Well, it is this way in our house, where he holds something of an elevated position due to his crumbling-in-the-face-of-tears attitude. And I remember my dad being the softer option, the one least likely to get his head bitten off. As Alicia points out, though, they don't want to be Dad; he is of less interest as a role model. Sometimes he is just collateral damage. They haven't spent thirteen years watching his every move and storing all the information up for their list of 'Mum's weak spots' have they? They are not entwined with Dad.

I think you have to monitor your girls with a sort of benign kindness to help them get all this off their chests. Each adolescent is different, so tweaks in response may be needed. If, however, the conflict reaches unacceptable levels and affects the whole family in a negative way then it may be time to consider the base health of the mum-daughter relationship. For this you may need to consult a mental-health professional (see the back of the book for suggestions).

The path to adulthood is rockier for some than others, and I have noticed huge differences in my girls in how they deal with tricky feelings or situations, which shows that no one-size solution fits all and you have to adapt your parenting to each child. I hope this all makes sense, I hope it makes you feel less alone and realise that there is no shame to be found in how awfully your daughter may sometimes behave towards you. I wish we talked about it more as mums, for there is comfort to be had in knowing others are enduring this stage too. And also comfort in telling other mums that they are good parents. They may in turn tell you the same thing back, and then everyone feels a little better.

7

Thank you, I really appreciate what you did for me, Mum

(Or, 'here, hold this')

Have you heard of externalising? It is a kind of teenage voodoo magic. How best to describe it? It's sort of where they say or do something godawful, but you cannot get cross or react or feel any of the feelings, because what they have actually done is the wisest, most sensible thing they can do. Stay with me, because this will make sense in a minute. Externalising is *major*.

So from the ages of six to eleven (which psychotherapists call latency) most children are generally calmer, more compliant and settled. They are usually easier; there are a few bumps, but hopefully nothing too catastrophic (and this book is not for the catastrophic, as I say in the Preface).

But when they get to around twelve, as I have said before, the brain gets remodelled. It is a bit like when the lid comes off a tub of marbles at the top of the stairs. This brain change prompts an emotional earthquake: a tidal wave of feelings, complex and raw. It's a lot for the young woman to wrestle with and sometimes it overwhelms her. The ripple effect is huge and your empathy and compassion will be their port in this unpredictable storm. This is the moment you need to dig deep and become emotionally available. This may not be easy, because this swirling turmoil of emotions is so huge and chaotic and hard to deal with that perhaps the only person your daughter can hand them to is you. You're ready, aren't you? Primed? Well, not quite, because you've just had this golden time of latency and you're wondering what the hell is going on.

In my daughters' early teenage years I was once bemoaning the terrible ear bashing I'd got from one of my daughters to an older friend. She wisely told me that of course my daughters threw all their horrors at me: it would be impossible for them to deal with such awful emotions themselves, terrifying for them to take all that on, so they turned to the only person up to the job, the one who loved them most, a grown-up who seemed emotionally stable and available.

'You should be proud of their outbursts in your direction,' she said. 'Otherwise they would have had to cope with that in their own heads. Which would have been terrifying. They will be grateful one day, I promise.'

The therapist Lisa Damour explains the theory of adolescent 'externalising' in her writing and in the times I have talked to her, she has reiterated that one day my daughters will indeed be thankful and appreciative of all the venting I have soaked up. Gratitude is not the reason to do it, but it's good to know they may one day recognise how much you love them even when they were not their best selves.

Let's go through it again, to really understand what is being asked and the magnitude of how upsetting it can be at times. What you may have is a newly made teenager fizzing with new feelings, many of which may be emotionally upsetting for both of you. Everything is a first for her. She may become intensely infuriated with any number of things, from the state of world politics to her locker being on the wrong floor at school and therefore ultimately responsible for her detention for being repeatedly late (please try not to be cross with her for being late).

What should she do with all this illogical fury, anger and confusion swishing about like the inside of a washing machine? Talk to her friends? Off she trots, but it turns out they are all crazy too, full of jumbled-up thought processes, waving their arms around hysterically as well, like manic octopus-people, glaring at passers-by with death stares. She can't rely on those nitwits, so she comes home and seeks you out in the kitchen (where you are quietly trying to remember the password to your online supermarket shopping account) and lets rip. Both of you wishes she had the willpower at least to wait until she's taken her coat off, but she hasn't, so you stand in front of this fire-breathing dragon and take the full force of her inexplicable fury.

Things not to do include trying to solve the problem (not interested) and asking her to calm down (she probably can't). She is externalising her feelings, and by doing this she is giving them to you to handle. She may think you are more capable of doing so. If you ask her if she wants actual practical help and she says yes, you may choose to step in then. If the venting is more their complaining about you or something you have done, you can always say, 'I have a different view of the situation, but carry on,' and just accept that your view is not relevant now because she has to get it all off her chest first.

You could also ask her not to 'get salty', as Damour rather beautifully puts it, and use kinder language, but it is unlikely to end well, so I often just walk away after the venting has finished, if I feel it is really unpleasant. All you need to know is they may just be handing hard feelings they can't deal with to you like a steaming pile of dirty washing. Sometimes they will tell you further down the line that they are sorry for all the things they said (yelled), sometimes they won't (maybe you should call your own mum now too and apologise). But they *will* be grateful one day, according to Damour. Just later on. When everyone has calmed down and adolescence has become a dim and distant memory (about the age of twenty-five, I am told). Hang in there.

'Mum, What's Wrong With You?'
Conversations with Teens

Her: I cannot believe you are putting all this pressure on me to revise to get good marks [declared apropos of nothing after a weekend spent on the heath picnicking with mates]. I mean, GOD, MUM, I just can't deal with it. I won't get over 60 per cent in anything and none of it is any use and I will end up just working in a frozen-pea factory because this is what happens to everyone even if they go to university, which I won't because I am not doing all this revision. For god's sake. You earn money and all you do is look at fashion, meet celebrities and write stuff no one reads, and it isn't a real job and you are rubbish at maths and can't speak any languages. You didn't even go to university. Have you packed my PE kit for school?

8

Who are all these people in my lounge?

Play dates stop around the age of eleven for most girls. You must never use this word again after that. It has taken a hike, just like 'mummy', 'mamma' and 'mumma'. And 'sleepover'. But the end of play dates does not mean you don't get to have a house full of wonderful young humans anymore, something I used to really enjoy when they were little. Quite the contrary. Teenagers have a hive mind. They move in swarms, drifting from home to home.

We became used to having a house full of them on a Friday night or winter weekend afternoons, when they would appear on the doorstep if they weren't on the heath, at the park, or wandering the shopping malls. They even came on holiday with us too, and we loved having such a fun gang with us.

I wouldn't usually see our temporary weekend residents until the afternoons, when they wandered into the kitchen with our daughters, all in their PJs. Always a happy surprise to encounter a new face rifling through your cereal cupboard.

But I think they're just lovely en masse. It's like being in a wonderful sitcom called *Testing Out New Personas* or *Hit and Miss: An Experiment in Finding Your New Identity*. It makes for a vibrant time; the energy in the house fizzes and crackles. There's a certain aliveness that comes with adolescents that feels like fuel for the soul. I swear it evens out wrinkles a bit.

You learn lots of new words while they are around, and how to use phrases like 'cancelled', 'man says', 'spill the T' and 'do be', as in 'this do be the worst cup of tea you ever made'. It's how I discovered 'dabbing' in the last days of 2016. Remember that? The house resonates with a wonderful youthful spirit and happy outrage. They have furious debates about everything from climate change (all Gen X's fault) to the disgraceful price of a large cookie in the school canteen. They can argue about both with extreme enthusiasm and commitment. All of it is a delight to witness quietly from the side lines, when you are allowed to, and a powerful reminder that much of Gen Z is a force to be reckoned with. They have been dubbed the 'philanthroteens', and a survey during the summer of 2020 found them to be more likely to donate to charity or become volunteers than previous generations. They do give a damn, and I find them impressively literate about world events and willing to protest for causes they believe in.

I love watching them all entwined over each other on our sofa, chatting, though sometimes they just sit silently together, all glued to phones. They leave their socks everywhere, and teenage girls have a circular attitude to clothing: it seems to rotate between households, and many (mine included) hardly buy anything new because of their commitment to sustainability and determination to save cash.

How wonderful it looks in these moments of calm to be between the vulnerability of being a child and the possibility of being an adult, and all the power that will hold for them.

Not every teen, though, will bring friends in big groups home. This doesn't mean she doesn't have any; she may just feel that her privacy is hers and she's more comfortable being able to leave a gathering and come home to her room than she is having her room flooded with other people. Personal space can be extremely important to teenage girls, some more than others. And what their friends think about everything is super important. They are working out who their tribe is and how they want to interact. I think the only time to worry is if their behaviour changes dramatically, for example, if they once brought people home and then suddenly no one appears. A socially isolated teen with no friends is unusual, and you may want to chat to her school if you think your daughter is without peer support in this way or that perhaps she is being bullied. Teen-girl friendships can be complex and we have witnessed behaviour both good and bad among our daughters' peer groups.

I'd say that few things make a teen girl more miserable than issues between friends. I try not to interfere immediately, as going into solution mode isn't usually what is needed. Instead I try listening to them talk about what's going on and ask what, if anything, they need me to do after that. But I don't make any specific criticism of the other girls involved, as you don't know what is going to happen next, and both your daughter and a troublesome friend are changing – they could be completely different people a week later.

I think quality is better than quantity when it comes to teenage friendships, and always try to work out what is the normal kind of conflict between girls and what has tipped into bullying. It is perhaps about defining what is simply one-off teenage rudeness or aggression and what is actual bullying that is happening consistently over a considerable period of time. This is what you should be looking out for in your daughter's life. I remain curious about any changes in my girls' patterns of behaviour and hope I am as attuned to the changing nature of their friendships as I can be without interfering.

It is worth pointing out to your daughters the difference between being popular and being liked. A smart career coach once explained it to me: girls who are popular may not be liked but they wield power. They may want status and perhaps use it to fulfil something within themselves. Other girls are often in awe or frightened of them and stay in that tribe because it is safer to do that than be on the outside. This can be hard for you, as an adult, to understand. It might be that your daughter stays in the thrall of an unpleasant popular girl because to remove herself from the clique is impossible; she would have to change her whole daily routine, perhaps, and that may not be at all easy – or attractive. If she herself is being bullied, either in person or online, you could encourage her to be more assertive around this particular 'frenemy', or talk to her teachers and devise a strategy the school can establish among the friendship group.

I always tell my three girls, though, that it is OK to be angry out loud about something that is upsetting or affecting them and that it is OK to call out bad behaviour. Being assertive is not always seen as a good quality in females, but you can encourage it in your girls. There is an excellent book on this by Marisa Porges called *What Girls Need*. Porges was a leading counter-terrorism expert in the Obama administration and often worked predominantly with men and she emphasises the power of giving girls the authority to show their emotions out loud. I liked the tone and spirit of the book and do hope my daughters feel the force of their female power.

When it comes to bullying in teenage, I do not think you should talk to the girl who is the bully or her parents. I have witnessed many furious mums intervene this way, causing all manner of problems for their daughters and usually making the situation worse. If your daughter is being bullied, she probably feels powerless; if you take control you may worsen that feeling. She perhaps needs some owner-ship of what is going on, to have her own ideas of how to tackle this problem practically, which you can ask her about and support.

But do check the facts. Are you being told the whole truth? Does the school's version of events match what your daughter is saying?

It could be that your daughter is in fact the bully. If she is, why is she behaving like this? You should not blame or shame her though, because she may be unhappy in an area of her life at home and you may both have to face up to that. Talk it through and perhaps seek professional help – the school may be able to point you in the right direction of a therapist, group or online resource. It is hard for parents to think their child may be the one whose behaviour is unpleasant, but the bully is always the child of someone. And bullies can be helped with the right understanding of why they are behaving this way.

The website Ditch the Label is a useful tool for those aged between twelve and twenty-five who are being bullied. Try to keep your lines of communication open at home: bullying takes so many forms that it can be good to talk about them so your daughter can spot them. The insidious silent treatment is one of the worst, alongside being excluded from a group's activities. And today this may happen in person or online, with some bullies sending appalling voice notes to girls they are persecuting, or picking on them during group-gaming sessions, so try to make your adolescents aware that anything said on social media or sent to them is evidence of bullying that can be shown to adults. It's your job to help teach them about what a healthy friendship looks like from a young age so they can hopefully navigate all this themselves with resilience and good self-esteem. We've been lucky so far not to have experienced any examples of extreme bullying with our children. This may be due to their particular friendship groups or the level of support at the schools they all attend but I have supported mums who've been through this and it is heartbreaking. Please refer to the back of the book for specific support services.

When teenage friendships are working well, though, they are glorious to watch. Having our house filled with new voices, male and female, often offered a moment of optimistic calmness in between all the other friendship stuff that goes on. And nothing gives me greater joy on a Friday night than seeing a thousand pairs of giant trainers lined up in the hallway, coats thrown near, but obviously not on, the coat rack.

However, you'll need to prepare for this teenvasion, as my husband and I call it. And that will mostly mean catering to it. For teenagers are eating machines. Even if you spent the equivalent of a small country's GDP on the weekly shop, the evening after it has arrived, they will open the cupboard doors and say, 'Why is there nothing to eat in this house?' their goldfish brains forgetting they've already eaten it all.

Especially if they have had friends over.

'May I help you?' I asked a rather tall, handsome boy I hadn't met before rummaging around in our fridge one evening. He was eating up all the 'bitsa', as we call it (bits left over after meals). I package up what is left after our younger kids have had tea in plastic takeaway boxes and leave it for teen foragers. This is a top tip and will save you a fortune.

'I'm starving,' he said to me. 'I haven't had anything since lunch.'

'What did you have for your lunch?' I enquired, without pointing out there is no official meal between lunch and dinner, though teens would favour one. 'A roast,' he replied.

We also noticed our teens had started to label food as theirs after a big shop or if they'd bought it themselves on the way home from school. I think this is a symptom of a larger family with constant visitors. They still eat your stuff, mind you. 'Ask forgiveness, not permission' is the teen default of choice with treats. And let me tell you, there is no disappointment as deep as the disappointment of getting your Cadbury's Fruit & Nut, that you have been looking forward to all week, out of the fridge (we are a cold chocolate family), only to find it is an empty wrapper. It's the same with juice or milk. They put that back when there is only a dribble left. This is to avoid the effort of rinsing things out to put in the recycling bin, which may be getting full and then they may be asked to empty it, which they can't do because, well, homework, hair masks, Instagram, watching *Friends* AGAIN.

9

The monster munch

(Or, 'what do you want for dinner?')

I am neither a happy cook nor a good cook so for me, the question of what to dish up for dinner became one of the most vexing of all when my daughters turned into teenagers and tea together would sometimes descend into an illogical and farcical power struggle. For us the 'What do you want for dinner?' question was a particular form of torture in early teens because it seemed to me that our girls would eat nothing and everything. Their choices changing faster than their musical tastes.

As they get older, adolescents start to eat meals out of the natural order of the day, routines change, and I noticed that sometimes those meals might consist of 'made from a packet' Betty's chocolate cookies followed perhaps by deep-fried vegetarian gyoza of dubious sell by date bought in the local corner shop, except these are not deep fried, they are mildly warmed in a frying pan by an impatient sixteen-year-old at 2 a.m. and then left on the side when it becomes clear they are disgustingly inedible. Be warned: the adolescent's road to culinary independence is a messy, sticky one.

But asking or planning or shopping for dinner may become an unexpected, niggly worry for those of us on what feels like twenty-four-hour food duty. While boys can be a bit fussy, it seems, from our son and from what friends say, they will mostly eat anything because they are ravenous all the time. Teenage girls, however, can sometimes morph into a sort of Mariah Carey crossed with Miss Piggy diva when it comes to the vexing 'What's for tea?' question.

The conversations about what my girls will and won't eat are often comical or infuriating. This is sometimes how it goes of an evening in our house:

'Do you want chicken [veggie/vegan/gluten-free/organic-only alternative] for tea?'

'What?'

'For tea. Do you want chicken/veggie alternative?'

'Why?'

Pause for parental sigh. 'Can you take your headphones out, please?'

'Why?'

'DO YOU WANT CHICKEN FOR TEA, FOR GOD'S SAKE!'

'What else is there?'

'Everything. There is everything else.'

'I don't want chicken/veggie etc etc alternative.'

'Do you want spag bol, pizza, fish, chips? Maybe some pasta and pesto?'

'No. Pasta and pesto, I'm not five. Why is there never anything to eat in this house?'

'I just listed all the things there are to eat.'

'I don't like them, you know that. What I mean is there is nothing I like.'

'What do you like? I will nip to the shop, then. Exactly what do you want?'

'I am not really hungry yet. Can we eat later?'

But obviously we cannot eat later, as it is already 8 p.m. and everyone else is starving. It feels like a minor thing, to mention all this to and fro over food, but for me it became infuriating trying to feed them well and at a reasonable hour in the hope they would eat with us and not drift away from the family. Eating together at mealtimes is a vital moment of connection for teenagers; it is the one common piece of advice given by all the mental-health experts I've spoken to. It doesn't have to be every single meal obviously and they should of course be learning to cook for themselves, but eating together is a ritual to preserve for family unity, it's healing.

Eating together can be a cure-all for fractured, splintered and tense relationships and a tangible goal for those families in crisis or undergoing seismic change at home. Holding on to family mealtimes, though, requires superhuman strength as the children separate off; sitting down to eat at the same time becomes harder because my teens get up so late and their weekends have no consistent timetable. I often cater to four different meals, in an attempt to keep everyone at our kitchen table at least twice a week.

Because of the importance of family meals, we made our kitchen table the epicentre of our world. Sometimes I think I love it more than I love my husband; it is the one thing I would save if the house was on fire. It's the beating heart of our family life, a quiet witness to the hurly-burly of our days. In the silence of the mornings, when I come down before everyone else is up, I think I can still hear the choruses of 'Happy Birthday' sung round it, the cheers of our Monopoly games, teatime tantrums, irrational tears when homework projects go wrong. It's where the girls revised and where my husband and I have sat for millions of hours, wondering if we are in fact the worst parents in the world in the storm of giant teenage rows.

It's where I threatened to leave my husband when he kept secretly restocking the drawers with Quavers during one of my healthy-eating binges; indeed, it was the scene of my pompous 'processed ham causes cancer' diatribe (the jury is out in our house), but this table is where once or twice a week we all eat together, a ritual I will not let die.

But if you have a twelve-year-old girl right now, you should know that even if you had Madonna's private live-in chef taking personal orders every single morning and preparing freshly made sushi that has been flown in from Fiji that day, there will come a moment when she will say: 'I cannot eat this. You know I don't like carrots [insert name of veg she has been happily eating since the day she first had solids]' – unless she is at someone else's house, in which case, she would eat cat food from the cat's bowl to be polite.

I have learned to let a lot of the wrangling over dinner remain as relaxed as possible and let them either shop with me and pick their own things, or I get their food choices in writing via texts. This also teaches them about budgets and the cost of the stuff they are eating.

You could go all hard-line and do the 'I am not your personal chef. You will have what we cook, young lady, and that's that, blah blah blah' speech, but this means they often won't eat anything good, which puts them in a dreadful mood. Or you hardly ever eat together, which is not good for family relations: it is a lost connection. And feels to me like an unnecessary row to have.

Also, let's face it, you love them and want them to be happy. Life is little caring steps, cuddling them with other stuff that isn't actual cuddles. And, besides, they have probably eaten half a bag of Doritos on the way home from school, so tea together is a chance to get a small amount of goodness into them. I like to give them a choice, and I am not moaning about the way they handle it here, simply offering you a version of the future that could turn out to be yours even if you have an adventurous eater under ten right now. Both mine ate more or less anything they were given before the age of twelve. Food makes them happy; it's better than buying them 'stuff', and being a teenage girl is hard, as we have already established, so your patience would be appreciated perhaps, even if it doesn't feel appreciated at the time. Maternal kindness isn't particularly tricky to display around food, just frustrating at times.

I realised food's potential as a battle zone when they hit thirteen and so I started to leave stuff lying round the house – nuts, fruit, those almost-crisps wheat things – as though I were living in a forest with small animals, to get some goodness into them (I was still slicing apples, for god's sake). Saying nothing about the teatime menu sometimes works, as they may absentmindedly eat what you serve up before remembering they have signed a charter somewhere with other adolescent females to make as much fuss as possible about everything. I may also just add another tiny dinner detail here for your amusement. The 'Why did you call me down when it isn't even on the table?' flame-thrower.

I noticed some teenage girls can play an odd cat-and-mouse game about coming when you call, 'Dinner!' It involves three or four goes before they slide into the room, having first had a shower, called their friends, lain on their beds waiting for a hair mask to sink in and rearranged the photos on their wall. But if they get to the dinner table after being summoned and the food is not immediately there on a plate, they might display Oscar-worthy dramatic outrage. Incredulous that you would waste their valuable time in such a way. This makes them sound rather spoilt, doesn't it, and perhaps it will be different in your house, but in the end they will potentially make a fuss about everything for all the reasons I note in the following chapters, so try not to take it personally. It's mostly just funny to witness this quirk of teen behaviour. No biggie, as they say.

Our kitchen table is the venue for their ever-changing foody demands or dietary experiments. One minute they are vegetarian, then vegan, then vegan on Mondays, veggie during the week and vampire carnivores at the weekend, or vegan unless it has pepperoni on it, which doesn't count, I don't know why.

Around 25 per cent of eighteen-year-olds are now vegetarian, according to a 2019 YouGov survey, and apparently nearly half of all vegans are aged fifteen to thirty-four, and there has been a reported five-fold increase in vegan takeaways in the past three years. We aren't big meat eaters as a family so veggies and vegans are welcome around these parts.

I interviewed nutritionist Sarah Dempster on the subject of adolescent diets when my fifteen-year-old first went veggie. Dempster advised me to remain curious about my kids' food choices and talk through what they imagine a vegan or veggie diet would actually look like before they try it – wise words to bear in mind. Teen girls often have a low intake of calcium and iron, and a vegan diet can reduce your intake of B12, iodine and zinc, so they may need supplements. And she suggested we frame the conversation around gradually cutting down on meat and dairy rather than cutting it out or trial it a few days a week so they see the reality of what they will be eating.

As a parent you can deliver all sorts of rules around food, but I have found teens will usually go their own way. Plus, conversations around food can suddenly become more loaded with teen girls, and perhaps it is best to avoid that emotional trigger of good and bad foods.

I swore I would never talk about my body in a negative way as a mum in front of my teenage daughters, when it came to what I ate; but this is a tricky promise as a woman (we will explore this in a later chapter). And we all make mistakes, don't we though, as mums around food? I don't think you can always stand by while they are devouring a giant pile of sugary crap for the third time that day without mentioning there may be better choices, but I have not always made that point in the most delicate way I could. My daughters, though, will rightly call me out if I come anywhere close to body shaming.

I have been lucky at home not to have experienced any issues around food with my teenagers so far, but I have interviewed young women with eating disorders and their mums, and their stories were heartbreaking.

When I spoke to the veteran nutritionist Jane Clarke, who has worked with hundreds of women over the years and whose experience in changing mindsets around food is invaluable, she was emphatic that you cannot flick the eating-disorder switch in adolescents simply by talking negatively about food. It is much more complex than that, from a mental-health and neurological point of view. If your daughter is beginning to restrict her diet in her teen years or becomes extremely specific about what she eats, however, do talk to her about the reasons behind this, as it could be a sign of an eating disorder developing, for which you will need professional help.

Eating disorders can be extremely difficult to treat and I have enormous sympathy for mums coping with this. But I don't think you can avoid any potential issues simply by avoiding talking about food either and it would take superhuman strength not to mention diet at any point as a woman in the Western world. However, you can promote a healthier attitude to food as a mum by mindfully keeping your negative thoughts to yourself when it comes to your own diet and body image.

I try to avoid getting into any power struggles around food and if I don't want them to eat it, I don't buy it. But we have a relaxed attitude to snacking at ours, with a chocolate collection Willy Wonka would have been proud of, and despite the rest of the world being seemingly in the grip of a wellness epidemic, I didn't really know what a chia seed was until I hit forty-five and had to address a massive iron deficiency myself, not least because it had made my hair fall out (very common in midlife).

But I have a friend whose most poignant memory of her childhood is her dad saying, 'A moment on the lips, a lifetime on the hips,' to her aged eight. She is fifty and still having fat-free yoghurt with a glass of hot water for breakfast. Maybe it's best to forge a middle way on the food chat and define it as being about feeling healthy rather than always linking it to weight. And encourage them to stay fit and get outside as often as they can.

As the years have rolled on, both my elder daughters have taken to cooking for themselves in between family meals with us; this started when they were around fifteen years old. This was all fine, and cooking for yourself is to be applauded, but the giant mess they make is infuriating. Tidying up sometimes goes on all evening when they do it themselves. And while I am pretty bad at loading a dishwasher, try putting anything in it after a teenage girl has had a go.

Also, rather like dogs, they cannot seem to judge portion control and nothing is returned to the fridge. Odd combinations occur. Nutella may become a default spread on everything, unless you stop buying it. They conduct all their cooking with their headphones in, chatting to their friends, so a million splintered conversations occur across the kitchen during its busiest time of the day. I spend a lot of time answering questions their friends were asking on the phone that I couldn't hear and wondering what the hell was going on.

They will leave one fish finger in the packet, rendering it useless for any further sandwiches. And I can never understand how they stand over the hob prodding the one frying pan that still has its non-stick coating with a metal fork, while eating a Twix, before enjoying a gorilla-sized pasta serving. The kitchen pings to phone timers all going off at different times for rice. It's often chaotic during teatime as a consequence, meaning we adults often have to eat later, when the teens have finished making the kitchen look like it's been ransacked by starving hordes. But it is also wonderful to watch them learn how to feed themselves, and I reckon every teen girl should leave home being able to prepare her dinner before she goes out into the world. My eldest makes a brilliant signature dish: spaghetti carbonara, which has stood her in good stead on campus at university. She was surprised by how many students couldn't cook when she first arrived. And I'm teaching my son as we speak, so he can master a few pasta recipes before he too leaves us. There is a wonderful website called Dinner: A Love Story, which offers simple, easy-to-follow recipes for teens to learn, and YouTube is awash with veggie or vegan cooking videos made by teens themselves if you get stuck for ideas on this weird and wonderful food journey.

10

Spoons, bananagrams and telly

The importance of rituals

Rituals and routines are the glue of family life, the anchor during the unpredictable adolescent years. Create and cultivate rituals and all is not lost. Find connections with your teen daughter through these rituals, and do this at all costs, because even the smallest of connections may make her feel safe, loved and cherished in challenging times. Be quietly vigilant around her, notice her likes and dislikes, and make the effort to nurture the rituals you have together from childhood or start new ones. It'll be different for everyone and different for each of your daughters. This could be as simple as making her a cup of tea at the same time each day (even if she only grunts a thank you in return) or finding a TV show she might watch with you – keep trying to engage on anything you can talk to her about. Gently, softly persist in this quest.

We cling to habits and rituals for safety and reassurance in the Candy house. Family dinner, restorative brews, local (short) dog walks, spoons (the best card game in the world), Bananagrams, Monopoly;

the simple regularity of it all secures us as our unpredictable teenage agents of chaos ricochet around our domestic world.

There is a brilliant Scottish word, 'thole', which means the ability to endure extreme hardship. We all need a bit of parenting thole during the adolescent years, when our children push us to the limits, busting out of that comforting blanket of family routines, kicking over the sandcastles of our beloved home-grown habits as they go.

What once warmed them now repels them because they're often obliged to do it with you, so you have to adapt the rituals as time flows through family life. This is, of course, easier said than done when they refuse to be in the same room as you or feel they are being constantly persecuted for infringements of 'the rules'. BUT please try hard, really hard, to engage with them, no matter how awful you feel they are being, or you are feeling.

One of my favourite routines as a family is telly watching. As a child of the 1970s, I love all telly. For a while during your parenting adventure you lose your chance to watch TV or see films because you are knee-deep in kids' viewing, but that moment after the early years, when they finally realise what is going on in a film, is joyful.

As the years strode on and we became a family of six, accommodating the telly watching to suit all ages became trickier. Nowadays we don't sit down together more than twice a week, but I try not to let the sixteen- and eighteen-year-olds drift off into their rooms to watch things alone on their laptops. We didn't allow TV or laptop screens in bedrooms until they were sixteen for this reason. Some nights it is good for them to have the space away from you, but a regular schedule of TV-together time may keep you all connected. Ditto listening to music.

This takes patience in the teen years, because if you have ever tried to watch TV with teenagers, they are frustratingly similar to toddlers.

There's a brief moment some evenings of our group viewing when I am optimistic that everyone in front of our telly will stay quietly sitting down, but one of them gets up just as soon as the chosen programme starts to put the kettle on. A giant row about tea-making then occurs, as in, 'I am not making one for everyone.'

The smallest child secretly wanders off to find snacks under cover of the chaos. Then we all sit down again and the boy one gets up to fetch a bag of pretzels and opens the bag across the floor before the chorus of 'For god's sake shut your mouth when you eat' begins.

The crunching continues intermittently and the two teen girls will start a mumbled conversation, which gets gradually louder before one of them says 'Whatttttt?' at full volume, finally noticing Dad and I glaring, while the telly is silent and on pause.

One will then conclude: 'The trouble with you, Mum, is you need it to be completely silent to watch the TV, which just isn't realistic. You need to compromise.' Before all this starts, you will have waited forty minutes for the teens to come out of the shower. Sometimes halfway through, one will say, 'Pause it I need to go to the loo.' Then twenty minutes will pass before you find her sitting on the loo on her phone, or that she has forgotten she is watching telly with you and wandered back up to her room. TV with teenagers is exasperating but necessary. This is what I mean by keeping connections.

Occasionally my husband implores us to let this one ritual go, so he can get to the end of at least one *Bake Off* without the bickering. And maybe he is right, but I find it particularly helpful after we have had an argument or some terrible teenage dispute has occurred. I have also discovered that while she is at uni my eighteen-year-old watches the shows we all used to watch together so that gives us something to chat about when she is away. A connection kept, even in absence.

The good thing about telly as a parenting tool is that you are simply sitting with them, not asking anything of them, and that can be a good, nurturing parenting skill. Even if you don't want to be there and cannot stand the programme on view, I advise you to stick with it. Of course, the context is that you also do other more interesting things together outside the house too but for simple-parenting box ticking, telly is a good one.

I also try to engage with them when they are playing video games on our telly (more on screens later). Now that they can interact with friends online via video games, I think it is healthy to know exactly what they playing, but I am glad they get to do this – it's helpful for them. Don't demonise this activity in case you encourage them to keep it secret. Many video games can be perfectly acceptable alongside their other activities as long as they are not played obsessively for long periods of time. We set some limits and negotiate that in advance. My girls loved their games until about the age of sixteen, though my son seems much more committed. With our eldest two we were in the dark about the new world of gaming but now we know more, we have set firmer rules for our nine- and fourteen-year-olds. No games in their rooms, time limits (no playing after 7 p.m.) and for us to be able to see who is playing if we ask.

When it comes to family board or card games, though they may refuse to play as often as before, you should try and keep the ritual going. Sometimes no one will agree on which game to play in our house, and then one wanders off halfway through and our two younger children become infuriated that the game isn't being taken seriously. I am sad to see these family pleasures peter out in frequency and become less a part of our life as our teens are looking for not-so-subtle signs their childhood is over and they are ready to go. But hang on in there, grapple them to the table if you can. All of this is subtle communication you want to be with them, that you are there, no matter what else is going on. It's non-confrontational, non-critical, occasionally tactile love in action. Unconditional and enjoyable. Cherish the moments, but don't let them happen by accident. These are team-building exercises, which are too important to be taken for granted in family life.

'Mum, What's Wrong With You?'
Conversations with Teens

Me: Could you just tidy up all the plates, cups and other food stuff you left all over the floor in your room please, before the dog eats the Blu Tack or dark chocolate and dies?

Her: Oh, for god's sake. [Sigh that goes on for twenty minutes. We wait.] Why do you spoil everything?

11

Oh Christ, have we been burgled?

Or, 'walk on by, nothing to see here'

This is the biggie, isn't it? The horror of horrors. The thing so many mums rant about when I chat with them. This unites the mothers of teenage girls perhaps more than anything else: the mess. So I am here from your future to tell you to let it go. To walk past. To ignore it, open a pack of biscuits, put the telly on and pretend you have no idea what is going on behind her bedroom door.

There have been times when a full nuclear-waste-proof biohazard suit was required to go into our eldest's bedroom. I just cannot describe some of the revolting filth I have seen, because I would have to put a giant trigger warning out to the universe for practically every trigger there is. And while our younger teen is a little cleaner, or perhaps more of a germophobe, she is so frightfully disorganised that there is no way of finding anything in her room. Even if it was as big as the abominable snowman, it would be lost forever in that bottomless pit of tangled stuff. You might think I am exaggerating if you are at the younger end of the teen years or have bought this book in preparation for the forthcoming tsunami of mess headed your way, but on the life of our dog, I am not. You will be revolted, surprised and disgusted.

Many renowned psychologists have explained to me that mayhem in teenagers' bedrooms is to be expected and tolerance should be shown. It's their brains again. All the neurology points to them not being able to actually see the mess like we can, hence it doesn't bother them. It took me a while, but I began to realise the experts were right: I could understand what they were saying. And, of course, our girls' rooms are their private domains and really should be none of our business. Closing the door really is the only option, unless you like shouting, rowing, sighing, crying or moaning from dawn until dusk.

So now I more or less just leave mine to it. Sometimes I insisted they bring the washing basket in their rooms to the machine to make this easier for me on the laundry front. But they often just shove everything from off their floor in and who wants to spend an hour sniffing it all to see what is dirty or not? So it has become rather hit and miss. Ultimately, I just left it. It wasn't easy at first, but, rather like pairing everyone's socks, I realised it would be an endless 'to infinity and beyond' task to get the rooms tidied up and all the washing done properly. May as well just give up – you have my permission.

I did object when their rooms got so bad it looked as if a burglar had been in, ripped off his clothes and decided to have a lengthy shower involving twenty-seven towels, but I cannot say this was helpful on my part. This was mostly during lockdown when they were learning in their rooms and space needed to be cleared. However, their rooms continued to look like they were living with Zuul, the ectoplasm-spewing fridge-ghoul from *Ghostbusters*, even after sporadic interventions from me or some enforced tidying. They have no shame or remorse about the titanic mess or the hoarding of mould-filled crockery and flasks. And there are some hygiene situations that I feel an A & E nurse used to Friday nights after pub-closing fallout would find disturbing. But I know it isn't their fault. Please believe that and brace yourself for it in the early years of teenagerdom. As they get older, they do clean up a little and they do prefer a dry towel, but it will still be a bit of a mess either way.

How bad can it be? I can still hear you asking. Well, let's look at it this way: if you were to compile an advert suitable to appeal to a teenage lodger it would read something like this:

Wanted: slow-moving, chaotic individual who never flushes the toilet and sits in front of Fortnite for hours at a time. Would prefer house-mate who talks loudly all the way through murder-mystery films, favourite TV soaps and who says 'It wasn't me' or 'What's wrong with you?' at least six times a day. You should have what is best described as a relaxed attitude to personal hygiene. Must allow dogs to lick your face too.

Don't apply if you have ever thrown an empty crisp packet in the bin or managed to get dirty washing in the dirty-washing basket. Do apply if you like a long lie-in, have never used a hoover, make an enormous fuss about spiders, love to squeeze the toothpaste from the middle and enjoy a loose relationship with the truth. You will fit in if you take the batteries out of remote controls in communal areas for your own personal use and have never replaced a finished loo roll with a fresh one.'

I interviewed mum Janey Downshire, a family therapist and author of *Teenagers Translated*, about the giant mess because so many mums seemed excessively worried about it when I talked to them, and she told me to relax. 'Close the door on your way past,' were her exact words.

There should be rules around mess in family spaces and keeping these rooms clean and tidy, because my girls' mess often spills out into bathrooms, and the safety of other younger siblings is some-times a concern. I make the expectations of tidiness in the rest of the house clear and, actually, my daughters have always been respectful of that.

But their own room is their business, whatever gender of offspring you have. I breathed a sigh of relief when Downshire told me the last thing I should do is clear up. I'm not a trained zookeeper; I don't have to put myself through such trauma. So no imposing of my highly efficient mess-reduction systems on them, no nagging them every five minutes to clear up. Basically, don't rescue them, because they need to resolve the issue themselves and, besides, it is one less thing on your domestic to-do list. When people say don't sweat the small stuff, I think a messy room is the small stuff they are talking about. Pretend it is a crime scene and walk away – nothing for you to see here.

And it is no use lecturing and lecturing them into sense around this. Trust me, I have wasted hours of my life doing this. Girls, much more so than boys, I have found, pretend they are listening when they are not. They may nod in agreement with your sensible logic around keeping rooms tidy, especially during exam-revision time, when they are under extra pressure to know where a pen is but they aren't taking any notice at all, in reality. They simply don't enjoy being told what to do: it makes them defensive and contrary (it makes us all like this sometimes, doesn't it?). And the majority just don't care what their rooms look like, even if they pretend to be taking in your forthright opinion on what it should look like. You may be having an intense and extreme reaction to the mess, but your daughter is not. Yours is an adult reaction, hers is an adolescent one.

Occasionally I notice one of our teen daughters will clean up of her own volition. It's spontaneous and often a little half-hearted, but she does do it. Oddly, if Dad asks, they are more inclined to sort out their floors. And when our eldest set up her own room on campus at university, I noted down the line that she was pretty tidy compared to her bedroom antics at our house.

On the parents-of-teens Facebook groups I recklessly joined in my search for help during darker times, I noticed the trend in the US is to remove the door as punishment for a messy room. This seems the cruellest reaction to something so minor, doesn't it? The fervently religious appear to be particularly in favour of this gross invasion of adolescent privacy.

Teenagers are building their identity, coping with school, peer groups, new emotions and a changing body; the last thing on their minds is tidying their room. And no, it is not a sign of disrespect or some kind of flouting of the rules of gratefulness, it is probably that they simply don't notice the mess. If they do, it doesn't bother them and right now they have bigger things to deal with. Their rooms are spaces of safety for them; don't disturb the fabric of their new, evolving life by interfering here. This is an exciting period of change for them and sometimes I think it is an honour to be part of that. Other times I'd just like to be able to see the carpet and pick up the piles of dirty washing without stabbing myself with my one pair of good nail scissors, which are tossed carelessly into those piles, but that's not really that important to them either, is it? Sure, it would be more logical to keep desks clear for homework or to have some general sense of order, albeit a more chaotic one than an adult may opt for, but in the big scheme of things, a messy room is not causing the biggest of problems, unless they seek you out and ask you to help them tidy it. You can of course ask if they want that kind of help but mine never have. They resist it with fury.

Sure, you can keep an eye out for the stuff they lose in the mess that you know they will need when you intermittently pop in for the dirty plates. But there are more important things to disagree on, more important ways you can help. I try to view the mess as a sign of independence. I cannot touch my daughters' stuff any more because they are no longer children. They are learning to be independent and that is a good thing. You don't have to approve of all the ways they do that.

So my advice to you is take a deep breath, wash your hands after you've collected their grubby washing and all those tea cups and plates with odd crumbs on them, and close that door until they are eighteen. Then you go into an empty, tidy room after they have left you and you'll stand there sobbing your heart out at the marks on the wall where their pictures used to be, wishing you couldn't see the carpet and that this room was once again filled with piles of empty plastic bags, till receipts, dirty pants, smelly oversized trainers, half of Depop's denim offering, the dog's missing lead, many of the belongings you've been looking for in the past five years and a dog-eared Christmas card from Grandma when they were five.

12

Finding other mothers

(And why other people's teenagers
are nicer to you than yours)

When my eldest first started dating her then seventeen-year-old boyfriend, he would spend much time with us at home. He was delightful. Six feet of smiley pleases and thank yous. He said good morning cheerily, washed up his dishes, replaced finished loo rolls with new ones and put the lid back on the jam. He would even chat about what he was going to do that day, sharing information freely without complaining about infringement of his human rights. 'Why,' I would hiss to Mr Candy, 'are other people's teenagers nice to us while ours talk to us like we're trying to sell them PPI? They're like terriers and my eldest's teen boyfriend is like a lovely Labrador.' When I congratulated the boyfriend's mother on raising an adorable young man, she said she had no idea what I was talking about, as he hadn't spoken to her since 2015.

Meanwhile, the mother of my second daughter's best friend tells me our teen is the politest of visitors. 'We adore Grace,' they say, going on to describe her as 'a ray of sunshine' and 'the perfect house guest'. She seems to be this Opposite Grace at their house: not just more polite, as we all are at other people's homes, but with an entirely different personality to the one we know. I think teenagers like to show off their best behaviour in other people's homes because they like to bask in the glow of praise from someone else's parents, which they maybe find more valuable than our glow, and perhaps they have that secret feline thing where they love to get the praise in front of the friends who live there. An adolescent one-upmanship? My more optimistic theory is that teens who feel secure at home have to test their developing personality on the people least likely to reject them for bad behaviour – that's you and me.

Lucky us. I'm occasionally inclined to introduce a code of family conduct, insisting on more friendly behaviour at home, like one of those posters that have obvious 'In this house we . . .' mantras on them, but I don't because my teenagers, like yours, are a glorious work in progress. I have instead decided to see the humour in their grumpy ways – after all, they won't be living with us much longer. 'My only crime,' I tell them when they're at their most disagreeable, 'is to love you.'

What I did do when I realised other people could be the key to getting the best out of my teens was put women around them who they will talk to and be open with – godmothers, and younger, cooler female friends of mine who could guide them. 'Other mothers', as it were. I hope this has been helpful to them. Grace's amazing godmother Nina takes her for lunches, cinema trips and all manner of outings where she is, by all accounts, chatty, positive and pleasant company. They watch horror films together and text each other all the time. Grace rarely texts me.

The theory of 'other mothers' is well known and widely used, especially in places where an actual village does raise a child. It's something to consider around the age of twelve for your daughter. In his book *Raising Girls* the renowned Australian psychologist Steve Biddulph calls them 'aunties', and they are often older, wiser women who perhaps have more time to be consistently available. Godmothers are good, as are sisters-in-law or non-judgemental grandparents. I've been lucky to have a mother-in-law whose caring nature and surprisingly modern attitude to life has been an invaluable source of comfort for my eldest teen. They get on incredibly well and Grandma Pru is a wise source of loving advice (and well-cooked lasagne with peas).

And as working parents we were only able to do our jobs by employing some wonderful childcare professionals over the years and have been lucky enough to have kept in touch with our nannies, and they have proved wonderful younger voices for our daughters.

It's never too late to introduce these 'other mothers' into your daughters' lives officially or unofficially. But I think if you do, you must keep out of the relationship. What happens between them is nothing to do with you. Meanwhile, at home just make sure you pass on to the mums of visiting teens how lovely they are in your company; it's a reassuring thing to hear on the days your daughters are perhaps not being their best selves. And other people's lovely teenage daughters are often a reminder of how amazing teenage girls are in general. This is comforting.

13

Pixel and Duke:
canine love stories

(Or, side by side)

When our eldest was five we got a dog. I come from a long line of
dog loons, so much thought was put into this commitment. My
grandparents showed Dalmatians at Crufts and we often had several
rescue dogs in the small Cornish bungalow where I grew up, alongside a menagerie of other animals that people had abandoned. But
I'm under no illusions about dogs; to me they are canines, not humans
wearing fur coats, as many dog fans believe. I love all dogs but I
don't let any lick my face, because they lick their bums. I don't
romanticise the dog–owner relationship. They do not understand
what I am saying.

So I thought I knew what I was getting into when our eldest
persuaded me that a dog would be the perfect addition to the family.
When we first got Duke, an Airedale puppy, I was suspicious about
the size of his giant paws and extreme exuberance, but my husband
ignored my worries when I mentioned them. During my childhood
my family nurtured mixed-breed rescue dogs with many issues to
deal with, so we went for a pedigree, hoping it would be a simpler

beast as a family dog, easier to train perhaps. This one will be more normal, I'd thought. Well-behaved, even. But my initial suspicions about our Airedale were proved right: it turns out I know a huge, rebellious nutcase when I meet one.

Our dog was enormous. It was like having Champion the Wonder Horse in the house – with four small children. The fact he had the IQ of Jedward wasn't his fault, nor was the fact he was diabetic, which made him a bit incontinent and meant he needed to be injected twice a day with insulin. The fact he was extremely naughty, however, was his fault. We had three dog trainers try and tame Godzilla the Canine, one of whom said the most he could do was teach him to sit. He failed. Duke was loveable but such hard work, and when the children were small it was a step too far. 'Don't get a dog,' I'd tell anyone who would listen at that time, after he'd stolen and eaten an onion whole with unfortunate consequences, too awful to go into here, or jumped into the lake in Regent's Park again overturning the pedalos. But Sky, my eldest, adored him. She is a dog loon. She'd lie on his bed, gently stroking this giant dog as he slept. He sat at her feet as she began revising for exams; he provided hours of entertainment and didn't show a flicker of temper as the smaller children pulled his tail or poked his various orifices. He was so naughty, though, we were known locally as 'the family with that Airedale'. Sky would get furious if I shouted at him. She wouldn't hear a bad word about him – it was true love, and when the end finally came for Duke, Sky's bravery was unbearable but impressive to watch. She was fourteen, he was just ten, blind and by now completely incontinent with a tendency to epileptic fits (much of it due to his diabetes). He'd lived a long time despite his condition and on the day the vet asked us to bring him in because he was in too much pain to go on, Sky was holding his dinosaur-sized head as he was put down. I was so proud of her. She asked to be there and we respected her wishes.

The timing couldn't have been worse: exams, puberty and the death of your dog – we didn't factor any of this in when we got him. You might want to check the timeline of any dog-buying plans. We spent a year animal-free, revelling in the lack of work he'd been associated with but missing him terribly. A big dog with young kids is ill advised but what I didn't know was that a dog with teenagers is invaluable; it's almost a must-have and should be prescribed by the experts. Three years ago we got Pixel, a miniature version of an Airedale called a Welsh Terrier. She is a little dog, so when you want to remove her from a situation, you can pick her up, which does make life easier if your dog is a little unpredictable. She's the noisiest, messiest and often worst-behaved member of our family, but she is also now sort of the main character that holds our family life together. Sometimes when connections are lost, she is the one who re-establishes them. I hadn't realised how many of our domestic rituals and group conversations revolved around our smelly, energetic fur ball. Any worries I'd originally had about adding the extra responsibility of a dog to a household already busy, with two working parents and four children, now seem incomprehensible. All our children love her, but the teens are particularly attached. She is like the fifth child, the fourth daughter. If you are thinking about adding a four-legged friend to the family unit with teens, my advice would be: don't wait another minute. Apart from the unconditional love she gives, there are extra benefits for those of us with older kids. As your children grow up, a dog doesn't just stave off parental loneliness, they also encourage adolescents to spend more time at home. My eldest daughter loves that dog so much, I sometimes wish she would look at me the way she looks at Pixel or the Little Barkatron, as we call her. As Nora Ephron once wrote, you have to get a dog when you have teenagers so that at least one person is pleased to see you when you get home. And it turns out that a small dog gently snoozing on your lap is the most comforting accessory for long hours of A-level revision. We also used our little terrier as a safety net for our son when he started wanting to go out on his own at the age of ten. I agreed to let him walk to the nearby shop – if the dog accompanied him. The most-used phrase in our house of a weekend is 'take the dog'. She was our focus for the day during the summer of lockdown too: the 6 p.m. dog walk was something we all took part in as our hour out of the house. And as I explore in chapters 20 and 26, side by side is the best way to talk to teens during difficult times, and the dog walk is the perfect moment to do this.

Owning a dog is one of the best forms of family bonding – we lap up her non-judgemental attention, her genuine joy at seeing each of us every morning and the lovely sense of belonging she creates. She won't come when she is called, she is hell-bent on barking her way into the record books and we are now known as 'that family with the noisy Welsh Terrier'. But she is vital for our teenagers' mental health. She's the matriarch, and much of our daily life revolves around her. We're lucky to have her. As someone once said, dogs are not our whole lives, but they make our lives whole.

'Mum, What's Wrong With You?'
Conversations with Teens

Me: Take your keys when you go out.

Her: I don't need them.

Me: Take them in case we are out when you get back.

Her: What is wrong with you? You *never* go out.

Me: For god's sake, just take your keys.

Her: I have lost my keys.

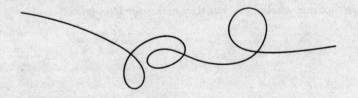

14

No one told me about pre-drinking

When you tell people you are hosting a teenage birthday party at home, they will fire out unforgettable horror stories unprompted. Rather like the way parents load you up with gory birth tales involving forceps and episiotomy stitches the moment you tell them you're expecting.

Everyone warned us. Mums and dads with older teens felt compelled to regale us with tales of trips to A & E clutching lifeless, drunk adolescents, drug-induced comas on bathroom-floor tiles and orgies on your youngest's Fireman Sam duvet.

We felt people were exaggerating but took the hint and downgraded plans for our eldest's sixteenth party at home to a 'gathering'. It was a pre-lockdown summer, and we agreed fifteen people could attend, there would be a guest list that I could tick off on the door, and no one who had heard about it 'on social media' would be allowed in. It would be manageable and, as far as these things go, civilised. My eldest happily agreed to it, no doubt planning other things out and about that we were not party to.

My husband now refers to the gathering as one of the worst nights of his parenting life so far. It was one more thing to add to the list of 'I didn't see that coming'. Another 'It was all such a shock' anecdote. Like childbirth, you don't believe the stories until you are in the story.

But it wasn't shocking just because of all the tipsy tomfoolery; it was shocking because it induced a melancholy parental grief I would rather not have experienced so viscerally on a Friday night. There is a raw sadness seeing your beloved little ones being so grown-up. I can't save your soul from this sadness, obviously, because you're either going to host a party that goes wrong, go out and come back to find you've accidentally hosted a party that has gone wrong, or pick your teenager up from a party that has gone wrong. I don't make the rules; this is just what happens.

I have a friend whose daughter's party ended up in the newspapers after the mum returned from a night away to find everything ruined when hundreds of uninvited guests arrived, and another remembers the night her daughter swore she was having a quiet evening in with a few mates, but when she returned, the house had been ransacked and someone had cut holes in all her husband's suits, as well as nearly setting light to their bedroom. All the wine had been drunk and the kitchen was wrecked. Another tells the tale of her sixteen-year-old triplets promising on their grandfather's life that they had not had a party, after being left home in charge overnight for the first time, only to have the neighbour pop round in a state of shock to talk about the huge party that had occurred the night before.

When teens first start to get together, no matter how small or large the group is, when alcohol is involved, it usually goes belly-up, as an Australian friend of mine is wont to say.

I do have some titbits of advice, though, that can save you from some of the more extreme elements of the teenage party. If you've got a tween right now and know this lies on the horizon, I can soften the edges. Or you can just keep saying no, which really is the only way to prevent any possible disasters happening in front of your eyes.

Firstly, I am telling you about pre-drinking, because no one told me and even though it seems obvious, I had not factored it in when we put out some low-alcohol bottles of beer for guests, thinking we were being liberal, understanding parents helping our teen look grown-up, yet restrained. Sky was the last one in her set to turn sixteen, the youngest in her year, in fact, so everyone else would be older and be used to beer, we assumed innocently.

Our teens had been having the odd glass of wine, fizz or beer on special occasions from the age of fifteen, and in the UK sixteen-year-olds can have wine with family meals in restaurants. We'd hoped that allowing them to test their limits would prove useful; we didn't want to be like the parents who banned sugar, only for their kids to go mental at other people's birthday parties, wolfing down Haribo like Bez on a night out at the Hacienda in 1995. On the other hand, we didn't want to be 'party parents' and completely accept teenage drinking from the age of sixteen onwards, because if you do that then you remove the excuse your teens can rely on when they want to turn a drink down: that their parents disapprove. It is a tricky line to tread. So, if you feel our party tips would be useful, then here goes:

Don't do glass bottles. Cans are, of course, more sensible. You know this!

Hide your own booze. The teenage friends who've been coming over since they were born will just head for your bottles of booze with a distinct lack of fear, as if helping themselves to custard cream biscuits, so familiar are they with your home, and in their inebriated state their politeness guard is down.

Do supply as much water or soft drinks as possible. Oceans of it.

Whatever time you start, your guests will be no doubt be tipsy or something on arrival. This is pre-drinking. A fellow mum told me I should take all bags and coats on the doorstep and then frisk those bags and coats for bottles of booze. I smugly did this, but it was a waste of time, as it seemed to us that most of the drinkers had drunk all their booze before they got to us at 8 p.m. – they were safeguarding against this parental safeguarding.

We said we'd stay upstairs out of the way, watching telly with the two younger siblings, but I estimate we spent eight minutes upstairs the whole evening. Most of that time was spent making a list of things I should have done before anyone arrived: this included fencing off the ancient trampoline, hiding the kids' bikes, putting cushions at the bottom of the garden steps, removing the old toddler scooters from the shed, ditto Frisbees, and ordering double the amount of nibbles (enough is never enough).

Teenagers find their inner toddler when fuelled by even small amounts of alcohol. This was most unexpected. At one point our tiny back garden (and remember there were only fifteen of them) looked like one of those soft-play centres, as huge bodies in hoodies hurled themselves around, fighting over a three-wheeled Barbie scooter and flinging the dog's ball at each other's faces. We had to police all this efficiently. I think every single one of them fell down the steps at some point, falling loosely, though, in a soft, child-like way, thank god, otherwise it would have been a broken-wrist count of about twenty-five. I was handing out plasters in the same way I did when they were five.

And you should also know that the most helpful teen, the one that calls you by your surname in a polite, respectful way, will probably be the most sozzled.

As a helpful drunk myself, I recognised this early on, mostly because this only works until you fall over. I encouraged one teen, who I'd never met before, to sit down quietly. That was easily the most helpful thing he could do, instead of ricocheting off the kitchen cupboards offering to help tidy up while continuously going into the coat cupboard to search for a loo.

You'd be surprised how easy it is to lose count of teens; it was like herding cats, trying to keep them all downstairs. At one point I felt like a character in a Monty Python farce. Doors were opening and shutting as teens in various states of inebriation chaotically came in and out of rooms. Two adults is not enough: I had to rope the-then eleven-year-old in to shout 'clear' every time he checked a bedroom for a guest.

Do remember it is best to provide non-tomato-based foodstuffs for those who overindulge and pebbledash your loo later on.

For safety, and to avoid angry parents calling the next day, we made sure everyone left in pairs. We put one pair into a cab twice, but they kept getting out the other side and coming back in again.

The responsibility of getting other people's tipsy toddler-teens home was overwhelming. And it may be just the London tribe, but I found the most inebriated teens were the ones whose parents regularly told me they were lucky because their youngsters 'weren't really interested in alcohol or drugs'.

I lived in fear of taking the blame for a teen that had overindulged, if her parents believed she was an angel. They might be furious with her but they would no doubt blame us for getting her into the state in which she arrived home.

This shows perhaps that we cannot assume we know anything about the newly forming adult characters of our own children either, as they go about discovering life outside the safety net of home. What boundaries will they be pushing, risks will they be taking when we're not there? Brace yourself for this realisation.

We started getting requests to go to parties when our eldest hit thirteen. It felt too soon but was of course inevitable, teenagers like to go out and socialise, this is normal behaviour. Play dates were replaced by invite-only parties, where they were sometimes being asked to pay to go in. Who pays to go to a party? '*Everyone*, Mum. What is wrong with you?'

Some parties, we were told, 'started at 10 p.m. and would be on the heath'. 'Outside, on the heath, in October?' '*Yes*, Mum. What is wrong with you?'

Requests to go out were thrown at me as I was on the loo, on a work phone call or involved in any other activity, which meant I could be bamboozled by confusing fact-free conversations.

'So-and-so is having a house party. Everyone is going. I have to be there. It's in Essex. Somewhere.'

Often there is no who, what, when to these parties. One was actually a two-hour Tube ride away and would have involved staying overnight 'next door to the party at another house'.

My Friday 4 p.m. phone calls at work from my early teen girls became so predictable my colleagues could have answered them for me.

'What time does it end/will there be booze, boys, bouncers? Is an adult going to be in the house? Who is going? What is the postcode? Do the parents know about this? Really? So if I rang them now, they would be OK?'

'Why would you do that, Mum? What is wrong with you?'

You need nerves of steel as party world begins, plus the ability to quiz your adolescent as calmly as Agatha Christie's Poirot and the emotional strength to set some boundaries around it all, not because you don't want them to go (although of course you would rather they be Velcroed to their beds throughout this distinctly terrifying time). No, you do want them to go forth and have fun, but you also want them to think about the practicalities of partying themselves, because the general last-minute nature of all of it is probably the most terrifying thing about it. The lack of planning, their lack of thinking around it – all caused in part by their evolving neurology, which makes them more prone to taking risks but having no adult skill to judge the severity of the risk.

I would often utter 'no postcode, no party' and this would encourage our girls to at least find out exactly how far away they were going for a party they were only really half-interested in being at.

In the early teens I'd talk to as many parents in my daughters' gang as possible on party nights, because some of them had teens who were better at planning a night out, and some had older siblings happy to drive them, stay with them and collect our stray teens. It would be about finding and sharing as much information as possible.

I didn't ask for access to our girls' phones because it felt like invading their privacy and I hoped my more liberal approach to going out would encourage them to share more. And I believe it did. They would be open with details of things that had gone wrong sometimes, or volunteer enough information for me to form a picture of who, what, where and when, which made it easier to say yes or no to the party in question. I worried that we should have issued an out-and-out ban on drinking and not just made it known we didn't like them to get drunk, but in these times I just don't think that is realistic. I discovered offering to host the pre-party meet-up (more of a female thing than teen-boy behaviour) meant I got to meet any new friends in the mix and could observe the mood of the evening before they went out.

All of it, of course, requires triple the patience of anything else you've ever done, because inside you're desperate to shout, 'No, no, no! Go to your room and watch *The Gruffalo*!' but you have to remain non-critical or judgemental (or silent in your critical judgement) because you want them to feel they can tell you things when it goes wrong and call you if they need you. But you also need to set some boundaries with consequences if they break them, because as I have mentioned before, teenagers without boundaries may worry you don't care enough about them if you don't set them. It's for everyone's peace of mind, you are not being a 'cool mum' if you let them work all this out themselves, you are, in my opinion, playing with fire.

We set some ground rules: locations had to be divulged and a time of return adhered to, but this time was open for negotiation during the planning of the night out, because I felt they had to have some input into everything. That way they felt more in control and less likely to rebel against hard-and-fast rules, which every expert will tell you may create a culture of secretive behaviour. Sometimes we got it right, sometimes we got it wrong. I hope we made them feel they could help set the rules, but I also hope they knew there were boundaries that kept them safe. And consequences for overstepping those boundaries.

When I interviewed the writer Neal Thompson in 2018 about his two sons' issues with smoking cannabis, he told me his biggest regret about parenting was that he wished he'd learned to 'worry less, and breathe more' earlier on in the teenage journey.

'You think you can muscle your kids through teens into adulthood and that when they fail, you have failed too. They make their own decisions. Failure is a necessary part of the process; they learn through failure,' he told me. The best thing he did with his two rebellious, skateboarding boys, he says, is teach them right from wrong. 'The rest is up to them,' he added.

A harsher curfew can work to some extent if the partying gets out of control and warnings are not being heeded, and while grounding was an effective deterrent for breaches of the agreement with our second child, our first was not always put off by the threat of them. Sometimes I wish we had come up with more ingenious punishments when ours did something potentially dangerous, like maybe ask them to read *Crime and Punishment* out loud at breakfast or try to explain how FaceTime works to an elderly relative (the true definition of patience and punishment). The novelist Jackie Clune once told me she asked hers to watch her dance to her favourite song in the kitchen as a punishment. It's an effective deterrent: 'They never make it to the end before promising not to do whatever they have done again!'

Ultimately this bit of parenting a teen reinforces the overarching rule that patient, non-judgemental love plus boundaries may be the best combination for looking after your maturing children. It's really the theme of psychotherapist Philippa Perry's bible on raising children, *The Book You Wish Your Parents Had Read (and Your Children Will be Glad That You Did)*. You have to calmly state your limits before a boundary is crossed, which may push you beyond your limits, after which you'll react with frustrated anger. And the row that then ensues may shut down all form of communication, which can be unhelpful in the long run, and the road ahead is definitely a long one.

The thing I knew would tip me into furious rage would be worrying about where they were and not knowing how to get them if anything went wrong. For me, the drink, drugs or, indeed, sex weren't the issue – it was the fear that I couldn't rescue them from danger if I didn't know where they were. We tried to explain our limits clearly and with honesty before the girls reached them. Again, sometimes it worked, other times the grey areas caused problems. I would say midnight is the cut-off point for me until they are sixteen, because I can't handle not knowing when they'll be back after then. Even when my eldest hit eighteen and was still at home, I insisted she gave us a rough idea of her return time and text us when she was on the way home.

At times I followed Philippa's advice and I didn't make it their problem, more my problem, which they were helping me with, for example, reassuring me of return times. I hoped that would work better than saying, 'If you don't get home by midnight, you'll be banned from going out for a month.' Often these more severe threats are impossible to carry out anyway and cause a diabolical atmosphere at home for weeks if the breach occurs. But perhaps if you make it about you, then you're setting a boundary defined by your feelings and being honest about that. And boundaries make them feel loved: they are a sign you care about them. If you cannot set boundaries or, worse still, you encourage the partying in an attempt to be a friend rather than a parent it will be scary for your children: they may well feel lost. (I have witnessed this so many times and find it inexplicable behaviour on the part of the parent; please avoid it if you are tempted.)

This is such a confusing time – for them and for you. Much experimentation will occur and I am afraid I cannot offer a hard-and-fast set of parenting rules because each teenager is different and they develop at different rates, so you will have to use your instinct. I always hoped something as simple to understand as 'I don't like it when I have to worry about you in the early hours of the morning' is an easier problem to solve for them than weighing up whether you'll carry out your more extreme threats of curfew for infringements of rules. Perhaps trying this out is less of a battle and more of a conversation? And you can of course answer 'let me think about that' to any partying requests that worry you before deciding what to do. A little time to consider makes both parties think about the request more thoroughly.

But sorting it all out in advance helps head off a possible row. My husband sometimes finds it hard to set boundaries; and would often agree something else after the initial agreement about return time had been set. We had long, tense discussions about this early on, after I'd read a few books about teens that strongly advised against trying to be their mates instead of their parents. He realised he would have hated being told what to do at this age himself and it somehow worried him we were saying things like, 'Unless we know the address, you won't be going, because it makes us nervous not knowing where you are,' to the kids.

So we also had to be honest with each other about what we needed from our teens to ensure we defined our boundaries together and didn't use all sorts of spurious reasons for wanting them home, which weren't entirely true and generally amounted to us subconsciously pleading for them not to grow up. Maybe that is what you are doing sometimes when you find yourself in a more dictatorial place around partying and going out?

Through all this I think I learned that I did trust the girls to be as sensible as any teenager could be while wanting to experiment and have fun, and I did *want* them to have fun and I did want to be able to say 'I trust you will make the safest choices for you' and leave them to make those decisions. I accepted mistakes would be made.

I knew how stubborn they could both be as well, and saw no point in setting non-negotiable boundaries, no matter how tempting that was, coming from a childhood of non-negotiable boundaries myself. It would have made me feel safe, as it was learned behaviour, but would they have dug their heels in and felt we didn't trust them and perhaps rebelled more?

It's like you're both looking over the top of a cliff and you, the adult, is saying, 'Step back, you might fall. It looks terrifying!' and they are saying, 'Wow, the view is amazing! Can I jump? It'll be fantastic.'

There was one point, though, when I realised the teens were sometimes looking for a way out of a party they'd agreed to go to. So it is important to have firm boundaries or they cannot rely on you as an excuse to get out of things that frighten them and save face with their peers.

They'd make it sound oddly dangerous, waiting for me to refuse them permission to go. I noted there were nights where they'd rather stay in but said yes because they felt they should under the peer pressure of FOMO. I had to try and work this out without directly addressing it as an issue, and save face all round.

We agreed they should text 'I'll be home soon' as code if they actually wanted us to come and get them early in a dire circumstance or from somewhere they felt uncomfortable. We also downloaded a black taxi app so they could swiftly remove themselves from any unwanted situations and we could track its movements. This was paid for by part of pocket money at first, then I realised that for our own peace of mind we would just pay for it, which is what you do as a parent if you can, and I know we were lucky to be able to afford this and that we lived in a city where this is possible. I often worried it meant they had a cushion to fall back on, one I didn't have as a teenager, which made me think more about the places I went and the hours I stayed out. But those were different times: I grew up in a rural place with no mobile phones. It isn't comparable and though it is hard not to compare, you cannot really do that for your teenager. And they are not you: they are all so different and unique that you have to adapt the rules for each sibling on the going-out-and-getting-wasted front. Often they would club together for an Uber, or perhaps get a lift from an obliging parent, but it all came from good communication.

Ultimately we had to let go. We had to trust them and let them find the edges of their own adventures, as we did when they were younger and crossing the road alone for the first time or getting the bus home from school instead of being picked up. But gosh, it required a deep breath, and you should know that just as their weekend social life ramps up, yours has to wind down, since you're on call Friday and Saturday now for party-related emergencies.

And they just disappear on weekend evenings after the age of about fourteen. They are gone as soon as it hits twilight. In later teens they come back in the early hours (our yappy dog is a sign for us of their return). They stay up later after they return and cook abominable food combinations or drink your holiday liqueurs, thinking you won't work it out (I mean, no one in their right mind has limoncello any more, do they?), and watch TV. Side note: you need to brace yourself for the later teen years when you are greeted with a massive mess in the kitchen on a weekend morning after late-night partygoers come home and decide fifty packets of chicken Super Noodles are the thing to have right now. They'll cook them and forget to eat them after falling asleep watching *Finding Nemo* on telly (true story) then they take themselves off to bed, leaving a greasy noodle-water film over every surface.

So, back to the sixteenth birthday and there were never two more exhausted parents than us when we finally ushered the last guest out of the house at 1 a.m. We didn't know we'd actually had quite a tame evening until we caught up with friends who'd gone out for dinner the evening their teenager had a gathering for her sixteenth. When they returned half the hall carpet had been pulled up, there was pizza on the kitchen ceiling and all the plants in the back garden had been thrown at an upstairs window. Crates of beer had been drunk, as the cellar door had been forced open. The thirty people they agreed to host had turned into at least a hundred and carnage had ensued.

My husband and I often wondered if the offspring of teetotal parents were perhaps less likely to get as drunk as they could at a party. Maybe for them booze was not something that they worried about experimenting with, peer pressure or no peer pressure? I don't know any teetotal parents so I cannot answer this.

But our girls were pretty disapproving of us having a drink in their early teens for some inexplicable reason, and they started to give us the condescending adolescent side-eye every time we poured a second glass of wine. My Dry Januarys seemed to cause them much mirth.

Yet I have friends who smoke in front of their children, which I find shocking, and friends who won't have a coffee after midday in case it sets a bad example to their teens. I wrestled with the dilemma of the teens seeing us tipsy. While I am not an obsessive partygoer in the manner of *Ab Fab*'s Patsy Stone, I do like a good night out and I would wonder if they were influenced by us occasionally staying up with friends to dance round the living room to ABBA (the shame of the ABBA probably worse than the drunkenness).

I interviewed the US psychologist Ann Smith about this. She wrote *Overcoming Perfectionism: Finding the Key to Balance and Self-Acceptance* and is a specialist on counselling children with alcohol issues in the family.

I was reassured when she told me a certain amount of parental guilt is a sign of love, that 'good enough' is better than perfect when it comes to being a mum or dad.

Ignore your judgey adolescents, she said, because you cannot bullet-proof their childhood, but you can do your best to make growing up a 'satisfying' experience for them, a goal I love the idea of.

'You can still be you,' she added. Her mantra is to focus on the now, the process of parenting today rather than the outcome of all the effort put in. And, personally, I decided to be relaxed around the issue of my teens occasionally drinking or witnessing us doing so. My main worry is smoking and, more specifically, vaping, because of the health risks, which I thought were more quantifiable and felt more dangerous to me (I mean, I know you could say the same about booze, but as a non-smoker this felt an easier argument to have. I suspect we all have different opinions here).

Zoë Bailie at The Mix website and charity told me the issue around vapes isn't that young people will see them as a gateway to illegal drugs or even as actual cigarettes, but more that they become a 'psychological crutch' and a habit hard to break. If your teen is vaping or smoking, she advises keeping the conversation open and make sure you consistently rebuff the myth that some things are safer than others.

Part of me worries that it is irresponsible just to let them work their own way through the kind of experimenting we perhaps did when young, because I have written many features about addiction and interviewed many addicts so I know how hard it is to recover or indeed get professional help to recover. But I am not inclined to look through knicker drawers or school bags in search of evidence of teen vaping: the invasion of privacy feels wrong to me though I have met many mums who do and see this as justifiable behaviour. But, if you find something, in all likelihood you'll need to 'fess up to some pretty atrocious rule-breaking as a parent too. Some parents are comfortable with this (the old 'under my roof' explanation) but I am not, I feel privacy is extremely important for teenage girls and there is no excuse for going through their stuff secretly.

The good news is that statistics show fewer and fewer teens are smoking. However, the urge to experiment is still there and while there is little information on vaping among teens in the UK, it is known that numbers of young e-cigarette users are rising in both sexes. It is too early to have any exact science on the long-term effects of vapes and although it is recognised as being safer than smoking, it is definitely not 'safe'. All you can do if you know for sure that your teen is vaping is explain why it upsets you and guide them to read about the fears many medical experts have on the long-term effects of such a habit.

As the girls have gone through their experimental stages I have found a more open approach from me, i.e. neither critical nor judge-mental, seems to encourage an honesty we had not expected. Perhaps patient and focused listening around this issue and a less hard-line view of life as a teenager may be a good path to tread?

All I know is that threatening your daughter with punishments may not have the desired effect: she may focus on the threats rather than the fact that lung cancer is a killer and smoking is one of the most unhealthy things you can do in life. Your chats could be more about the risks she is taking, not the way you'll punish her if she goes down that route. In fact, I have never threatened any kind of formal punishment for overindulgence of this kind. I always felt their focus would be on defying me rather than avoiding putting themselves in harm's way if I did that. Experimenting with things like vapes may be part of teenage developmental behaviour.

Indeed, many adolescents hate authority and will do the opposite, so try to bite your tongue – if you can – while setting reasonable boundaries around their behaviour in the home and communicating your feelings around vaping, smoking and drinking.

Remember, everyone's circumstances are different. Please don't judge other mums during this time, or other teens; avoid comparisons to the behaviour of other teenage girls you know and focus on your teens. It is heartbreaking to see a family in crisis because of teens' behaviour around drink, drugs and smoking, don't add to anyone else's stress on this. Just be vigilant: just keep checking in, quietly and calmly. Observe what is going on with your daughter. You cannot and will not know everything about her life, but each day is a chance to connect with her and give her the space to talk to you about anything she is worried about. And once again, don't expect the worst, as catastrophising helps no one.

And now at least you now know about pre-drinking. You can thank me later.

'Mum, What's Wrong With You?'
Conversations with Teens

Me: I've managed to get the laundry done, wash up, strip the beds, walk the dog *and* do thirty mins YouTube exercise this morning. What about that?

Her: What's your point, Mum? I have done sixteen years of being Epic. What about that?

15

Going out out

Ski mask the slump god and generation Xanax

If you are the parent who shouts, 'For god's sake don't get a tattoo,' every time your teen goes to Westfield shopping mall, this chapter may be uncomfortable reading. But stay with me, because we know adolescents may be inclined to take risks without evaluating the consequences in a way adults are not, and so we all know drugs may come into their world at some point, whether at parties, ye olde festivals or, more latterly, the playground, where you may have read that Generation Xanax has been germinating. I am hoping this chapter will put an overactive parental mind at rest. It'll at least help with your WAT face, as I call it (Worried All the Time).

Obviously, between writing this and the book coming out, all the drug slang will have changed and so undoubtedly will the drugs being bought, sold and taken. For example, a few years ago I had never seen those little silver helium canisters that litter the roads so routinely. Now I absentmindedly kick them out of the way as I pick up dog poo on our daily walks.

A survey published in 2019 revealed that teens aged eleven to fifteen are less likely to drink and smoke, but one in four have tried drugs, and many studies imply teenage girls may be more susceptible to trying drugs because they perhaps fold quicker under peer pressure. Drugs like marijuana are often more powerful than when we were exposed to them many moons ago, so we are, of course, right to be worried. I can't offer you reassurance that if your little one tumbles headfirst down a hedonistic rabbit hole that they will come out unharmed, because the circumstances around each teen are different and, to some extent, we have to hold our breaths and see what happens, but my experience so far appears to have been similar to that of the majority of our parent peers. But I have felt the heartbreak of parents who lose their teens to drugs either temporarily or for what has felt like the longest time. Vigilance is your strongest weapon on the drug front line at home.

I first started worrying about drugs in the days when music festivals were the summer rite of passage for teens. Mine would give me a seven-minute warning to book tickets out of the blue for these mass gatherings. I'd be instructed to get in the phone queue immediately before tickets sold out for events like Wireless, Boardmasters or Reading.

My two eldest, then aged fourteen and fifteen, would tell me with serious urgency that they desperately needed to see a list of bands I'd never heard of (Ski Mask the Slump God, anyone?) or they would risk becoming social pariahs. Plus they just loved music, couldn't get enough of it. After a rigorous conversation on the chores they would need to do to earn the price of their tickets (or after pocket money and birthday money had been handed over), we would call the tiresome hotline because 'that's what everyone else's mum is doing'. They couldn't do that themselves, obviously, because they had to go to school: for some reason I was always on this phone line before school.

When festivals became a thing for us I rang Fiona Stewart, who owns and runs the Green Man Festival in the Brecon Beacons, in a mild panic about drugs. She has worked in festival land for more than twenty years and had sound advice. Firstly she recommended we google any event our teen wanted to go to without us by typing in the name and the word 'incident'. Obvious, really, I just hadn't thought of it. And whether Covid-19 affects the format festivals take in the future or not, there will be events or places your kids want to go to that you should probably google in advance.

Then you can try to have a calm chat about the event and the incidents with your teen in a low-key, non-fearful way. Perhaps make them aware of the risk, should they choose to take it. Fiona pointed out most of these events are designed for adults, most even expect under-18s to be accompanied by an adult. Make yourself aware of the risks, check the programme thoroughly and absorb site maps.

Her most memorable piece of advice was to let your children know that if they buy drugs from people at such events, or anywhere, really, it has probably been smuggled up someone's bum at some point. Could that horrify them enough to say no to drugs sold on the streets, to not buy things from strangers in crowds? I hoped so, but a niggle in the back of my mind always remained. If I had smuggled drugs up my bum then we are definitely safe – my daughters would never touch that – but a stranger may not bother them so much.

The consequences of their actions can be less obvious to our teens than to us, and when talking about drugs, you can try to get them to focus on the possible outcomes of their behaviour, but at the same time be careful not to exaggerate. Regaling them with tales of horrific heroin overdoses or stories of teens who've died after smoking one joint is not a deterrent. I think it probably has the opposite effect and makes you look like you don't know what you're talking about, tempting as scaring the wits out of them may be. And there is no specific scientific evidence that a so-called milder drug is a gateway drug to another more dangerous drug – so many factors are at play here, with teenagers' reactions to drugs or propensity to try them. Several of the experts I talked to cited many reasons children become addicted to drugs, based on their environment (rich or poor), circumstances, personality and neurology. No one thing is to blame. But try not to assume the worst and wave every terribly sad drug story involving teenagers under their nose every day. Also, many teens are at that stage of not really believing parents when they talk about facts. So perhaps it's better coming from someone they are slightly in awe of rather than their idiot parents.

School warnings of drugs are often dismissed out loud without a second thought, though I do think some of the actual facts do slip past the net of denial. We felt that it was good to tell them how scared we were of them taking drugs, to set some kind of family code on it, to register our disapproval of it, because we were frightened for them.

And yes, you need to remind them constantly that taking drugs is against the law and the consequences of that cannot be ignored for their future. But teenagers are in a strange limbo world of new-found freedoms – they want to try things. And they may be susceptible to peer pressure too. Especially when they hit sixteen and are legally allowed to do a lot more than they could before. Ultimately what you're trying to do, according to Mandy Saligari, an addiction counsellor I have spoken to several times about adolescent drug use, is stop a habit forming. You can't control your teens' exposure to drugs or, indeed, control your teen (that's impossible and not something you should be aiming for), but you can highlight the dangers as you see them, ignoring the eye-rolling as you do so. Just make sure you have the correct facts when you do the talking.

At one point, fearful of all the headlines about antidepressants like Xanax being used by teenagers to relieve anxiety during what they perceived as tough times, I watched a video on the website Vice, where a drug dealer was interviewed.

117

I wish I hadn't, and I had to keep repeating the mantra 'don't always assume the worst' on a loop in my mind. In the video he explained how pupils bought the pills for anything between 30p and £3 from him to alleviate 'the stress of anxiety'. It puts them in a calm bubble, he said, describing the zombie-like influence of the pills he sold on Instagram.

Drugs like Xanax may be perceived as less dangerous by teens, like weed, but users build up a tolerance and have to take more and more for it to have the desired effect. 'I see it take the spark out of their eyes,' the dealer told the young reporter quizzing him. He went on to explain that it is very hard for a parent or friend to see if their youngster is taking this drug, as there is no paraphernalia to discover covertly hidden in underwear drawers and no immediate change of behaviour is obvious.

Saligari told me in 2018 that pupils see Xanax as a low-risk chill pill and share them between each other after buying them online, a retail community I marvel is consistently allowed to exist. I mean, if a teenage girl who cannot work out how to shut a drawer properly can work out how to buy 'Xans' online, then surely the police can nip in and shut it down? If you suspect your teenager is taking this kind of drug, Saligari advises a 'shoulder to shoulder' approach rather than a more confrontational one. Be calm. Tell them they don't seem themselves. You need to be vigilant enough to spot this and ask why that might be (not every twenty minutes, though, they won't like that).

She told me that generally, in the world of young drug taking, the paranoia phase around what they have done kicks in the next day and that may be the best time to tackle them on it, not when you immediately suspect them.

'Comfort and support their conscience to teach them what they know,' says Saligari, 'Rarely should you stand between a teen and their conscience; that is the most valuable teaching opportunity there is.'

Once when our eldest, then fourteen, fibbed about where she was and I found out by accident that she wasn't on a sleepover but at a huge party, miles away, I discovered a rare inner patience. Her dad and I calmly called her and, without yelling, explained we knew she was at a party and as it was 1 a.m., we'd like her to come home to us immediately. She was instantly apologetic rather than defensive. No words of judgement were exchanged in that moment. The next day she explained everything and we felt she'd been truthful; she was incredibly apologetic and tearful about what she'd done. I like to think her conscience intervened after we'd explained how scared we were about her going to a big party without our knowledge. To be honest, I think she was glad to be rescued from such a full-on adult party, but the incident underlined for us the need to keep confrontation to a minimum in the heat of the moment or she might not have come home to us, and without knowing where she was, we would have been powerless to get her back. 'Trust their conscience' feels like something a very gullible parent would say, but Saligari is an expert and she has counselled parents through the hell of teenage drug addiction, so I am inclined to take her at her word.

I went to see the US therapist Dr Brad Reedy when he came to London in 2019 to speak about teens and drug use, interested in his different theories on how to help them. He specialises in an unreg-ulated form of wilderness therapy for teen addicts and is something of a contrarian when it comes to adolescents. I had a light-bulb moment listening to him speak, though, and enjoyed aspects of his book *The Journey of the Heroic Parent*.

In it he advocates a more hands-off approach to parenting than is currently the trend in Western culture. If you want to raise resil-ient teens, he advises, you learn to take care of yourself first and not expect them to make you happy or proud.

Reedy says Gen X focuses too much on their children's well-being rather than their own. 'We set them boundaries based on what makes us feel comfortable and happy as we parent,' he said in his talk. 'This makes them feel subconsciously responsible for our unhappiness, which is unfair.' By taking care of ourselves and attempting to iron out the psychological creases of our own childhoods and minds, we are better able to set firm, unemotional boundaries that protect our own children for their benefit rather than make us feel good about our parenting.

'You may be protecting your child from you, not the consequences of their own behaviour. They [adolescents] can work that out for themselves,' he says simply. Again, rely on their conscience.

The gist of his talk was how we complicate their lives with all our own emotional baggage, which means that, for those unfortunate enough to become addicts, so much more is involved than just their behaviour. It's a tricky message to untangle, but it's certainly worth considering reading his books if you are experiencing issues with drugs and alcohol and your teenagers. He advocates relieving your offspring of the huge burden to please you with good behaviour. Something they will rebel against at some point.

It made me stop and think and become much clearer about boundaries for my teens as they headed into this more dangerous grown-up territory. Reedy says we become too attached as parents, too controlling of the outcomes. 'Be a person, not a parent,' he concludes.

So our foray into the world of drugs is an ongoing experience.

You cannot protect them from everything and you cannot, as I have said, assume the worst. You have to try to keep a lookout to sense any changes in your daughter's behaviour, to know that if she does end up in trouble you may need to see your GP, talk to her school or find a mental-health professional to help her. Again, this is a time to keep your connection to her, to constantly and quietly check in with her, to maintain some of those rituals at home and to make sure you keep an eye on her schoolwork and what is happening with her friends, without interfering. Always the lightest of touches.

Who knows how it will pan out for our two youngest, aged four-teen and nine as I write. But we do have the older two to refer to when it comes to all this, rather than our own experiences, which are just not helpful. Ours have never asked us about our drug taking, though it is a question I wait for. A well-known friend of mine once told me she had had to sit down and tell her two young teenage girls about her cocaine-taking days of youth after the press threatened to reveal it. She said they weren't shocked, mostly embarrassed and confused as to why she was telling them.

'They appeared to make no judgement,' she said. 'Rolled their eyes, kept scrolling on their phones.'

In the end the paper didn't run the story and for many years the girls teased her by calling her 'the cocaine kingpin', as in, 'Tell the cocaine kingpin her tea is on the table.' The point is they weren't shocked; they didn't judge; they found it funny. 'I don't think they believed me,' she said. A part of her had illogically hoped they'd find Mum a little bit cooler. We all wish that sometimes, don't we, given they tease us mercilessly about lack of street cred. My eldest once asked if I could come to a pop-up drum and bass night with her, called 'My Nan Loves Disco'. A little confused by the invite, I thought it was because she didn't want to go in the door on her own, but she was so desperate to get to this club, she would resort to taking me.

'I get in free if I take my nan,' she said with a straight face.

'Mum, What's Wrong With You?'
Conversations with Teens

Me: Can you shut the kitchen drawers after you've used them, please. I keep bumping into them.

Her: Nagging. Is that what your day job is? That's the job you do, is it? Nagging me. All. Day. Long. I can't cope with you, Mum. It's too much. If you keep nagging me, I just won't do it. Can I have ketchup and gravy with that mash? What? Why are you looking at me like that? What's wrong with you?

16

A French farce

Holidays with teenagers

When we had four kids under ten I used to look at families vacationing with teenagers with envy. One day, I'd think, we'll travel light too: no buggy, no bottles, no bottoms to wipe, no deadly car-hire baby seats to complain about, no constantly asking waiters if they could warm milk up or do 'spaghetti bolognese without green bits in it'. We'll be able to stay out late, wander famous museums together, enjoy exhilarating water sports and chat about our day over exotic local cuisine.

But it is not quite like that, sadly, and I often want to call my parents, who took us camping in Cornwall every year until I left home at seventeen, and apologise for my behaviour.

With my kids I dreamed of being able to show them the bits of the world I loved, a 'to-do list of awe' that I could give them as part of our family's history. Everyone on *Desert Island Discs* is always talking about wonderful holiday memories from childhood, as if those holidays significantly shaped them. But holidays are another of those rules of retrospective appreciation for teens: they simply cannot enjoy it at the time, only the memory of it later on.

It's the Saturday before New Year's Eve, 2019. The last one of the decade, and we're on a family trip to France. The six of us have come away because I know that as our eldest two are sixteen and seventeen, this is the final New Year with us all together, ever. I know not just because I know in that melancholy way one starts to wonder 'Is this the last time?' about everything as they grow up, but because they tell us every fifteen minutes. They won't allow another one to occur 'ever', they promise.

There is, of course, much moaning about agreeing to a trip with the word 'family' in it, but by some fluke most of their friends are away too, so they are not missing out and we have not condemned them to a fate worse than death: a weekend away with mum and dad and their younger siblings.

It's not just the end of the six of us going away, it is the end of the six of us full stop, for next year Sky leaves home. Henry has just turned thirteen; his vanishing is almost upon us. And my little one, aged nine, has already started to shut her bedroom door on me. The weather is sunny when we arrive. The city, Bordeaux, is pretty. There is enough to do for three days to keep us moving. It's all good.

On day one we head out of our small hotel and walk past a circus and hear the lions roaring. 'Imagine if one escaped!' Mabel, nine, says. A long conversation follows about who it would eat first. Everyone concludes it would be me. 'You're the slowest,' they agree.

'And the largest,' my son adds, already cutting his teeth on the ritual teenage humiliation of the mother. Lions revere the female. Humans do not.

In the cathedral Sky goes into the confession box after I explain what it is for and that she has to ask for forgiveness for something she feels bad about, and she mutters, 'I stole all Mum's cotton buds,' referring to a huge row we had some time ago in which she vehemently denied going into my bathroom.

Each morning over a buffet breakfast the bickering starts as we discuss an itinerary for the day. Someone has to win. Their choice of activity must be made. They take each discussion on where to go and what to do as a personal slight, accusing you of favouring one over the other. In reality they don't really care where we go or what we do.

It is, of course, lovely to show them new things. I didn't go abroad until I was sixteen and that was for a school trip. I never went abroad with my parents because it was too expensive, so this feels like a wonderful privilege to me. And it is good to be with them away from their friends, to get them out of their rooms, frankly, and in retrospect they always speak happily of our holidays. But teenage awaydays test your patience due to their reluctance to show any sign of approval or enthusiasm for anything. This is frustrating and tiresome. I am painting this picture as a little warning of what is coming your way, for whatever you offer teens on their journey through life doesn't really matter, because you have reached Destination Ungrateful. So many mums ask me why their teens suddenly refuse to acknowledge the lovely things their parents do for them, and they feel aggrieved; this is a waste of your energy because all this is perfectly normal and there's not much, if anything, that you can do about it. Just roll with it.

As we walk around this beautiful Gallic city on the river in the sunshine, they mutter 'Why are we going here?', spontaneity is banned (god forbid you change the agreed plan) and they question every route and demand exact times for the amount of walking. No. 2 is particularly keen to know specific distances and why she has to wear a coat over her t-shirt (it is January; frost is on the grass).

They either try to walk some way away from us and we often lose them in the sightseeing crowds, which still induces the same panic as if I'd lost the nine-year-old. Or they walk exceptionally close to me, criss-crossing in front of me as they go, and asking me to hold all manner of things they have brought from their room. Pens, an orange, a book, hair bobbles and water. Teens cannot go anywhere without litres of water. But they don't hand me their room keys because they've lost those. I always used to wonder as I watched parents of teens on trips why they would be carrying backpacks. *Surely they don't need any paraphernalia?* I would think, with jealousy, looking down at our buggy. But I know now they were carrying gallons of water.

Grace is taking French GCSE this year. Her teacher tells us she is good at French, so good, in fact, that the teacher wonders if she has French relatives. It's a fluke, but the teacher praises us for letting her watch French films with subtitles and conversing with her. Neither of which has happened. I don't speak a word of it.

But she can read French at speed and has been listening to a podcast in French on the plane over. Yet in France she will not speak French. She must remain loyal to the rule book of contrary teenage behaviour.

The following scene perhaps best sums up the teenage brain. The scorpion and the frog-like logic they all display for some inexplicable reason, that horror of showing pleasure in their parents' company.

We stop for lunch at a lovely market full of tourists. The eldest samples a ham baguette and sits down to start her lunch before anyone else has got theirs. She never waits to eat. It is as if this is a solo trip for her, so self-contained is she. No. 2 is a bit cross; the walk was a few hundred metres longer than we said it would be and she feels we tricked her 'into walking miles and miles'. I don't know what else she had planned, but this is most disagreeable for her. The sun has finally come out and now she chooses to put the hood and zip up on her giant puffer coat.

Henry has ice cream. He doesn't want anything else and deems a baguette 'too French'. But No. 2 is still in shock after the horror of her accidental trek and inexplicably refuses lunch. 'There is nothing here,' she says, pointing at the massive indoor market packed with food stalls spreading as far as the eye can see. The mum from a nearby family smiles at me with sympathy.

Dad and I get some chips and a beer and settle down, and she asks how we can eat in front of her when she is so hungry. I get up and take her into the market again. She wanders behind me shaking her head at every option offered. Long after my chips have gone cold and the beer is flat and we have now walked almost as far as we did to get here, the delicious smell of food overcomes her. 'That,' she says, pointing at a baguette. She wants that, and some ham sliced from the stall next door. I speak no French, but, remember, we have been told she is practically bilingual. She refuses. I point at the bread but the French adolescent manning the stand pretends not to understand me and offers me a croissant. Grace shrugs her shoulders and stands with her arms crossed as I mime baguette and have a comedy conversation emptying my purse for the stallholder to take any payment she wants. I hand the food to Gracie with fury and she says, 'God, that was so embarrassing. How can you behave like that in public?'

When we get back she confers with her siblings about how embarrassing I am. 'She was waving her arms about everywhere and the woman had no idea what she was talking about. She just shouldn't talk to anyone from now on.' It is the first time she looks happy that day. And from thence on acts as if nothing has happened. The four of them laugh at me.

At dinner we try to chat about our adventures, but the two teens remain unenthusiastic. Instead they show us TikToks they like.

But when we get back home, I often hear them telling friends about the things we did in Bordeaux with great enthusiasm. They recall it with fondness and joy. They may have gone on holiday with the wrong people, but they are at least reminiscing with some enthusiasm.

Because teens are on a quest to separate from you and define their own identity, voluntarily going on holiday with you goes against that quest. It's obvious, really.

Trips come with new rules; I would become infuriated because we had to accommodate their ability to take three hours to leave a room for a day trip into our planning. When they were at the early teen bickering stage, we had to start agreeing in advance to a seating plan for plane trips, taxi rides or car hire, because the four kids became a squabbling nightmare. We tailored our trips to be much more active, especially if there was no wi-fi, and it required a lot more itinerary planning because they hate surprises or spontaneous long days relaxing (ironically). My best bit of advice on travelling with teens is go for the breakfast-included option. A good brekkie appears to be their favourite meal of the day and would distract ours from our 'no screens until early evening' rule on more exotic holidays. I mean, who spends a fortune to go abroad and look at their phone all day?

But you just have to ignore the moaning, the side-eye and the grumpiness that can accompany you all on holiday, because taking pleasure in retrospect is such a teenage trait. Grit your teeth through their inexplicable fury as they pack for a family trip, and at that cloak of boredom they wear wherever they go and the moaning about the wi-fi (a friend's sixteen-year-olds once booked themselves on a train home in the middle of a half-term staycation because the wi-fi wasn't good enough).

Because it isn't a waste of effort and money. They just can't show you that you have made them happy as they separate from the family tribe. Other members of the cult would disown them if they did this, but you have made them happy, trust me, you have. You've given them happy memories, which is what parenting is really all about.

'Mum, What's Wrong With You?'
Conversations with Teens

Her: Why are you always coming into my room unannounced? Go away.

Me: It's 7.30 a.m. – you asked me to wake you up.

Her: Oh, for god's sake, what is wrong with you? That never happened.

17

Phonegate, screens and the screams

Towards the end of 2016 I instituted what was then referred to as a 'digital sunset' in our house. An electronic curfew that saw my two eldest daughters hand their mobile phones over at 9 p.m. every evening. They were thirteen and fourteen. I had done much research into teenagers and the effect of screen time on their lives for a feature I was writing for a national newspaper and concluded that screens weren't the demons they were often painted as but that moderation was key. And some boundaries were needed.

Back then most mums around me had either gone for total prohibition or unlimited access. No other generation of parents has had to deal with smartphones, unlimited twenty-four-hour access to the internet and social media, so myself and other parents of a mostly Gen X persuasion felt like we were making it up as we went along. In the UK now almost half of ten-year-olds have a mobile phone and those aged between fifteen and twenty-four spend roughly four hours a day on them. This will of course have increased since the pandemic when screens became an even bigger part of young lives.

But, dear god, from the moment our digital sunset started at home I endured what we now refer to as the Incredible Sulk; it went on for months and was upsetting and exhausting.

My two teens threw everything at it: whining, screaming, raging, heavy silences, the thousand-mile stare, villainous sarcasm, demonic hatred, sighing, evil dictator side-eye, constant low-key resentment. They hid their phones, smuggled them into their rooms and demanded sleepovers, knowing they could spend more time on their phones at someone else's house.

All this I felt was a dramatic overreaction, but they maintained a concerted effort to get their phones back at night-time. It was as if I'd kidnapped a beloved puppy. They weren't just cross I had taken something that belonged to them, they were emotionally bereft, and neither my husband nor I could understand this reaction or their addiction to a small metal gadget.

I wish we'd had the foresight to remove it at 9 p.m. (as we now do for No. 3 and will do for No. 4) from the moment we had given the phones to them; this should have been the rule from day one, in retrospect. But like all parents we make mistakes. However, I persisted with the curfew because my instinct on it was overwhelming.

I did it to relieve my girls of what I saw as the almost constant pressure to communicate. And I did it worrying about what they were looking at online after 9 p.m. I also did it because I had read about the plasticity of teenage brains and didn't want to affect the developing neural pathways negatively.

Mostly I wanted to forcibly remove them from the 'he said, she said' debates among friends, the teenage girl 'dramas' that seemed to rage through the early hours, a time when nothing makes sense to anyone. They appeared to have no control over it themselves, so I felt the need to step in as the adult in charge. One morning pre-the digital sunset I'd noticed my eldest, then fourteen, was upset from a group conversation that had, to my horror, occurred at 1 a.m.

She was unsettled, too young to work out that the language of social media, texts, WhatsApp, Snapchat is different. Too young to know that cowards and bullies thrive in a virtual space, saying things they would never dream of saying IRL. And too young to see some of the more disturbing images I felt complacent social-media companies had allowed on their sites.

I told my daughters that I'd review my 'medieval rule', as they dubbed it, after a few months. But when we talked it through again the following February, in 2017, I refused to change the 9 p.m. cut-off because I felt nothing had changed, even though they were both older.

I wasn't my maternal or personal best during that conversation and resorted to the imaginary book of bad parenting with the worst line: 'Because I said so.' They refuted any experts I quoted and accused me of making the risks up and controlling their lives, trying to keep them babies. They said it made them feel left out of their friendship groups – their friends were apparently allowed unlimited access. They said I didn't trust them, and they were right.

Lack of trust is extremely upsetting for teenage girls. If you don't trust the new identity they are building, then why should they? It may have disturbed them to feel this way but even knowing that, I stuck to my guns, to the boundary I had set. We had horrible conversation after horrible conversation and I didn't listen as well as I should have, but my mind was full of scare stories of self-harm, online bullying and grooming. There were even lower moments when I ended up snatching devices that wouldn't be handed over, appalling parenting on my part but I was frightened and so was my husband.

There were no 'soft conversations' to be had about screens, I felt, because it all came from a place of fear: a fear of the horror stories about the online world and the basic parental fear of not knowing exactly how the hell any of these gadgets worked and no real information on their long-term effects. Now I know that some of that fear was misplaced, though I believe I was right to stop them accessing their phones at night even though it got me into trouble with my girls in other ways.

My daughters were blamed at school by the daughters of fellow mums who followed my lead. And other mums disagreed with such emotional turmoil at home (I felt many just couldn't face disciplining their daughters around phones, the gadgets had a strong hold over families, and especially over parents who feared confrontation and rejection). Some parents felt judged for not instituting the 9 p.m. curfew and became defensive when I saw them. When teens came on sleepovers I made them hand their phones over at 9 p.m. too, and endured the angry stares and rude sighs of other people's daughters. My two claimed I had made them pariahs, which made me feel terrible.

We went to hell and back during this screen-time debate with our two eldest, both of whom we allowed to have mobile phones at the age of twelve. It would have been better for the harmony of the whole house sometimes just to give in. As they got older and we felt they were mentally resilient enough we changed the handover time, and at sixteen, they were allowed their phones and laptops in their rooms after 9 p.m. first at weekends, then during the week. By then they had started to occasionally self-moderate. It was a surprise but now and again they would pop their gadgets in our kitchen cupboard where I had been storing them and potter off leaving them behind if they felt that had been on them too long of an evening.

But I am not anti-screens, nor anti-social media, far from it. Perhaps the tale of the woodcutter and the axe is a good way to view this generation's ongoing and contentious screen-time debate. The woodcutter can use the axe to fell trees and fuel a village or he/she can use it to murder everyone in their beds. This is the same with screens, the internet, games, social media. I think the focus should be on how we all use them, how we moderate ourselves and how we get the best value, because I love being able to see my children delight in what they learn, and their new connected way of living with friends, their access to new music, to film, humour and history.

On almost everything else I am not so inclined to be rigid about rules but for this I think rigid boundaries need to be defined the day your daughter is given a phone and renegotiated with her over the years. Consider how screen time and all that goes with it affects your daughter in particular. This means you may have to look at what is going on in her home or school life and possibly make some reassessments, because the environment and developing personality of teen girls is the background to how they feel when they use their screens, what they react to and what influences them adversely. We may need to ask, what else is going on that would affect what she chooses to see or do on her phone or laptop? Who is influencing her choices? And you could observe if her behaviour is changing as a result of access to social media or prolonged gaming.

A teenage girl's need for affirmation on social media may come from how fragile she is in the real world, how her neurology is developing as her brain undergoes rapid change, what her underlying personality is. So perhaps those diet ads may affect her more than others, so stay extra vigilant and remain curious and engaged with her. Talk to her about what she is looking at, ask her how it makes her feel. Keep your connection with her. If you suspect your daughter is struggling with what she is seeing online, perhaps seeking out the darker side of social media, then get the help of a mental-health expert to help her find a way to deal with it.

Screens are here to stay. They will become increasingly advanced, and those toxic algorithms that scare the hell out of us on social media are ever more sophisticated, so our job is to help anchor our teens in real life and encourage them to stay in the more positive parts of the internet.

And I have to say that without the screens, lockdown summer of

2020 would have been even more of a disaster for the mental health of our young people. Teens need to stay connected to their social circle and I think we must always let that happen, in person or not.

When I interviewed the neuroscientist Sarah-Jayne Blakemore in the middle of that summer, she told me she felt screens were invaluable in supporting the mental health of teens struggling with being isolated from their friends. Screen time allowed them to separate from their parents, as teens must do and to stay in touch with their peers and the social world they wanted to be part of.

So: setting boundaries and encouraging moderation is the key to healthy screen use in my opinion. It all sounds simple, doesn't it? But it's more complex and emotionally loaded to put into practice in real life. However, this is the one element of parenting I don't believe is negotiable, for a teenager will rarely voluntarily stop looking at their phone. They just won't, even if they are awake to the addiction, awake to the manipulation of their minds by social-media big business, awake to the knowledge it may be dominating their thoughts negatively. You are the one who has to step in here. And if you intend to help them moderate their use you must moderate yours. Teenagers can sniff a hypocrite out a mile off. Mine are always comparing their screen-time notifications to mine, it gives them hours of mirth, but it does remind me that the rules apply to everyone but the dog in our house.

My husband plays Scrabble on his phone, for example, which he thinks gives him a get-out-of-jail-free card but saying, 'I am playing Scrabble,' is no excuse after 9 p.m. when you are asking your teens to do what you don't do. Ditto me and social media.

When they first got mobiles, I asked my daughters to use them only in plain sight. And no going to bedrooms for prolonged time on a phone alone and they were not to be used at the kitchen table while we ate. My aim was to stop the phone from becoming an emotional crutch or the only way to entertain them and I hoped removing it would then give them pre-planned catch-up time on their phones to look forward to later on. I wish we had held off longer, to be honest, and not given them smartphones until the age of thirteen, but I am not sure that is feasible today and, in fact, our almost-ten-year-old has a smartphone with parental locks on it now as a result of her summer in lockdown. The need to FaceTime her friends privately trumped everything.

We made sure we still enjoyed outings as a family with no phones with our eldest teens and that being outside was as important as inside activities. We didn't over-schedule or go mad with the activities to 'keep them off their phones' as some parents told us they did, as I felt that would create more tension, so while I clung to my 9 p.m. rule, we just remained persistent about getting them out and about. Having a dog really helped with this. I guess what we were trying to do was stop the dopamine hit of the social-media likes becoming a habit, to give them real-life alternatives to phone life.

At home we kept asking, 'Do you think you have enough time on that?' as they played computer games with each other and remotely with friends. They would usually say no, but at least they had the question hardwired into their brains, the message being we thought they had had enough. That may have worked, or it may have constantly implied we thought screens were bad. It was hard to know what impact constant worried focus on phones on our part had, but I hoped we'd made the point that we were sensibly cautious but generally accepting.

We talked to our girls about social media. We investigated social media, looking at every platform; I am a frequent user of most platforms for personal and work use. We asked them to think about it, but we didn't ban them outright, we didn't follow them on any platforms, we didn't ask for the passwords on their phones because they had complained about lack of trust and this was a way to show I did trust them. Again, in retrospect, I wish we had asked for password access at the beginning of their journey and I have made it clear with my nine-year-old that we need to have password access from the get-go. Though we did verbally agree with the two eldest when they got the phones that they would allow us one-time access if we felt they were in danger. We turned the wi-fi off if things got heated about screen time. And if phones were lost or screens broken then they had to save up to have them repaired or wait for birthdays for a replacement.

We chose to believe they weren't putting nude pictures of themselves on Instagram or making plans to meet cyber friends who could turn out to be grown-up paedophiles pretending to be Fortnite addicts. And I took the phone away as a form of punishment for rude behaviour that I felt was caused by being on a phone too long. And I took it away if other boundaries, curfews and the like, were broken. Inevitably, this caused volcanic eruptions.

I talked about 'revenge porn', as it was dubbed early on, and the new up-skirting crimes making headlines. I showed them how I once traced a job applicant through her open social-media profile, one which didn't present her in the best light. I tried to be an ally on this front, explaining that I knew they could be impulsive, as teens are, but acting on impulses to post inappropriate pictures, for example, may have a long-term ripple effect. We brought all this into the room to discuss and I tried hard to sit and listen to them. At one point I asked a much cooler, younger friend to follow one of my daughters on one social-media account but realised that this 'secret tracking' was a hopeless tactic, for how would I confront any activity I deemed unsuitable? It was a mad idea and ill judged.

We chose to believe the risks were the same sort of risks faced by every generation as a new development comes along, a modernisation of the way we live, and proceeded with caution, but gradually welcomed technology in rather than hiding from it in fear or judging others for their choices. We discussed the heartbreaking headlines about the negative effect of too much screen time or social media on teenage girls and I always asked their opinion because I was aware that they were often seeing this upsetting news on their Snapchat channels as well. But we still had more arguments over phones when our daughters were between the ages of thirteen and sixteen than anything else in their lives.

Ultimately, you know your child; what is good for one may not be great for another. While one young girl can look at a curated life on Instagram or Pinterest and feel absolutely no FOMO, another looks at it and is driven to despair. Undoubtedly, more regulation is needed by tech companies to stem the tide of disturbing images online, to stop what can feel like a tsunami of free pornography reaching young audiences, but there is some reassuring evidence for parents worried about this online world.

I interviewed Suzi Godson, an experienced adolescent mental-health expert, about the effects of screens and exposure to social media. A therapist, she set up the award-winning app MeeTwo, a peer-to-peer app for young people in crisis situations. Through a moderated site they can post messages of support for each other, share experiences and get professional help from content on the app. Thousands of teens use it. When I asked her if she would blame social media for the deterioration of young people's mental health and the increase in adolescent anxiety, she replied forcefully, 'Absolutely not,' confirming that to her knowledge there was as yet no clinical evidence that social media causes mental-health problems.

'I know this is not what parents want to hear,' she explained. 'It is easy for us to blame the new kid on the block for issues we see our children going through.'

Godson says that on one occasion she was researching the reasons for more than 3,000 posts on the app and noted only twelve mentioned social media. She says that the thing young users were most worried about was their parents' relationship, especially whether they were going to split up. Anything that fractured family life. I am not blaming parents, but simply asking everyone to be aware of all the factors that affect teenagers most; those factors drive them to delve into different worlds on their phones, where they could be at risk in some way.

A study by Professor Andrew Przybylski and researcher Amy Orben at the Oxford Internet Institute in 2019 found that there is little to link social-media use and an adolescent's satisfaction with life. In fact, at the time of writing this, no smoking gun has been found from studying thousands of teens globally over the past few years. Things may change as more research is done but be wary of those scaremongering headlines.

I am well aware of the cult of perfectionism that social-media use can feed, but again, perhaps it isn't the platform, perhaps it is how a teenager uses it. To be clear, I am not in any way undermining the severe effect of using these social platforms may have on some young women. I would hate to play that down, because it is heartbreaking for many parents whose daughters have been sucked into a spiral of pressure and negativity, which can dominate their lives. There should be tighter guidelines and stricter controls over what adolescents get shown in their feeds by these tech businesses which were allowed to ride roughshod over all of us in an unregulated way for too long. I am all for that, and the pressure must continually be applied to them to take more responsibility. But they are here now and there are many threads and discussions on social media which have been truly beneficial for young women. I think the body positivity movement on Instagram for example has helped reshape the way adolescents think about themselves and the young activist elements of social media are to be applauded in my opinion.

All this is here to stay so what is your plan? Work it out before you get your daughter a phone. Do your research. Websites like YoungMinds and the NSPCC's Net Aware can help you find out more about what is going on and the practical side of this technology (but it is not rocket science – you're probably on Facebook, so you'll be able to look at the other platforms with ease), but use your instinct when it comes to each of your daughters. Keep communicating in a non-confrontational way.

And while we are on the subject of social media, can we talk about informed consent? When I interviewed the parenting guru and psychologist Steve Biddulph about his book *10 Things Girls Need Most to Grow Up Strong and Free*, I was a little cross with him. He had sent me two emails beforehand that had upset me. Best known for the bestseller *Raising Boys*, Biddulph had rebuked me for allowing pictures of my children to appear in a newspaper. He chastised me for my columns describing my family life when the children were small. I was stung by his words – because he made valid points. He accused me of not thinking it all through properly from the children's point of view, and now they are teenagers, it is clear he was right. I made mistakes, I regret them, and I would do things differently if I were to do them again today. This is a digital age: the information is never not out there. I have come to a certain peace with being a journalist who writes about family life in a way that is designed to provide help for other parents, with tips from experts in order to make everyone feel as if they are not doing this alone. Which is indeed what this book is for. I am, of course, aware of the irony of writing about privacy here while talking about my daughters' lives. I have shown them the book (generally they are not that interested) and gained what I feel is a happy balance around everyone's permissions around privacy now, but what Biddulph highlighted for me was this contentious and continual debate around informed consent, which affects us all as the Facebook generation. I am as big a lover of a baby picture as the next person, but sometimes I see posts of family life I know will come back to haunt those in them when they are teenagers. This is a sensitive subject, entangled as it is in all sorts of emotional complexities around why we post things on Facebook in the first place.

Why do we share what we share? Is it for us, is it showing off, is it simply family fun or is it a deep-seated need to prove something about our parenting? I don't know any of the answers, I am just saying think it through before you hit send on the posts on social media. It's worth pausing to consider what your children will think of your posts when they hit the teenage years and their privacy is such a sensitive part of their new identity. Even if they approve anything you share, can they be giving 'informed consent' at such a young age? We cannot pretend our activity doesn't have a legacy or that there isn't some lasting ripple effect caused by us releasing details before our children are old enough to give informed consent. For example, what kind of pressure are you putting on your children if you only ever post stories and pictures about their successes? Are you creating a narrative, without their permission, that will be painful for them when they are older? Taking some time to consider why you post what you do could be helpful.

When I wrote a jokey weekly column about my offspring as small kids, various details were changed and the columns ran out of sync with the events described, but I shared too much of their lives and intruded too much on their privacy. I was comfortable at the time with the level of personal detail, but I acknowledge now, thanks to some gentle probing from Biddulph, that I had not properly considered how they would feel about this being in public. Today, my children and I chat everything through: they tell me what they will and won't want written about, and they have contributed to columns I've written. We feel OK about it as a family, but it is not for everyone. I don't cast any judgement on what anyone else does, but maybe just give it a second thought.

I think one of the good things about the new online world we are all guinea pigs for is that it forces us to talk to our children about the more difficult subjects to chat over with them – things like sex and drugs. It makes us communicate with them, gives us a point of connection, and that is healthy. So if you can help your daughter create a social-media content bubble that supports her and makes her feel good, then that has to be the way forward, and if not, you could perhaps ask someone else she respects. Go with her on this new journey into the tech world, but remind her that nothing online is private. Even if her account is private, it can still be shared. And turn to experts if you are worried. But don't demonise her choices or she will become secretive and that won't be helpful.

SUGGESTIONS FOR DIGITAL BOUNDARIES

As the first generation of parents navigating this journey, we are perhaps the generation of parents charged with setting rules around this. So, to recap here's what we did at home, which may be useful for you. Experiment and see what suits your family best but don't side-step your responsibility on this subject and be emotionally prepared for how unpopular setting guidelines will make you.

1. Rigid rules from day one: Start with hard-and-fast rules that can be negotiated as she develops and matures. It is so much tougher to retrospectively set boundaries as we did.
2. The digital sunset: No phones in rooms after 8 p.m. from the start. First all the time, then just weekdays, perhaps at around the age of fifteen or sixteen. Then renegotiate as and when YOU feel comfortable your daughter can handle late-night internet access.
3. Set parental controls on the wi-fi.
4. Don't immediately replace broken, lost devices: I see this

a lot and by doing it you are reinforcing their view they cannot live without their phones. Let them endure this pain; but you will have to as well. It won't be pleasant. But as I have said before, we CAN do hard things. This is one of them.

5. Consider a digital contract as a family: Something like the one parenting website iMOM provides, which is a printable contract with rules around phone and/or social-media use. Dr Bex Lewis, who specialises in digital culture and communication at Manchester Metropolitan University, recommended this to me in May 2019, and it means you take some responsibility as a parent for how much you use your phone too. We didn't stick to the contract, but just talking about it made us all aware how we rely on our phones and how their use affects everyone in the family.

6. No phones at meals, no phones on dog walks, no phones for family game time: We find these guidelines helpful in our house. Work out what you can realistically dictate, expect and maintain. I would put the phones in a cupboard as it meant they couldn't see them and still be subconsciously distracted.

7. Eye contact is crucial: Don't have conversations with your teens with your phone in your hand, keep the eye contact. Put your phone down.

8. Set time limits with alarms for gaming: Our nine-year-old loves to play RoBlox but we agree on for how long she can.

9. Think about how screen time is affecting you: I know many mums who perhaps have a more anxious disposition who find social media stressful. Have you got someone you can talk to about how it makes you feel, can you reset your relationship with your phone? Step back and think it through. If you have suffered with mental-health issues, is

it making you feel good or bad when you engage online? Perhaps it has a negative effect on you but isn't affecting your daughter in the same way, so be mindful of this in discussions with her about it.

10. What is your daughter watching or doing online? It will always be worthwhile trying to talk to her about it even if she dismisses you. Demonising it could make her secretive so try to be curious and perhaps log in yourself and find out what teenagers are watching. YouTube was a brilliant discovery for me and my nine-year-old loves it. But I researched the programmes she asked to watch and saw for myself. Make time to do that. You are not powerless here and it is always best to know about the things you may argue about later. Stay informed.

11. Get the passwords on day one. Then as time passes and you feel you can trust your daughter more you may not need the passwords. I felt it was an infringement of their privacy to have phone access but I may have been mistaken in that decision. We have always had the passwords of our two younger children's mobiles.

12. Always and forever: that is how I explained inappropriate pictures sent on impulse on the phone. That is how long they last. I think almost all teenage girls will send pictures they know in retrospect are wrong to send so there is little point in being furious if you find out, or 'shaming' them about their behaviour; better to remind them your fears are for their future not for now. How will those pictures look when they go for a job interview?

18

Your daughter is not your friend

(Repeat after me)

Making life easier for mums dealing with everyday, ordinary, expected teenage behaviour is the main aim of this book. As you may have guessed, I favour an approach that gives everyone, you included, the benefit of the doubt because, god knows, we are all trying our best, and this stage of parenting is so new to everyone that we are definitely going to make mistakes. I hate to offer hard-and-fast diktats based on the journalism I have done or my own personal experience, but I when it comes to mums being friends instead of parents to their daughters it is wrong. It is not a good thing when you hear mothers say, 'We're very close – she tells me everything.' That sentence makes me shudder. Your teenage daughter should not be telling you everything.

I know we all kind of secretly hoped we would be the 'cool' parents, the ones whose kids won't laugh at for being old-fashioned and dreary. I romanticised about happy shopping trips, romcom movie nights, rainy Sundays in art galleries. I looked forward to a whole cultural life with my girls as they grew up. I did not anticipate my role as Clown in Chief. I anticipated fun times, not being-made-fun-of times. And at many points through their adolescence I tried overly hard to enforce some mum-daughter bonding. Once I took the girls to see a play called *My Mum's a Twat*. They were reluctant, arriving late at the Royal Court theatre. I chose this play so they could come with me and legitimately make fun of me and maybe see a play that appealed to them. It would still be a play and we would still be together. It would be cool, I thought (idiot).

Apart from secretly Snapchatting me reading the programme for the LOLs, there was no jolly post-theatre banter as I had hoped; instead, they were monosyllabic in their critique and angsty about having to sit so near me, even though they looked as though they enjoyed this poignant and funny one-woman play about dysfunctional mother love. I think they liked the cheese-and-onion crisps at half time. My desperate need to please was one of many anticlimaxes on the maternal-bonding front. But their behaviour was to be expected, a developmental phase so many go through.

Get used to this feeling because a parent can't be their teenager's best friend. Every expert will tell you that this is a bad thing. It is called 'parentification' – where mums and dads try to fill a friendship void in their own lives by inserting themselves into the social lives of their youngsters.

You can be friendly, for sure, but a benign, loving, stable presence is a more realistic but less exciting aspiration. Like an old sofa. I know, it's disappointing, isn't it, but I think you should abandon any 'best friends' dream you may have as soon as your daughter turns eleven.

I think we partly want to do 'friend' things with our girls because we want to make them consistently happy, to keep them entertained, but in his book on raising teens, *We Need to Talk*, the child and adolescent analyst Ian Williamson concludes that a style of parenting has evolved today that defines perpetual happiness as a teenager's inalienable right. This view trumps the more traditional belief that your job is simply to prepare your child for adulthood as best you can. According to Williamson, it doesn't do to be 'matey' with your teen. You want to be leading or coaching them rather than being part of their new world. You have to be the grown-up, which made me feel slightly cheated of a fantasy mum-daughter relationship I had in my head. That will come as they get older, and I see flashes of it with my eighteen-year-old, now that we can go out for dinner and have a glass of wine together, more adult experiences, but it wasn't to be during adolescence. Be patient.

It's obvious, of course, but as soon as they start to head into adolescence you can enjoy doing things with them instead of the relentless 'entertainment to occupy' mantra of childhood, it feels as though you want the fun side to be more fun for you too. Less going on inflatables on seaside holidays and more doing things you actually like doing. But you are dealing with so-called 'queenagers': it should not be within their remit to be fun alongside you. Frankly, parents are the last people on earth they want to have fun with, because you are not their actual friends. You are the ones they want to cross the road to avoid talking to, but they have the unfortunate problem of living with you (and loving you, though they hide that for a few years). And you joining in is not what they envisaged: it won't help them form an identity during this time or become independent, which is much healthier for them than pleasing you. If they are doing this with you instead of their peer group, you should encourage them not to and find out why they aren't with other teenagers. Don't be one of the mums that says 'I'm lucky, she wants to spend all her time with me' because this could be a sign your daughter is struggling to form her own identity. Teens need their tribes; they need other teens around them, not adults.

The mum-as-mate route looks tempting because it may keep them close, but you are not equals and they are no longer children.

Hierarchy is important: it can help set clear boundaries and may give teenage girls something to lean against as they wrestle with their developing minds. Boundaries are a place of certainty. It's OK to have a close relationship with much communication, as long they can still look to you to set boundaries and to stick to your consequences for poor behaviour. If they can tell you personal and intimate things then that is all well and good, but don't expect to know everything.

The words 'mum' and 'cool' cancel each other out. It's your mumness they are rejecting temporarily or indeed laughing at on social media sometimes. Even those mums who spend hours making TikToks with their teenage daughters must be aware of that: it isn't laughing with – it is laughing at.

You should stick to being with your own friends or find a hobby that takes you away from your children for small amounts of time and removes the temptation to wade in and be a dominating part of their social life. I am now at ease with becoming the main star of *Carry On Parenting* for my teens and obviously acutely aware that while they can make fun of you, they take themselves super-seriously, so you cannot, under any circumstances, make fun of them. I now accept that sometimes all I am good for is providing petty cash or locating lost lip salves.

All is not lost though, because some lovely moments of shared memories happen in adolescence and you can still be close to your daughter. The emotional connections you crave as they get older are possible; it is just that sometimes they are often spontaneous – and so all the more delishly surprising. Watching *Queer Eye* together with my eldest; walking fifteen kilometres around Florence on a mum-daughter weekend with Gracie, then aged fifteen, but more the lying-in-bed reading while she slept beside me before sightseeing; swimming in the ponds on Hampstead Heath together; making pasta with a pasta machine bought in Oxfam; getting ice cream in the park; letting my eldest do my make-up; listening to 'Africa' by Toto in the car and singing along; everyone agreeing they have no idea who is listening to Coldplay; moving snails off the pavement together so no one treads on them.

Your parenting should bend around them in new ways as you strive to keep the connection with small gestures, perhaps. For example, as we know, I am not a happy cook; in fact, I hate it, if I am honest, but I know my eldest loves to cook. When she was small, she'd pound the pizza dough with her little hands on our wooden kitchen table, refusing to hand it over until it was just the right consistency. It delighted her, and I notice that over the years, in times of stress she'd make chocolate cupcakes or experiment with giant bowls of spaghetti creations. I think it made her feel grown-up and it made me feel immensely proud of her ability to make things. So while I fantasised about taking her to art galleries, what she really liked, aged fourteen, was a trip down the baking aisle at Tesco's. If we were feeling particularly 'bougie', as she'd say, we'd go to Waitrose and splash out on gold icing pens – art of a form, I guess. It's then that you become the kind of parent who realises the huge value and infinite joy of doing small things with great love. They have friends. What they need is more important: a mum.

'Mum, What's Wrong With You?'
Conversations with Teens

[Driving]

Her: Mum, are you going to indicate?

Me: In a minute.

Her: You should do it now.

Me: I will indicate in a minute. [Said sternly. I am the adult, after all.]

Her: This is not the right way to drive. You aren't even looking in the mirror. Mum, you are a really dangerous driver.

Me: I am a very good driver. [Said in voice of Rain Man – reference that is ignored because it is from the 1990s.]

Her: So why are you driving so slowly? I need to get there on time. Can you even see everything properly? Are those glasses strong enough for you? I am going to be late if you don't hurry up, Lorraine.

19

Anxiety

What's the T?

There have been many occasions when the mum of a teenage girl has taken me quietly to one side after finding out that I write about parenting and told me stories like the one below.

A woman in her late forties recounted this to me one evening after a panel event I was taking part in on adolescent development, as we sipped warm white wine.

In the early hours of the morning her fourteen-year-old teenager would tiptoe out of her own bedroom and creep into bed with Mum. Dad would have to move to the spare room while his daughter would lie down in the darkness with her back to her mother and begin to share her fears. She whispered to her mum that sometimes her feelings were like hundreds of small butterflies swarming all over her; frightened, she would suddenly find it physically hard to breathe. She felt as though the butterflies were her worries flickering around her. They were overwhelming, terrifying, and she didn't know what to do. Next a feeling of dire panic and dread would sweep over her, she said.

The mum in turn was scared: fearful of what to say or do, desperate to fix the problem yet without fully understanding the problem or knowing how to help her daughter cope. Like many of us this mum felt unprepared. Had something serious happened to her daughter that she didn't know about? So many thoughts would run through her head as she quietly listened to her little girl, who as a child had seemed so confident and jolly. This mum was also concerned that her daughter's behaviour could be a sign of a developing mental illness, depression perhaps, and was worried what the next steps might be: self-harm? An eating disorder? Suicidal thoughts?

The mum looked quite desperate as she told me this story and asked my advice. All the headlines about the epidemic of anxiety gripping this generation of teens weighed heavily on her mind and she wondered if her daughter's behaviour was unusual and perhaps a sign that something had gone desperately wrong, a question many of us ask at this stage of mothering. I sympathised greatly because I had seen flashes of what I would describe as overwhelming anxious thoughts and feelings in my own daughters. And I had likewise read all the upsetting headlines about the perilous mental health of young people today. This mum was essentially asking what's normal and what's not. How exactly do you tell what is ordinary-teenage-girl 'sadness' and what could be a clinically recognised anxiety? How do you help your daughter navigate her new, more grown-up, emotions? And when should you turn to a professional for help?

As I chatted to this mum I tried to help her put her fears in context and explain, as I hope I do in this chapter, what you could look out for when it comes to anxious thoughts and feelings and how you can support your girls if they are sometimes finding growing up a challenge mentally. There *are* ways that you, with reassurance, empathy and compassion, can help your teenager develop mental strength.

Firstly, though, we are right to be concerned by the headlines, to note what they report and be vigilant. Every expert in adolescent

153

mental health I have spoken to confirms the same thing: the world adolescents live in now puts more pressure on their mental health than any other time in history. There has been an unacceptable rise in mental-health issues among teen girls. Many external factors are contributing to this as well as factors at home. When I volunteered with Shout, the crisis text line, I witnessed the story behind the headlines first-hand. I saw text after text from children in desperate domestic situations who were self-harming or struggling with many forms of anxiety, not to mention many texts from teens and children in what would be described as less extreme situations but who were suffering similar levels of anxiety.

According to an Office of National Statistics report, there was a shocking 67 per cent increase in teen suicides in England and Wales between 2010 and 2017. And an NHS survey published in 2018 found that one fifth of young women between seventeen and nineteen in England have resorted to self-harm or tried to kill themselves, and one in eight 11–19-year-olds have had some form of mental disorder. We also know that NHS support is fragmented in the UK and hard to access for many, which no doubt makes us even more nervous and fearful for our children.

Running alongside this, I think, is an ever-expanding wellness industry that seems to promote the idea that a life free from anxieties is possible, which is unrealistic nonsense in my opinion. No one can be happy all the time, can they?

However, while we do need to be mindful of all this, we also need to avoid catastrophising outcomes for our daughters in advance. There is so much conversation about anxiety nowadays, in the media and among young people themselves, that many parents are jittery, continually on extra-high alert for signs of emotional turmoil and often overly keen to leap in and try to banish bad thoughts or negative feelings immediately.

You must remember that your daughter is a teenager and they

are at times going to feel sad, overwhelmed and down. That *is* normal. You cannot fix this. Similarly, we should avoid using the word 'anxiety' purely negatively in conversation, because there is such a thing as healthy anxiety. We all experience it and we all benefit from it – it can help make us more resilient. To avoid everything that makes us anxious would simply confirm those fears: in psychological terms, 'avoidance' may not be healthy for the anxious mind, as it can feed, validate and reinforce anxious feelings. Anxious feelings are an alarm system for us. They tell us something is about to happen and that we need to work out how to deal with it, plan for it and cope with it.

Many girls today may feel an intense stress to achieve academically. Exams in particular may cause teens to worry or feel extremely anxious, for example. This is not an unusual response, though, or indeed a bad thing. There are many stressful situations where you need to feel anxious; parents do not need to go into overdrive trying to stop their teens feeling these feelings every time they occur. However, if your teens' response to the stress of something is completely out of proportion with what therapists would call the 'perceived threat', if her negative and frightening feelings are dominating all her other feelings and dragging her into a darker place than either of you recognise, then maybe that is when they do need extra support, either from you and teachers or a mental-health professional. Remember, though, that every girl is different. I think we are all somewhere on a scale when it comes to feeling all the feelings, with some of us more anxious, more emotionally fragile perhaps. This doesn't mean we are unable to cope, it's just that we'll need more support or a different kind of support from those around us.

Most mothering at this stage boils down, I think, to communication and active listening. I tend to talk about forthcoming events that may make my daughters anxious in advance in a gentle, inquisitive way, offering help if they need it and letting them know I recognise their fears. I will ask what they feel they could do to lessen their worries. In a way you are tilting them in the direction of the thing they fear to help make it less frightening, as we all know once we've done something we had been anxious about doing, we may feel less anxious about it next time.

It should of course be borne in mind that while anxious feelings and behaviours are a normal reaction to stress they may also be a symptom of several types of disorders, including generalised anxiety disorder, panic disorder and specific phobias. It is complex and symptoms will be different for each person. The reality is that the majority of teenage girls will feel anxious at some point; it is not unusual for them to be overwhelmed by fearful thoughts and feelings. They are on the brink of enormous change: their bodies are being transformed and people look at them differently and react to them in a new way. It would be weird if they weren't fearful and didn't occasionally feel helpless and hopeless as they walk away from the warmth of their childhood. Every step forward in the hinterland between child and adult is a new one, so anxious feelings and thoughts are understandable. They could learn from these emotions as long as you don't automatically step in and rescue them, or solve their problems all the time. And they may then begin to feel stronger and more able to deal with anxious feelings. Of course we find it hard as loving mums to sit with their discomfort, we struggle to cope when they seem inconsolable, but sometimes they have to go through those hard feelings and we should let that happen without panicking or overreacting. We do need simply to sit with them as they experience this.

Most of the mums who ask me about teenage girls and anxiety want to know what specifically they should be looking out for to indicate if the changes their daughters are showing in reaction to stress are to be expected or if they are something more serious.

To gain more clarity, I interviewed an experienced mental-health professional in the summer of 2020. Over the past few years I have got to know Dr Fiona Pienaar, a mental-health clinician of many years' experience and chief clinical officer of the charity Shout and the organisation Mental Health Innovations. She has counselled many families and I turn to her, a mum of two grown-up children and one of six children herself, if I need sensible specifics for our everyday parenting lives. If it is not unusual for teenage girls to feel overwhelmed emotionally occasionally, or sad and anxious, then what is the key to seeing if something more serious is going on? I should note here that of course, every teenager is different so use your instinct with any advice I or anyone else offers.

'I advise parents to look for changes in their daughter's behaviour,' Dr Pienaar told me. 'You should know her best and you will expect some ups and downs at this developmental stage, but if your daughter has noticeably different patterns of behaviour, that could be a sign she is struggling.

'It's noticing if these emerging patterns sustain over some time and are starting to impact on her ability to socialise as well as interact with her family, attend and enjoy school or college and focus on her school work and studies; in other words, the anxiety is starting to affect her daily life and her relationships.

'As they get in touch with their independence, they need to know you have got their backs, you are watching out for them. So be vigilant, notice if she becomes stuck in her room for extended periods of time (although retreating to the bedroom is not unusual in itself for adolescents, perhaps she may not normally be this withdrawn), or if she loses contact with her peers. Socialising and feeling part of a group is important in adolescence, so if this is not happening, then you should start to check in with her.'

Dr Pienaar's number one piece of advice – and it is one I return to again and again in this book – is to keep up communications with your daughter. There could be what Dr Pienaar calls a sense of hopelessness and helplessness among teenagers struggling to cope with growing up; it may tip into anxious feelings and stop them in their tracks. It is hard for a parent to witness this, especially if you do not feel equipped to deal with it, but remember you are not trying to 'solve' this: you just need to be available when they need you and observant of their behaviour, not to be fixing the problem. She may well work through the feelings herself if she knows you are there in the background for her. Letting them learn how to deal with those thoughts themselves is crucial, I think, and I sometimes watch my daughters move from an anxious place to a more resilient one without any help. If I step in to solve their problems immediately, I notice it sometimes confuses them, because I have given them more thoughts to take on and process.

When my eldest daughter first started revising for exams she would occasionally become overwhelmed if she didn't understand something. During her tween years, I would sit down with her and try to solve the problem, often bringing out my Post-its and all sorts of possible solutions. However, I began to see that this really wasn't helping, it just increased her frustration and stress. I realised I needed to step back a bit, even though I was desperate to stop her feeling so wretched. As she grew up, I learned simply to be in the kitchen with her as she revised. I noticed she began to develop her own coping strategies, ones that suited her practical nature. For example, she would get out her miniature sewing machine in between bouts of revision and make all manner of things, and it seemed to calm her down. Giving her space to sit with those tough feelings potentially helped her find her own way to a coping mechanism. God knows why she picked sewing because I'm no Kirstie Allsopp, I can barely stitch a button on, but maybe she had watched her dad – in times of stress he always turns to working on something practical too.

I believe there is much to be said in favour of mums modelling the behaviour they hope their daughters could display, which means talking about your worries and showing your girls that despite those anxieties you are going to deal with whatever you fear anyway. It's the same with failure, isn't it? The cult of perfectionism that now seems to be prevalent among girls may demand your daughter aims to be a high achiever but if she sees you getting things wrong, making mistakes, it will help reassure her that failure is OK. It is sort of anti-perfectionism training and it could help downgrade anxious feelings to ones of disappointment, which may be easier for her to handle.

Most importantly we should maybe try to reframe the conversation by saying, 'My daughter is anxious,' rather than concluding, 'My daughter has anxiety.' Only a medical professional can diagnose that, and there was a point, mid-2018, when I wrote about a worrying trend brought to me by an NHS nurse specialising in digital mental health. This psychiatric nurse told me she was noticing a rising number of parents diagnosing their teenagers as having mental-health ailments, often going so far as to inform the school of it after googling symptoms.

It is, of course, terrifying and heartbreaking to witness your child in emotional pain. I can understand how some parents may turn to such a label to make them feel they are not to blame for any issues, or that they can then give themselves permission to seek professional help, a path forward.

A better course of action may be to communicate with her first rather than leaping immediately to anxiety as a 'diagnosis' or trying to 'fix' her problem. Finding out from her what is really going on could be the beginning of helping her become more resilient. It's all about building or rebuilding your connection with her. Listening without offering solutions.

I would also prepare yourself mentally and physically for this stage of the parenting journey, because you may need to work hard to reconnect if you have a daughter who has withdrawn into herself, as some adolescents do. You'll have to learn not to take the knockbacks personally. Some teens are so reluctant to chat it's like hugging a hedgehog but you have to persevere past the spikes because some potential mental-health issues are no respecter of background, wealth or family stability.

As a mum you will have to brace yourself for going back in again and again with a uncommunicative daughter. Slow down and be more curious around her. All is not lost, even if you feel like you're talking to the wall. Dr Pienaar recommends reinforcing the rituals of communication constantly. All those rituals you had when she was little – sitting on the bed, chats over breakfast, walks together, things like that – you need to maintain or softly reintroduce. This is about simply being with her, without any goal or agenda. No problem solving. It can feel oddly ineffective as a remedy for the anxiousness a girl can feel, but I have seen it in action and the relief of a rebuilt connection is immense. Keeping her company is a great parenting strategy, as it's not pressurising her to do or be anything.

We often lose these rituals as our children pass out of the tween period into the teenage one but try to keep them going – or pick them up again. If you are in a room together, initiate the chat. Prepare to be rebuffed because few opening remarks come teenager approved. Be patient. And although trying to initiate rituals from scratch in the teenage years is harder, it's not impossible:

'It is never too late to connect with your daughter; don't give up. They'll see you persevering and that in itself should tell them how much you care about them and their well-being,' Dr Pienaar tells me when I express the hopelessness I encounter from some mums whose teenagers are beyond even one-word answers.

'It is always worth trying, and it may take time to put this habit back into your life, but you can. Opening sentences may have to come from you. Start with, "I notice we haven't been talking for a while. Perhaps I haven't been the best communicator or the best listener, but I'd like to try again." Let them see you will make space for them.

'They may not step into this space until you tell them you want to reconnect again. Until you verbally tell them you really are there for them. And don't give up, this takes time – if you don't get anywhere at first with a chat, maybe leave them a note in their room.

'You might have to break whatever cycle of behaviour or communication you are in, perhaps rethink the way you have been interacting with them. Go sit on her bed; tell her what you are thinking and feeling. Don't make it all about her and what you feel she is going through – make it about you to start with. Model the communication you are looking to nurture with her.

'They are changing; they are supposed to be different when they become adolescents, so you may have to change too, change the way you are with them. I always suggest inviting your daughter to go out with you, just the two of you. Go and have a coffee or go for a walk. Spend some time together. Perhaps talk about how you would like things to be different and that you're interested in hearing what she thinks and what she would like from you. The emphasis should be on how you want things to be different, not how you want them to be different or that what your teen is feeling is wrong.'

If you don't think you are connecting with your daughter maybe she can talk to someone else? Ask her who she would feel comfortable voicing her feelings and thoughts with.

I always think that, no matter how bad one day has been, tomorrow is a new day and you can press reset. Take a step back and sense-check the reality of what is going on to avoid panicking. Find a calm place for yourself around your worries and somebody you can talk things through with when you might be struggling yourself. Your mental health is important too.

Clinical psychologist Dr Malie Coyne has written about the self-kindness parents may want to learn as they nurture a teenager who is perhaps more anxious than most. She points out that children need to put their trust in you as they face what is often a 'manageable threat' and if you want to be there for them you may need to quieten the critical and possibly panicking voice in your head which tells you that you are doing something wrong, the voice that may blame you for your child's negative feelings. Self-compassion may make you more able to model the ways your daughter could deal with stress.

And perhaps we can also be aware that looking to blame any anxiety our daughters are experiencing entirely on one thing may not be helpful. Our teenagers today are living in a world where they may feel under pressure to be connected all the time but I notice time and again that many parents blame declines in mental health solely on social media. I have been guilty of it myself. But to blame it alone for your daughter's anxiety could mean you miss the root cause of what is going on at home, at school, or with her peers. You may miss other important clues to what is affecting her mental health. More safeguarding for young people should be undertaken by the big companies, as I discuss in chapter 17, but the way the online world influences your daughter will be different from how it affects other teens. Parents could instead be more mindful of supporting their children's online behaviour, communicating around how it affects their particular child, what it makes her feel. It may also be the way this world is used by your teen, and your teen's own psychological make-up that is triggering her anxious thoughts.

Then there is the fact that, according to family psychotherapist Suzi Godson, the most common causes of anxiety are the same today as they were many years ago: family breakdown, toxic friendships, parental problems or exam stress. Letting their parents down in some way, for example, can be one of the main fears of teenagers leading to stress on their mental health.

In therapy Dr Pienaar will often encourage parents who seek help around the subject of anxiety to use other words to describe their daughter's experience of it; words that refer to her feelings and thoughts, not her 'condition'.

'Adolescence can be a time of phenomenal vigilance for mothers,' she acknowledges, 'but if you're talking with your daughter about anxiety, perhaps you can guide her to talk about what she is specifically feeling and what her thoughts are, because your body can have such strong reactions to your thoughts and emotions. If she is feeling anxious, it may affect her physically too.

'Encourage your girls to increase their vocabulary around their thoughts and feelings. Are they anxious or are they scared, sad, frustrated or worried instead?

'In therapy we invite and encourage clients to talk about their feelings and thoughts, so that they are no longer trapped in their heads or felt in their bodies, or acted out in their behaviours, but are witnessed by someone who is empathic, someone who cares, observes and listens. This alone can be a first helpful step. You too can do this as a mother. Learn to listen with focus and with depth.

'If your daughter cannot voice her thoughts and feelings out loud, perhaps she can write them down in the privacy of her bedroom. She may feel they are private or that they are too much for you to deal with. Naming them can help relieve the pressure. She can even crumple the paper up and throw it away.

'Also ask, "What thoughts are going round and round in your head?" and let her speak. Don't interrupt or pass judgement or promise to solve the problem she may be talking about. Really just listen and acknowledge those feelings and those thoughts she is having.

'This is why communication is so important: it shows you are open for them, that everything can be transparent and not hidden.'

So many things can influence a teenager's mood and propensity towards anxiety or anxious feelings: the circle of friends they may mix in, schoolwork, adverse childhood events such as divorce or perhaps family trauma, and you will see that each of your daughters has a different need when it comes to coping with or avoiding more negative emotions and feelings. Body image and how they feel about their own looks or physique can be a major factor in the anxiety teenage girls experience. As they create their new identity, they are also looking at where they align themselves sexually. There is much awareness of choice around this today, which can perhaps make some teens confused emotionally. You are dealing with a complicated set of emotions and developments and will need to offer them reference points, such as books on those subjects you may not feel able to discuss expertly. Help them with a reading list or point them in the direction of vlogs or podcasts that could help them. You should also turn to books on the subject yourself if you are worried (there is a list for you at the end of this book), listen to podcasts and of course, seek professional help via your GP (or personally recommended private practitioners) if you feel for a moment you are out of your depth.

Really your main job is to be properly 'in the room' when you think your daughter is feeling anxious: not to be preoccupied, half-listening or even diving in with practical solutions to her problem. Just be present. The psychologist Lisa Damour refers to this as 'pot plant parenting', a phrase I love.

'Don't disappear into your own busyness' is perhaps the best advice I have ever received from Dr Pienaar because alongside this fear of a growing epidemic of anxiety runs Western society's need to be busy.

We live in a world of 'doing', but a world of 'being' may be more comforting to an anxious teenage girl. Dr Pienaar tells me it is sometimes the wealthiest teenage girls who are the loneliest. They may have everything they want materially but very little they need emotionally. There are those who don't see their parents on a consistent and regular basis, eating alone in their rooms, perhaps, or feeling their voices aren't worth listening to because no one wants to know more about them than their grades or their achievements. Stuff is no alternative to time, and your time is the most precious commodity for a teenage girl. This is why they are more time consuming than toddlers, so be ready to devote those extra moments, plan them in now if your daughter is in her early teens. The more the better.

I have personally learned that helping my daughters deal with anxious feelings is more about connecting, not directing. About soft, not hard conversations. Mother-and-daughter writing duo Sil and Eliza Reynolds describe this in their book *Mothering & Daughtering* as 'formless' attention. For those of us more suited to problem solving, this is often especially difficult to give, particularly compared to form-based attention, where we issue instructions – something we do when they are little (don't touch the hot oven, etc). We may sometimes get into patterns of behaviour and perhaps fail to switch from little girl to adolescent, or take a while getting used to this switch.

Sil Reynolds also explains that mirroring behaviour is a form of formless attention. For example, sitting with them or eating when they do. Having read her book, I feel a little guilty about the times I have sped around, ticking off things on a list after or before work when it comes to my daughters' needs. Not guilty about working, you understand – that's a waste of energy and illogical in my opinion – but guilty about not taking as many slow moments as I could between the work as they have got older. That critical voice inside me says I should have stepped out a little more. Carved out 'nothing' times with them and felt less pressure to occupy them with some fun activity. So perhaps find a spot in your day to slow down with your daughters, whether they are anxious or not. The other best piece of advice Dr Pienaar gave me was to remember to tell your teenage daughters how wonderful they are, something you see as they unfold if you perhaps make more opportunities to witness it.

'If there is an ethos of empathy, compassion and kindness around them, they will soak it up,' she adds. 'And you should say, "I really think you are wonderful," to your girls whenever you can. Tell them it is exciting watching them grow up, that it is a privilege to be alongside them. Never let them forget their loveliness, their uniqueness and their beauty. Tell them and show them you love them.'

DON'T PANIC, YOU GOT THIS: A RECAP

1. Don't catastrophise about the potential outcomes of anxious or stressful feelings in your teens. A rainbow of feelings is to be expected. If you want her to be happy all the time that may also put pressure on her to please you, which I don't think is fair. It's OK for her not to be OK sometimes.

2. Anxious feelings are a healthy response to what are deemed 'manageable threats' of daily life. Help her learn how to feel this feeling and find her own coping mechanisms. Talk to her about them.

3. If you are worried, look out for prolonged changes in your teenager's behaviour. You know her best. If she is behaving out of character? Is she withdrawing from her social circle? Look for clues that she may need support. Be curious not overzealous in this, though.

4. Communicate with her. Be direct. Tell her verbally you want to help if she would like it. Unpack her worries with her by actively listening to what she says and without dismissing any of her thoughts. Talking calmly about anxious feelings does not make teens more anxious. Ask her what she is feeling. If she cannot talk about it out loud, perhaps she could write it down. But . . .

5. Do not immediately leap in and solve her problems with practical ideas. Don't go into rescue mode. Explore her feelings with her. Encourage her to rescue herself.

6. Change the conversation: is it anxiety? Or does she feel sad, panicked, overwhelmed? What other words can she use to describe her feelings?

7. Become a pot plant: just keep her company. Don't do, just be. Plan your 'just being time' by being less busy yourself. This can feel ineffective but, trust me, it works wonders.

8. Is her environment helping or hindering her? Can you change anything in the house that may be affecting her negatively? Is she getting enough sleep, fresh air, good food? Could you encourage moderation of her social-media use or screen use in a non-threatening way?

9. Be mindful of exactly how sensitive your daughter is: some girls may find this part of growing up more of a struggle mentally than others. Is your daughter perhaps more fragile, more affected by things like noise, or chaos or hectic family days? Take a step back and be curious about her personality and adapt around her gently. Is her schedule 'too much'? Would it help to clear some of her activities out of her diary? She has changed and so you may need to change how you are with her and review her day-to-day lifestyle.

10. Self-kindness and self-compassion may also help you cope, and your daughter will mirror this by being compassionate to herself. Quieten the negative voices in your head judging your own parenting. Talk to other mums about what you are experiencing. Share your empathy and compassion. That way we may get rid of any shame around this issue and how we cope with it as mothers, or any guilt we may feel about what our daughters are experiencing. And other mums may have coping tactics you have not thought of.

11. Notice any physical changes in your daughter. The mind and body are linked and it may be you spot something that

could be a clue to her needing more emotional support even if she says she is fine. Be curious, calm and gentle when you talk to her about this, though, as she may not know how to tell you what is upsetting her.

12. Rituals and connections: find a way to keep those childhood rituals going in a new form, especially if you are in the tween stage. Tea and biscuits works for us, dog walks. Simple connections are super powerful with teenage girls. They show love.

13. Look under the bed: this is a metaphorical tip. If you focus on one thing that you feel is to 'blame' for your daughter's anxious feelings you may miss the real cause of her feelings. What else is going on in her day-to-day life that may not be helping? This could include your own behaviour. I once kept a diary for during a particularly difficult and tense fortnight with one of my teens and noted it coincided with a really stressful time for me at work. I may have been subconsciously bringing that stress into the house and unintentionally inflicting it on my daughter.

14. The long-term effects of the global pandemic on the mental health of our children and adolescents hasn't been quantified yet – but we know it has affected them negatively, severely in some cases. I have found the mental-health clinician and NSPCC trustee Tanya Byron most helpful on how to deal with the anxiety induced during the pandemic and urge you to check out her website for further guidance on helping your teens through this specifically. And the website Rethink has a useful list of how to access mental health support services in your area.

15. And finally, I often rely on the mantra of author Glennon Doyle when it comes to parenting teenage girls. Remember,

'we can do hard things'. Oh, how my teens roll their eyes when I say this, but it's true. Adolescents can be terrifically resilient and overcome many obstacles at this developmental stage. Applaud them for this. Encourage them to find their own way through. Tell them they *can do hard things*.

20

Teddies on the bed

Or, how could they?

In an unexpected turn of events when my daughter was sixteen, she went on holiday with her then boyfriend of five months, also sixteen. This was her first solo holiday without adults. Too many firsts for my liking, but we said yes, persuaded by the expert way she argued for the four-day trip to Cornwall. She patiently agreed to all the rules I concocted for the break. Eyebrows around us were raised. Our supposedly liberal attitude to her relationship was questioned. But she booked train tickets, sorted a food delivery to the rental cottage she was staying in and even bought a tide timetable to prevent me calling the coastguard and putting them on high alert. We had no logical reason to say no; we felt it would have been cruel and controlling to do so. The only real reason to refuse would have been fear. Fear that she was growing up too fast and no longer needed us, fear that he wouldn't look after her as well as we would. All the fears you could think of, really, but we felt none of them would have made it right for us to say no. Actually, I was proud of her independence and organisational skills.

Some friends thought we'd been reckless in letting her head off with her lovely boyfriend. That it was too soon for her to be doing such things. But we chatted to him and his parents, whose open-minded, caring approach was refreshing. My instinct was that we were making the right call for our daughter. This was something she wanted to do for herself and we supported her calm, thought-out and reasonably made request.

Now, if she had gone off with the teenage version of Keith Richards, I would have said no, or if she was in any way untrustworthy and liable to put herself in danger, we would have refused, but the night we FaceTimed the happy couple, they were drinking pint glasses of apple juice and watching *Cloudy with a Chance of Meatballs*, which is what our then six-year-old was doing too. It may not work for other sixteen-year-olds but for her – sensible, mature – it did. It felt right for us to agree to it.

I am not saying we found it easy, this transition from girlhood to almost-womanhood, because any which way you look at it, when your child becomes sexually active it can feel truly shocking and confusing. This is the line in the sand. The landscape of your relationship has shifted. And it can also feel excruciatingly embarrassing, even for the most open-minded among us.

I used to edit *Cosmopolitan* magazine in the early 2000s, so I feel I've always been able to have an open and honest conversation about sex and sexuality. But even I found elements of this part of the parenting journey uncomfortable.

I have, however, learned two important lessons and those are: never assume the worst and you cannot be the expert. You are Mum, so relax. You don't have to know the specific nuts and bolts. And you won't. The modern world of sex and sexuality is not something about which you will have all the correct physiological, psychological or emotional knowledge. Your views may be outdated, your language around it may be incorrect. But this doesn't mean you are powerless to support your daughter: you can source the information and research the sexual lives of young people. I turned to TV dramas, to books, podcasts and YouTube. Women like Dr Karen Gurney, or YouTube creators like Hannah Witton, Alix Fox or Dr Lindsey Doe, host of the podcast *Sexplanations*, helped. Sites like Brook, Bish Training, Fumble (run by young people) and Sex Positive Families gave me an overview (these resources and more are listed at the back of the book).

Conversations in our home about boys, love, sex, dating, contraception, puberty, periods and LGBTQ+ choices began before adolescence, probably around the age of eight. Indeed, I am having those conversations now with my younger two children.

As your daughters mature you can have a million satellite conversations, which will mould together at the right time when it comes to sex and sexuality. And that is a good way to approach this, according to the experts, for there is no 'chat', no one mafia-style sit-down to nail the details. Your daughters would honestly rather listen to you singing 'Club Tropicana' out loud than do that in their early teens, but after all those smaller chats the bigger stuff is less of a surprise. As we'd had these initial forays into the changes on the horizon (and I'd dropped off what I felt were helpful educational books in my eldest's room) it made it easier for us to go to the GP together to talk about things like contraception. I didn't tell her we 'had' to do this, I asked her if she would like to, given she was now in what seemed like a stable, monogamous relationship.

I can't claim to be a medical or psychological expert on the sex lives of teenage girls but here's what I have learned on my journey so far. This sensitive part of teenage development may require you to move from an old-fashioned mindset into a more modern one. It will almost certainly require you to be compassionate and caring. If you have a pre-teen or a tween now, you should really get moving on the love, sex and relationship jibber-jabber with them asap. Here goes . . .

CONSENT & PLEASURE

I introduced the concept of sexual pleasure early on in the chats with my daughters. I felt it was important for them to know and believe that sex should be enjoyable. I hoped they would be asking 'what do I want to get out of this, what do I like, what do I desire, what makes my body happy?' It was cringey when I talked about this with them, no doubt about it. But these were super short ad hoc conversations, often prompted by something we were watching on telly. The girls were horrified when I mentioned masturbation, lubrication or vibrators, literally horrified. One of them would run off mid conversation!

But I felt I would be letting the sisterhood down if I didn't plant this seed of an idea early on and let them know they may have to experiment to find out what they want sexually. I didn't take it for granted that they knew what they wanted. I think they were around fourteen when I started to discuss these details. The over-riding theme from me was that it could be about what *they* wanted, not just what their partner may want (male or female). They had control and they could refuse to do anything they did not want to do. As girls usually reach puberty before boys, they are more mentally and physically mature so I notice they often pick older partners (the majority of girls I know are in heterosexual relationships, often with older boys, so that is my context). But do these girls know how to ask for what they want in these relationships and are they confident enough to say no to what they don't want?

You may not feel able to talk about female wants at this stage, it may not be part of your conversational repertoire, if not perhaps you could point your daughter in the direction of the right information on this (there is a list in the back of the book).

It goes without saying you should only be this specific if your daughter expresses an interest in relationships and opens herself up to conversations about it, because many teenage girls aren't interested

173

in any of this until much later in adolescence and that is OK too. There are few chances for this topic to come into conversation so have information at your fingertips and have a plan on how you want to tackle it when such occasions do arise. Once again, though: you don't have to be the expert.

The reason I brought up the pleasure principle is because I don't think Western culture cares much about what women want from sex and I'm afraid to say there are still double standards. I think women who admit to loving sex and having many partners are still viewed more negatively than men with the same attitude or experiences. So I believe you have to call it out early on, to help change the narrative.

In my experience, few schools proactively teach girls or boys about female sexual pleasure: focus is instead still on the physical and the risk of disease or pregnancy. Until 2019, guidelines on sex education in schools in the UK hadn't been changed for almost twenty years meaning that even today in these supposedly more enlightened times many pupils may still be getting information from an outdated rule book as some teachers catch up. I cannot imagine orgasms, libido or desire taking up much room on the timetable. According to my two eldest daughters, it certainly didn't on theirs.

It may well be that this negative trope about women and sex is what your teens are seeing on the media they consume or hearing among their peer groups. And young boys are seeing more pornography than any other generation, so they may not be getting many positive messages about women and sex either. Not to mention that what they look at will undoubtedly affect what they ask for or expect from a girl sexually. Unfortunately, it may end up being your daughters who tell teenage boys that the graphic and often violent sex they see online is not normal and where the boundaries should lie.

A lot of this sexual exploration seems to happen via text and we – and our daughters – should be mindful about who is seeing those texts beyond the intended recipient. I think it is worth reiterating as often as you can to your daughters that some boys are also under pressure from peers to prove their masculinity via sex and may push girls too far because of this and they may share intimate moments meant just for them. Stating out loud what could be going on is helpful, despite the eye rolling you will receive (I mean, few teen girls want to hear their mum use the word 'sexting'). Try to speak calmly throughout, because panic is not a parenting tool that works. Do. Not. Freak. Out.

US author Peggy Orenstein's book *Girls & Sex: Navigating the Complicated New Landscape* is a useful read for you when your daughter hits about eleven. Based on interviews with teenage girls in the States, it delves into the mindset of the female adolescent, with stories from the teens themselves. It concludes that while they may learn the physical facts, the concept that they are entitled to pleasure is still some way off. This may be changing as we examine sexuality in all its forms more broadly, but for heterosexual teenage girls, the idea you aren't just saying 'yes' seems largely undiscussed, even now. That you can find sexual joy may not be something everyone has cottoned on to, despite a lot of great (and not so great) sex advice on social media.

But I have to say that listening to my daughter and her friends discussing relationships around our kitchen table or in the back of the car gives me hope, I am quite heartened by their confident and forthright approach. They seem to know where the boundaries lie for relationships or are at least learning fast. Perhaps I have more urban teen girls who are absorbing less traditional influences, but they are furious if they think a boy isn't being respectful. I can only hope they feel confident in expressing this fury in the right situations.

And there is now an army of young women on social media, who would be best described as sex warriors, bright shining stars in the ongoing war against online misogyny. Then there is the array of smart, spirited female writers bringing this subject to books, mainstream TV, film, music and theatre. Women like Florence Given, Flo Perry, Rubina Pabani and Poppy Joy. These new superheroes are spreading a more positive message with intelligence and subtlety and for that we can be thankful.

EVERYBODY IS DOING IT . . . OR ARE THEY?

In the early days of teenagerdom at our house we had a no-bedroom-doors-closed policy when a teenage boy or a couple came over because I quickly found out you need to be aware that other teens may be using your house as a meeting place because theirs is less available.

Perhaps we were seen as the more liberal parents? Who knows, the reality is I still have to take a moment when my now eighteen-year-old asks if a boyfriend can stay overnight. I cannot believe she is this grown-up already, it feels like only moments have passed since the days of crushes on popstars and hands being held at the bus stop after school.

I admire her confident chutzpah, though, I really do. I would never have been able to ask my parents about this so progress has been made, I feel. We did turn this request down several times at the beginning of her main relationship, waiting until we felt it was serious, had an idea of her boyfriend's personality and had a feel for what else was going on in her life at the time.

The boundaries you set will depend on individual circumstances, but it is good to set them. As I have said before, 'rules' will make your daughters feel loved and safe. My advice is to follow your gut instinct on the overnight-stay question and consider it in the wider context of the rest of your daughter's life. Can she handle it emotionally? When asked, you can always answer with 'Let me think about that': it's a helpful phrase that gives you both time to consider the issue and it shows her you have listened and that you care enough to think it through.

She may in fact be looking to you to set this boundary, to boost her confidence to say no to her partner.

You may not feel the same as we did and choose to say no to the overnight stay full stop, or no to boyfriends in bedrooms, door open or not. Boundaries are good to set, but when you do so, explain your preferences calmly and don't judge or shame her in any way for asking the question.

The choice is personal to you and I think as long as you can remain available for your daughter to talk to, whatever your decision, that is key to keeping a connection and possibly preventing her from becoming secretive and feeling unsupported.

What I have noticed is that some teenage girls dive headfirst into the pool of attention they suddenly start getting from the opposite sex. When I have talked to experts on this, the advice is to observe how much of their self-esteem may become tied up in the attention they get from boys and perhaps how much their status among their own peer group is reflected in their having a boyfriend. This new drama of girls who really like boys adds a layer of complexity to your parenting. It means you may have to look at your daughter's whole life; what else is going on in it that may be prompting her to focus so much on boys? Perhaps she is struggling at school and the idea that she is suddenly good at something else appeals to her?

If you are worried your daughter may be over-investing her time in relationships it could be useful to distract her or think about how else she could boost her self-esteem. I have a mum friend who found her daughter a Saturday job when she went 'boy mad', as she put it. The job occupied her and also made her feel independent. It also tweaked her circle of friends. Some parents do this with sport or other activities; it is a gentle nudge in a different direction. It may take a few different suggestions to shift a teeanger's focus, and it could also simply be a phase as things change so rapidly during adolescence. Basically, try not to immediately over-compensate for her new-found enthusiasm and observe her emotions around relationships with patience.

JUST KEEP TALKING (side by side, never face to face)

In my experience the key to supporting your daughter's sexual awakening in puberty is to be sensitive to the way your daughter wants to discuss this. My second daughter is more uncomfortable talking to me about the more intimate issues, so I have stepped back and instead found resources she can look at. She is likelier to turn to her older sister than to me but I still make it clear that I am available and reliable, that I won't panic and I won't freak out whatever she asks or tells me.

Gen Z give their love lives quite a bit of thought and they have a lot of information at their fingertips via their mobile phones, so it may be tempting to think they know a lot. However, I think they see a lot but don't always know how to process that information. You may need to help them understand what they see or read; you still need to talk or listen to them about specifics, to connect without being overly intrusive and invading their privacy. A family-planning expert once told me that, contrary to popular belief (perhaps perpetuated by parents who, understandably, find it almost impossible to talk to their kids about this), teens can deal with hearing specifics from their parents on the subject of love and sexual intimacy. They don't want to hear about you and your partner, obviously – that would cause spontaneous vomiting – but they may want to know you can be available emotionally and physically to discuss this most intimate of subjects. They don't want you to be alarmed when you see them holding hands or find them entwined on the sofa or snatching a kiss. They don't want to be teased about their new relationships, they won't like smirking or being generally made fun of, even if you feel this lightens the mood around the whole subject.

They may want to be able to ask questions. They may want you to be the 'askable parent'. Often your daughter may instinctively know certain behaviours in a relationship are wrong and may need to tell you about it, but she is unlikely to do this if she thinks she is letting you down, disgusting you or horrifying you in any way. And she wants to be taken seriously.

At first, I thought I was being too liberal with my daughters, but I think this was maybe a leftover from my own childhood. My parents never discussed such subjects and I may have been subconsciously berating myself for being so open because it felt 'bad' to do so. This was the message I took from the more repressed 1970s and 1980s upbringing. Check in with yourself on how your childhood may affect your attitudes to talking about sex and relationships. Just a thought.

If you stay calm and listen when your daughters ask intimate questions or describe situations, you are not saying, 'I approve of this behaviour,' you are being empathetic. From that, you can move forward to help her, even if you are perhaps upset or even angry about what she has raised. You can sometimes 'mirror' your daughter's emotions back to her, by which I mean you repeat back to her what you think she is saying but in your own words. This may help her understand what she is feeling and think more deeply about the situation, because she has to listen to the behaviour she has described or the permission she has requested. You are almost asking her to approve the request herself rather than giving her your opinion; it's encouraging her to talk it through out loud before you tell her what you think. Every situation is different but active listening, throwing questions back, may make her explore the subject she is discussing more thoroughly. Your hope is that she'll conclude herself that, say, sending nude pictures to her boyfriend when he requests them is wrong. Her reaching such decisions herself will be far more effective than you laying down the law on her behalf, I think.

Knowledge is power when it comes to sexual relationships and a happy sexuality is a gift you can give your teen girls if you do some research and learn where to point your daughters in the direction of more information.

Perhaps I can direct you to the Netflix comedy drama *Sex Education*, which was one of our parenting tools. It explores so many relevant themes around modern sexuality. I found it brilliant for teens of any age. I interviewed the young cast and the programme's intimacy coach, Ita O'Brien, who explained that everything you see on screen is based in fact or a real-life experience of a teenager. It is not exaggerated for dramatic effect.

It has all the correct information and language, although be ready for how astonishingly graphic it can be. We didn't watch it together, but all of us saw it and so used some scenes as jumping-off points for chats. Remember my advice, though: dog walks, car journeys, always talk side by side for these chats, never face to face.

The sex lives of teenagers can be messy. They make mistakes, they may lose their way, sometimes they may need to bring you stories that shock you or tell you about abuse or harrassment they may have suffered or witnessed. Until I wrote the piece about the scene in *Sex Education* portraying it, I had no idea how common sexual assaults on young women on public transport were; yet every young member of the cast I spoke to had experienced it and when I got back to my office at the *Sunday Times* every young female colleague in my team told me they had also endured it at some point, as I have too on several occasions. So, depressingly, it is likely that your daughter will one day need to talk to you about it – and she may not feel comfortable doing so if you have freaked out in the past about anything else intimate she has shared. Learn not to look shocked when you listen to these experiences. And being informed will help, knowing what's coming will help. I read something in Peggy Orenstein's first book, *Schoolgirls: Young Women, Self-Esteem and the Confidence Gap*, which I found comforting and hope you do too: there is 'magic in awareness'. She is so right. Even if you are just tiptoeing around the subject with your teen when it comes to sex and sexuality, you are at least aware, and from that good things can come.

GENDER IDENTITY AND SEXUAL ORIENTATION

Your teenage daughter's sexual identity is evolving and you cannot influence it. You have no idea what choices your child will make, who they will be attracted to, who they will want to be. Several of our friends' teenagers entered same-sex relationships, or decided they were bisexual in early teenage. Some Gen X parents, with the more traditional heterosexual narrative running through their minds, found this challenging to accept. But I believe you must try to open your heart to accepting your teenagers' choices in a way that supports your teenager. When I volunteered on the text helpline Shout, reading about the lack of parental acceptance of same-sex love was deeply upsetting.

Personally, I think it is truly one of the most damaging ways to parent, no matter what your beliefs. Such parental rejection pierced their children's hearts and made them feel unloved and, in some cases, ashamed. By causing these negative emotions in your child, you are potentially putting them in danger from themselves. Kindness should be the easier choice, whether or not you agree with or approve of your child's choice. Ensuring the good mental health of your teen surely is the most important part of what you do as a parent? Possibly you should find professional help and advice on this if you cannot support your child's decision, no matter how uncomfortable that makes you feel. Open your heart and mind to educating yourself about the LGBTQ+ community, and maybe talk to a counsellor or text Shout yourself to ask questions. If you still struggle, perhaps find someone with more empathy or experience around the situation to take on the responsibility of supporting your teen. If you alienate your teenager over their choice of partner, they may close down the line of communication between the two of you, and then they won't have anywhere to turn in times of trouble.

I think teenage girls who are in a sexuality minority, i.e. are anything other than heterosexual, may find it harder to be as open as they would like to be with their parents about their life, choices, feelings and behaviour. It is extremely stressful to be part of a frequently stigmatised and attacked group. Adolescence is stressful enough on its own, so to have this on top may well feed into any anxiety already present in your daughter and create an overwhelming combination of thoughts and worries for a developing mind to process.

In her book *Untamed*, the author Glennon Doyle reminds us that saying things like 'I love you no matter what' is not helpful if your daughter offers a choice that does not sit comfortably with you. Try not to say that because it may imply disappointment, an emotion your child may struggle to deal with at such a pivotal time in her life. Disappointing a parent is one of the main fears teenagers grapple with that can have a significant negative effect on their mental health.

Doyle advises us not to be 'expectations parents': parents who say they love their kids even if they don't meet their expectations, hence 'no matter what'. Instead, be 'treasure hunt' parents, she says, and encourage your kids to keep digging until they uncover their identity throughout adolescence. Also, for the sake of clarity, gender identity is separate to sexual orientation. Which gender your daughter identifies with will not define her sexual orientation (who she is attracted to). Using the correct language in these situations is crucial.

If your daughter brings you a choice you don't fully understand, agree with or expect, perhaps you don't tell her you love her 'in spite' of this but *because* of it? Congratulate her on her ability to choose a path for herself.

She is telling you who she is possibly becoming and that's a mature and wonderful thing. Be proud. Support her by being alongside her on her voyage of new discoveries and pleasures.

HEARTBREAK IS INEVITABLE

As we know, because we were all teenagers once, not all first loves are good experiences. When mums talk to me about their daughters' terrible partners and bad treatment of their beloveds, sometimes the mums' tales drift forwards into the future. Really, it is best to stay in the moment: your teen most probably won't marry this person, so there is no need to scare yourself with a story that won't come true. I also think, from personal experience, that you don't know what a good relationship is unless you've had a bad one. Remember: your daughter is learning a lot about herself by being in such a close relationship with someone else, isn't she? This is all going into her adult persona, shoring up her banks of future resilience, improving her instincts. It's all about listening to her – why does she like this terrible partner? Why did she pick him or her, what is it about them that appeals to her? You may never agree and you may want to shut the bad boyfriend's head in the door, but it will probably only alienate her if you cannot talk with her about relationships or if you show your disapproval time and again.

It is worth noting that when I have interviewed couples therapists, they make the point that teenagers will absorb what they see around them, meaning that how you and your partner behave in front of them may affect your child's view of what a relationship should be, or what she may 'endure' in a partner. One therapist told me it is common for teens to be worried about their parents' relationship because they may witness rows but rarely see their parents making up as that is often done behind closed doors. You are in many ways role modelling what a good relationship could look like so it's worth being mindful of that.

Teenage love is a wonderful thing to witness when it goes well. I would often watch wistfully as my daughter and her first boyfriend stood, arms wrapped around each other, in our kitchen cooking their breakfast together at 4 p.m., inseparable even for the minute it takes to take a teabag out of a cup. What a great start to her romantic life, I wistfully thought.

I was both a little bit jealous of their hope-filled new devotion and cascade of raw love, and a little bit scared about how doomed it was – how it would end, how we would one day say goodbye to this dreamy, six-foot young man, who loved my cooking and talked to me with polite interest and earnest kindness. He is part of our family history. When it did end as she turned eighteen, it felt brutal for us all. He was part of our lives for nearly two years then all of a sudden, he was gone.

The summer of turning eighteen is a shocker because, no matter how stable everyone appears to be in their adolescent relationships it seems that those with long-term boyfriends or girlfriends actually make a plan to part; they seem to know (at least the urban adolescents I have known) coupledom won't survive further education, or a gap year or whatever life holds away from the routine and world of school. Do bear this likelihood of a break-up and its aftermath in mind if your daughter has a long-term boyfriend before she hits eighteen and prepares to leave home.

There is much debate among the girls about how to end their love affairs; my mum-friend WhatsApp group was pinging through the summer months with 'it's over' chats, as we all felt a wave of sadness or, in some cases, relief that our daughters' first few steps into adult romantic life had come to an end.

It isn't always a smooth cut-off, and much drama ensues in parks and pub gardens during those sticky summer evenings. Some huffing and some sulking and then another round of tears as make-ups break-up again.

When our eldest was that age and her relationship with her boyfriend ended, I had known it was coming because anyone who has been a teenage girl in a teenage relationship will recognise the signs. But the tear-stained face of the girl you love so much, her little heart shattered into a thousand pieces, is unbearable to watch. For it is not just any old heartbreak – it is the uber-dramatic stuff-of-love-songs heartbreak. You may not be able to make their pain go away but you can just be there as they go through it.

Bella Hird, a family therapist specialising in adolescence, told me that the positive you can take from their distress is that this negative emotion is all part of the learning curve of getting ready to live in the real world as a grown-up. In these times, Hird says, you need empathy, not sympathy.

The American self-help guru Brené Brown has made a film explaining the difference between empathy and sympathy, which could be useful if you're tiptoeing around how to support a heart-broken teen. You will need lots of tea and empathy. You cannot make them smile; you can only keep reiterating that you know how awful this is for them, keep taking them seriously even in the more OTT dramatic moments and keep treating the emotional pain with the same care and attention you would a physical one. Love hurts, which is something we all know.

'Mum, What's Wrong With You?'
Conversations with Teens

[After a terrorist alert in central London while my eldest is out shopping]

Me: Can you text me where you are in case anything happens?

Her: Why?

Me: [sigh] In case anything happens. I'm worried.

Her: There won't be a terrorist attack. You don't need to know where I am at this exact moment.

Me: How can you possibly know when an attack will happen? You're not M from James Bond.

Her: Look, I just know. It's not on Snapchat; the news says it is just an alert. No one would attack Tottenham Court Road at this stage – they would go for where the politicians are. My friend says it won't happen and his dad is in the Navy. So you don't need to be so dramatic and make such a fuss about where I am. You can't track my movements every minute of every day, for god's sake. I am not a prisoner. And you really don't know anything about counterterrorism.

Me: Just text me where you are, OK?

Her: [Long, bored sigh.]

21

Her new body and body image

My job has meant that I have been at the forefront of the body-image debate, submerged, if you will, in our Western culture of 'lookism' for decades, during which time I have witnessed many changes in attitude and behaviour, for good and bad.

My decisions on magazine cover girls (many of whom I knew personally and had watched grow up through their own teenage years) will no doubt have influenced young female readers' attitudes to what is or isn't beautiful.

I've interviewed several experts on body image, delved into the books – feminist, medical and psychological – reported on the surveys and new thinking. I've also interviewed women whose looks came to define them in many ways (those cover girls, the supermodels, A-list actresses, athletes), as well as iconic feminists and plus-size campaigners. So as my daughters grew up, I was perhaps hypersensitive to and about the whole matter of body image, worried about not being able to set them up with a robust self-esteem and confidence around their developing bodies.

I also worked in offices predominantly staffed by women, where body talk was sometimes a self-critical rumble in the background of our day. Many women are on a constant journey to change something about themselves physically, which they often feel, inexplicably, will make every other part of their life better if they just get it right. Body talk is relentless in the world of women.

So after absorbing all this, computing it and rationalising it, you would hope I would have some answers when it comes to protecting your teenage girls from poor body image and any low self-esteem associated with it, that I could swoop in and throw a bulletproof vest over them and their emotions, but sadly I can't. I'm sorry.

The best I can offer when it comes to mothering teenage girls around body-image self-esteem is to suggest you go quiet. All chat about appearance, size, shape and looks has to stop. Not the listening to them when they talk about it, you understand, but just your talking about it. Your opinions on any of it. Your silence as their number one female role model is golden. Actually, this is true for girls of all ages, not just teens. And boys. Best to say nothing. Give their bodies no value. Instead give other attributes value while keeping your expectations around achievements in check.

But this advice to go mute is almost impossible to follow, isn't it, in today's world? The conundrum is context: our society places so much value on the appearance of women as a metric of good or bad that you cannot protect them entirely, even by being totally mute at home, because this conversation is not mute outside of your home. It is so complex that I don't know where to start unpicking it. What mum or dad can never comment on their daughter's looks? Sometimes things just slip out and we can tie ourselves up in knots. But even if you have spent your daughter's childhood telling her how beautiful she is, valuing her looks, now is the time to stop. Find her value in other things about her. Change the narrative.

Also, let's remember you yourself are probably hitting midlife, when body confidence becomes more of an issue again, like it was during your teenage years. If you are Gen X, then your body will be changing: hair loss, a thickening waist, adult acne, loss of collagen (all symptoms of the perimenopause). This may come as a bit of a shock to you, just as the new hair everywhere, the growth spurt, the puppy fat, the acne, breasts, periods often are a shock to an adolescent female. But now, more than ever, you have to stay calm and quiet. You may have a billion years of negative natter about it under your belt already, so in the presence of this new woman-to-be, who absorbs your every thought and watches your every move, you really must not talk about it any more. Therapists and parenting experts reinforce this advice. Resist the urge to comment on your daughter's looks or body, don't succumb to using the careless toxic language of funny put-downs or casual remarks about weight, skin or shape. Avoid commenting on what she, or any other female, looks like or is wearing; avoid comparison to other girls or siblings. Ask the significant male figures in their life to do this too. Try to stay quiet until your teen hits her early twenties, and even then it would be sensible to refrain from body talk, unless it is about her health. Keep the conversation consistently neutral.

I regret I didn't remain as quiet as would have been helpful, even when I knew I should. When they were little I said I would never use the D-word: diet. But as they grew older I did. They've heard me moan about putting on weight in midlife, about my wobbly four-pregnancy-stretched tummy, about the giant frown line down my forehead that makes me look permanently grumpy. The girls heard all this. And god, I regret it, I really feel shame and guilt about the possible effect this talk had on their own body image, and worried in retrospect about the effect it had on my then seven-year-old daughter and eleven-year-old son. I try to be less vocal about it all now.

I wince when I hear my daughters criticise their own healthy bodies, when they show embarrassment that they don't conform to

189

so-called normal standards, but until the society we live in, that they are growing up in, changes its definition of beauty, we are sort of stuck. It's bigger than all of us.

You might feel that perhaps by staying silent we are playing into the narrative that women have something to hide particularly as we age, but we can talk about it – just not in front of our daughters. I am not advocating denying something factual that happens to women, thus implying we are ashamed of ourselves, I just don't want to fuel the negative internal voices that adolescent girls are vulnerable to believing at this stage. Sure, they need information, but stick to physical facts that would be helpful for them.

If you have no issues and have a positive relationship with your body, good for you, but even if you have only uplifting things to say, please still say as little as possible; instead, look to giving value to other things your girls do, other personality traits rather than appearance. Be available to listen to their worries, though, no matter how trivial they seem or even vain or shallow (and teen girls will stare at a piece of skin in the mirror for days before announcing there is something cataclysmically wrong with it), but don't give an opinion, give facts and encourage talk of other things they do that you can praise and admire them for.

In 2018 I asked writer and activist Honey Ross, now twenty-three, who is a size eighteen, to write a piece for the magazine I was then editing about body confidence, given her intelligent and smart attitude towards it, which I had followed on her social media. She had talked about her parents' worries about her size and weight as a teenager and wrote 'How to Raise a Body-Confident Child' for me. Honey remembered that her diagnosis with severe dyslexia as a young child may have led to a reward culture at home around food, a debit and credit mindset that prompted her parents into hiring a personal trainer for her when she was fourteen.

She was at Weight Watchers with her mother during her mid-teens and at one point says she was 'a miserable size ten', joining her parents on the keto diet but still hating her body. She says she thinks that all of this was, in retrospect, an unhelpful way to deal with a teenage girl with body-image worries. But all of it came from the deepest well of parental support and love. It was only when Honey started to see women who were not slim on social media celebrating their size that she began to accept the body she was in, gaining, as she put it, 'hours of my life back not thinking about how awful my body shape is and demonising food'.

When I first read her piece, it was her thoughtful mother's defiant and loving battle to make her happy that struck me particularly as the most poignant part of this story. As mums, we want to give our teenage daughters the gift of body happiness, which I don't think is always entirely possible in our Western culture. The message that slimmer is better is so continually reinforced that it feels it is almost impossible to overcome, though strides are being made in chipping away at this culture of female body perfectionism, with a loud collection of more diverse campaigners who have their own platforms to help educate young women. I would urge you to seek out these new voices online. The singer Lizzo is a particular favourite of mine but allow your daughter to find ones that suit her.

I get all mixed up in the arguing around body image because I know so much is wrong, but I cannot put all of it right myself; I can only do what I can personally for my daughters (and my son, as boys experience this pressure too).

I spoke to Honey as I was writing this book to ask her how she thought her mum was feeling through the emotional years of Honey's adolescence and she says, 'I saw her pain.' She also admits it is hard never to mention body image at home.

'It is so difficult for mums,' Honey tells me over the phone. 'I felt there has to be a level where you can talk about it as a family. When my parents tried to avoid it, I was suspicious. My parents had not healed their own issues with food and body image, so when they said to me I was smart or lovely or funny and didn't comment on my appearance, I wouldn't believe them because there would be a level of distrust, because I knew they were on a diet themselves. How can you sell something you haven't bought into yourself? was what I was asking myself. So this conversation has to be in the room somehow.' And, as Honey points out, the bit of the problem that was toxic was society's attitude to her body, not how her parents dealt with it.

'My mum and I have always been close. I knew I could bring anything into the room and not make my parents feel uncomfortable or judge me, but society was always going to judge me. Mum-daughter relationships are complicated and tangled, and you need to navigate boundaries with each other. I found it helpful to see my parents' own vulnerability around this too, so I could see we were all growing together and the work isn't done overnight.

'Teenage girls are uncooked, half-baked beings; everything is so raw, so huge at the time, so when I look back, I see everyone was doing their best.'

Her best piece of advice looking back at her teenage years is that old failsafe of active listening. You may not be able to solve any problems, but you can be there as they confront their worries and talk about it. And step in if you feel they might need help from a professional therapist.

'Being listened to was the most important way Mum supported me,' Honey adds. 'She was present and open and honest about everything. I knew that she could cope with everything I was going through, and as a result I could see even at seventeen that parenting was a tough job, and once I had that empathy for them, I had it for myself as well. Mum made it clear she wouldn't dictate to me, that she would listen.'

Honey is an advocate of therapy for teenage girls worrying about this, if you can afford it, but a non-judgemental and unshockable parental attitude is generally always a help. To appreciate what else your daughter stands for besides how she looks and to show empathy around her body-image worries is your job. I think lurking is a good parental tip during the teen years, because they often want to talk to you at the oddest times and you just have to have an open door and be around. Perhaps the attitude you are aiming for with teenage girls and body image is an acceptance that everyone is different and that is OK. That they *are* normal as all these new things happen to their body.

Social media is often demonised as much as food in this debate but to do that is perhaps to misunderstand the internet. The body-positivity movement is huge, and now young girls can see so many different bodies (hurrah Lizzo) being celebrated on social media that they have something else influencing them apart from highly curated magazine covers, Hollywood films and TV shows that previously fed into adolescent thinking. YA books have pushed the boundaries on body image, popstars have been vocal about the need to accept a better range of body shapes, and models do now come in all shapes and sizes. I have put many of the new army of outspoken, activist women on magazine covers in the past few years and been proud to see how that has prompted a positive response from the young women reading the publications I edited. I wish I had done this earlier in my magazine career.

I think we are at the beginning of a body-image revolution in the media, but we need to keep thinking about it at home too. As Honey points out, a parent's job is also to see what our teens are looking at on social media, to help direct their attention to what is more accepting and relevant. To curate the feeds more. To support them in finding a positive bubble online.

She advocates talking to your daughter about what she is watching and listening to without judgement on her reasons for liking certain things.

'This problem is so much bigger than all of us,' she adds. 'Keeping an eye on who they follow and asking them if this makes them feel good or bad about themselves is helpful. Encouraging teen girls to follow accounts that make them happy and ignore others is a good thing for mums to do. These teens of Gen Z are warriors; they will back up behind something they really care about or believe in and that will help them form a healthy attitude to body image.

'Everything during your teenage years feels high octane; all the stakes feel so high to be able to find your community online is reassuring. The pressure on a teen girl to be normal is intense, so seeing other women like you makes you feel as if everything will turn out OK in the end. I think if you can, as a mum, help them find these girls online and you can keep putting inspirational women in front of them, then you are showing them it is going to turn out OK.'

And many young women I speak to make the point that they are very much aware of what is real and what has been digitally manipulated or changed to present a more perfect image in the media. We should not underestimate the ability of young women to make their own minds up too; indeed, we shouldn't patronise them by generalising about how they see other women, particularly famous women. And, of course, many other things feed into how resilient a teenager is around this subject, as I have said before: her neurological development, her environment, her particular peer group, her personality, issues or changes at home.

Personally I feel incredibly grateful that I seem to have been lucky with my girls around this issue; while they do sometimes talk negatively about what they see as their bodily imperfections these thoughts don't seem to affect their mental health. Did we dodge this bullet, I wonder? Or have I just not noticed it? Is it manifesting in a different way? I hope I have made myself available and I have not judged their choices.

I often wonder if maybe my field of work has meant I take for granted that they will express their identity in what they choose to wear, how they do their make-up and hair. I don't have an opinion; I just let them wear what they want. I sometimes wince when I see the leering face of 'white van man' as my girls stride off up the road, but I don't stop them dressing in any way they want to. I see fashion and beauty as a form of self-expression, even the piercings, which, truth be told, I really don't like. It is up to them.

My observations of my daughters are that they don't let it seep into their soul in a harmful or even meaningful way. They look at pictures on their phone of well made-up, line-free women with concave tummies and tell me they know it is not real. They berated me when I once had Botox on my forehead for a piece I was writing, asking why I was unhappy about the number '11' frown lines between my eyes, claiming I had let the sisterhood down. We had a fiery debate, I enjoyed listening to their views.

I hope I did the self-esteem heavy lifting during the early years so that when my girls became teenagers, the message that all sorts of 'normals' exist was anchored in. They certainly met a host of people from hugely different backgrounds at home.

But if you feel your daughter is troubled by her body image as a result of your behaviour and language around it, there is always time to heal; change doesn't come from blame. Change comes from awareness about what you may not have got right. Knowing that means you can move forward and talk about this with your daughter.

So many things can bombard girls as they develop, so remain vigilant and offer them the space to talk about body image without pushing them to do so.

For some young women it might be impossible to overcome society's body-image obsession easily and ignore the value put into looks, so those teens may need professional help. If the worry about body image is overwhelming and affecting their mental health, go to your GP for advice.

IDENTITY AND RACE

This subject is a book in itself; far too big a conversation for me to have in one chapter, but also too important to be left out. There are some excellent reading resources, which I have included in the back of the book, but I wanted to address how for mothers of Black and brown girls the world is littered with even more emotional landmines when it comes to body image and identity.

The area and city I live in is far more racially diverse than many other parts of the country. Yet, as a white mother to three white girls, my experience of raising a family is a hugely privileged one in comparison to the mothers of Black or brown teenage girls in the same environment. Only recently have young Black and brown teens seen role models on magazine covers or represented in other media they are influenced by, which would help them feel valued. I spoke to screenwriter and actress Sherise Blackman, the mum of two daughters aged thirteen and sixteen, about her experience as a mother of Black teens in London, and it is significantly more complicated and exhausting than mine.

Society often expects Black teenage girls to be more mature than white girls of the same age and they are often oversexualised in our Western culture. Many also experience racism from infant-school age on. Sherise tells me that all this can feel like an overwhelming combination of factors for a Black mum.

'I have to protect my girls more,' she tells me. 'I have to allow them to be their ages, not to be rushed into developing too fast. And to know about their culture and history, because it is largely ignored at school. As they grow independent, though, Black mums may have to remain as close as possible, to be allies for them, given what they face in society, which is a different and often more negative and stressful experience than a white teenage girl's.

'My girls cannot push me too far away as they mature, because they need me to navigate this time. I have been a Black teenager; I know what they are going through better than anyone else.'

She tells me her teens will perhaps be 'kinder to her' as they separate into adults than white teens are to their mums because of the unique experience of growing up in a culture that can make Black women feel invisible and can perpetuate the myth of 'the angry young Black woman'.

She adds: 'My best bit of advice for Black mums is to make your daughters feel as if there is no scenario in which you won't love them, nothing they can do which will stop you supporting them.

'It's exhausting sometimes and it takes lot of energy to be on high alert for my girls all the time. I need to be strong, to watch out for them and the unconscious bias they face at school and when they are out and about.

'I want them to remain "soft", though, not to bury the bad things they may experience, but to be able to talk about it with me and work out a good response to racism they may endure. And while things are changing when it comes to attitudes to body image, I still have to make much of an effort to find the right hair and make-up products for my daughters.

'There are more role models now I can offer my daughters, more high-profile Black women in society, so I can only hope this will be less exhausting for the girls when they are mums.'

Dr Pragya Agarwal, who has twin four-year-old girls and another daughter in her early twenties, has written a brilliant book if you are wondering how to talk to your children about race and understand your own biases. It will also allow you to be a better ally as you engage with your daughter's friends from different backgrounds. It's called *Wish We Knew What to Say: Talking with Children about Race* and when I spoke to her in 2020 her main piece of advice was to make sure your daughter knows where she is from, that she knows about her family background if she is not white.

'I think it is so important to connect girls to their racial ethnicity, to give them information about their ancestors,' she says. 'As the only person of colour at my school, I tried to fit in, but differences do matter. I spent much time talking to my eldest daughter about feminism growing up but I didn't talk to her explicitly about race. This is something I am doing with my younger daughters.

'Research shows some teens may reject their own racial identity if they don't mix with people like them, so you need to talk about this with your children, keep the information flowing and do not allow them to internalise racism. They must talk about it and feel comfortable with who they are and feel they fit in somewhere.

'The gender dynamics for Black or brown teenage girls are different from white girls; they are seen differently by boys, who expect them to be more mature, which is unfair.

'Talking to your girls about this is important. Never underestimate the impact on her emotionally. Society is becoming more open, this debate is being openly discussed, and silence won't be tolerated by new generations, but you have to be there for them as mum as they experience this.'

All parents should try to educate themselves around race so we can recognise where our biases are and be able to take part in conversations around the issue with our daughters in a modern, relevant way.

PUBERTY & PERIODS

When our daughters were around the age of eight, we began to talk to them about what would happen to their bodies during puberty. I bought the book *The Care and Keeping of You* for them and left them in their rooms, and while this book is a little old-fashioned we found it a suitable tween or pre-teen resource. I also think Judy Blume's novel *Are You There, God? It's Me, Margaret* is useful, even though it was written in 1970.

If you are a Gen X mum it may be that your own mother never had a conversation with you about periods. Mine, like many of her generation, was embarrassed and perhaps a little ashamed of having periods. She didn't tell me much, teachers told me nothing and my Cornish comprehensive school peer group weren't any better – between us, we knew so little.

When, at the age of twelve, I told my mum I had started my period she replied that it wasn't possible to start so early so we didn't discuss it again until the following month when it became impossible for me to muddle through without sanitary pads! I don't blame her for this attitude – she had been raised not to talk about it. Women had been denying what happens to their bodies for so long her attitude was not unusual.

Even now, though, we still seem to find it tricky to talk publicly about women and their menstrual cycle. Infuriatingly the taboos endure and according to the charity Plan International UK, one in five young girls in the UK are teased or bullied about their periods, a statistic that makes me both sad and angry.

I have spoken several times to Dr Shazhadi Harper about the menstrual life of teenage girls. Now a private GP after a career in the NHS, Dr Harper is a specialist in perimenopause and menopause yet who also treats teenagers struggling with the hormonal activity in puberty.

If your daughter is suffering from extremely painful, irregular or heavy periods, then you should take her to the GP as this pain may be a symptom of other conditions that need treating such as PCOS (polycystic ovary syndrome) or possibly endometriosis. Get it checked out immediately, she does not have to endure this and it is not her 'womb settling down' as one mum once explained it to me before I implored her to take her daughter to an expert. This assumption that women, even as teens, must put up with pain is unhelpful, to say the least.

Dr Harper, the mum of a teenage daughter herself, emphasised the importance of taking any level of pain your daughter is feeling during her menstrual cycle seriously.

'Pre-Menstrual Syndrome or PMS can have a big effect on a young girl's life. As her oestrogen drops in the week before her period, she is more likely to suffer from low mood, anxious feelings, irritability and perhaps have carb or sugar cravings,' she told me. 'For some these may be mild symptoms, for others they could be cataclysmic. They could affect schoolwork or exam results quite severely and, in some cases, could necessitate a mild antidepressant being prescribed for the time just before a period. These symptoms may completely change your daughter's personality. This hormone fluctuation is out of her control and some young women are desperate by the time I get to speak to them. We need to intervene as early as possible to support them.'

Dr Harper also told me that there is prescription pain relief medicine, such as mefenamic acid, which will not only remove cramps but reduce blood flow as well, unlike over-the-counter medication such as Ibuprofen, which will only help with the pain. Ask your GP about this. Some teenagers are prescribed the pill, which may help with all the symptoms of PMS, but you can also help your daughter by supporting her with diet supplements: Vitamin A, magnesium, Vitamin D and iron. I know of teenage girls whose hair started to thin due to lack of iron in their diet combined with heavy periods. And 25 per cent of women get diarrhoea during their periods, which makes life pretty intolerable.

Many young women use apps tracking their menstrual cycle today and therefore know when they are more likely to suffer from PMS and perhaps alter their lifestyle around it. I think we should also be aware as parents of what they are doing during the week before their periods, when effects of their hormones will be more intense. If they are any experimenting with drink and drugs, partying with

PMS, it may make the effects of those substances worse. It is worth highlighting that to your girls.

If your daughter suffers from anxiety then be aware that her mental health may decline when she has PMS and she may need extra support. If she cannot talk to you about any of this can she talk to another woman or perhaps you can point her in the direction of resources that can help?

Sites like HelloFlo and its accompanying book are great, if a little American in feel. One of my favourite sites, which is especially good for older teens, is Maisie Hill's, and her book *Period Power* looks at the whole cycle and the effect of hormones on every aspect of your female life. US gynaecologist Dr Jen Gunter's spirited TED Talk 'Why Can't We Talk About Periods?' may be helpful for you to find out the specific facts.

When my daughters were eight years old, I showed them tampons and pads. When they were eleven, we made them a little beauty bag of period necessities, and they took this to school each day just in case.

I also involved my husband, by asking him to chat with them about it occasionally, so that nothing was taboo in our house. I made sure he knew not to make fun of any element of this aspect of their lives – I have noticed that so many men of his generation have a default old-fashioned negative humour that focuses on periods as a way to demean women. Our son has in turn no doubt absorbed all the conversations going on around him and he knows a Mooncup when he sees one!

LET'S GET MOVING

Some teenage girls love sport, some do not. But a lot of them drop out of organised sporting activity when they hit puberty, which could have a negative long-term effect on their physical and mental health.

I work with a charity called Women in Sport, which encourages a more diverse attitude to girls and exercise and runs campaigns to get mums and daughters exercising together. For some girls, the traditional school sports aren't enjoyable because they perhaps are made to feel bad at it by traditional PE-teaching methods. Many adolescent girls, mine included, are given little advice on their developing bodies with regards to sport: no one but me, for example, mentioned a sports bra until my eldest was in her mid-teens, which I found a shocking omission.

Girls drop out of doing sport for many reasons and according to Women In Sport, by the age of fourteen, girls in the UK are playing half as much sport as boys. Judgement from their peers is cited as the main reason teen girls cross sport off their to-do lists and I also think school sport is often connected to a culture of achievement, which eludes many teenage girls. Sport doesn't just have to be about winning. We know regular exercise is good for mental health, so I think it is important you encourage your daughter to keep it up. It is tricky, because they won't always be keen to go outside. Ours joined the local council-run gym. Getting a dog helped us, especially at weekends, and even their friends joined in. A dog isn't an option for everyone, of course. Perhaps look to more enjoyable energetic activities for them than the ones schools offer: martial arts, ice skating (ours had a brief moment with this as we live near Ally Pally and its ice rink in London), boxing (my sixteen-year-old loved it so much that she set up a boxing club at school), dance. Or why not Park Run, which they could do with their friends, or even you? It's a free, sociable 5K run held in parks across the world every Saturday, for all ages and speeds. Make an effort to form a habit that involves movement before your girls become teens. I persuaded our nine-year-old daughter to take up football by encouraging her friends to do it with her.

Some teenage girls put a little weight on during puberty and exercise can help here too, of course, keeping them healthy. And while we should try not to attribute value to looks and image in our conversations, it is fine to talk to our daughters if we think they are not caring well for themselves. I think it is OK to say if you notice your child gaining an unhealthy amount of weight due to her bad diet or chaotic eating pattern. But the conversation is about her looking after herself and staying healthy, not about her being over-weight because it looks bad or because she doesn't fit into her clothes. In these circumstances you can offer alternatives to what your daughter may be consuming, and investigate other non-judgemental strategies around better, less-disordered eating, but talk about health, not size. They are still just working out what they like to eat, so patterns of eating change and their tastes seem to change too. It is not unexpected and should not become a huge focus of family life.

Make sure you explain this to relatives who don't see your daughters as often as you do; some from an older generation can make careless and thoughtless comments around size and weight. And of course, siblings can also be cruel when it comes to appearance, so be vigilant about conversations around you. If you are worried, perhaps an appointment with a nutritionist would be useful for your daughter to help her make healthier decisions. A friend of ours did this and the results were successful because a teenager will often listen to someone else rather than you. The school may work with nutrition-ists who can help and advise you about this.

THE SPOT DRAMALLAMA

One day their skin is still as soft as a baby's and the next it is not. The sudden invasion of spots took me by surprise with our first child, but it has since happened almost overnight to all our teenagers. Such a change will mostly be due to rapid hormonal fluctuations but as ever, if you are worried, see an expert: every child is different and needs a different approach to have happier skin.

Take it as seriously as you can because poor skin can affect self-esteem, so don't brush even the smallest of spot worries aside, as they can be a crippling source of anxiety for some teens.

Skin problems are extremely common; I had terrible acne as a teenager myself. I am in the fortunate position of having a friend who is a dermatologist and I took my teens for a consultation as soon as they expressed worries about their skin. This is a good route if you can afford it, because it puts everyone's mind at ease and they stop expecting you to cure things and an actual expert's advice stops your teens from buying all those cheap products that make the situation worse rather than better. It always helps if someone else offers the instructions too, because they watch so many social-media tutorials it's hard to keep them focused on a more beneficial simple routine unless an expert tells them in person.

Stress and anxiety can make inflammatory skin problems like acne worse, so bear that in mind, but if your daughter has acne on her back and neck, visit your GP and perhaps get a second opinion on the medication prescribed if you are worried as time goes by. A GP can also refer you to a dermatologist, so do ask about that.

According to my friend the dermatologist Dr Sam Bunting, teens should look for noncomedogenic make-up, as it doesn't block the pores (this will be on the labels) and develop a simple regular morning and evening routine around skincare. Masks aren't great for teen skin and neither is constantly poking your face with your hands, which I notice mine are always doing. Products containing retinoids can be used at night as they help exfoliate skin, according to experts. And anything containing azelaic acid or benzoyl peroxide will help reduce spot inflammation.

The Black Skin Directory is a good source of advice for Black teens, as is the *Guardian*'s Funmi Fetto.

Go to retailers who specialise in skin products and ask for advice, find product information on the internet with your girls and also keep an eye on what their peers are doing, as other mums often know things you don't and can share advice. Around 85 per cent of teens will suffer bad skin at some point but if they don't make it an issue, then let them deal with it themselves; only step in if they ask for help.

'Mum, What's Wrong With You?'
Conversations with Teens

Her: I cannot eat this raspberry. The pips are not right.

Me: What do you mean, the pips are not right?

Her: There are too many pips, Boomer. And this banana has gone spotty.

Me: What do you mean, 'spotty'? Have an apple, then.

Her: What? Are you joking? What is wrong with you? You know I don't like them when they are this red. Why is there never any food in this house?

22

Dads: a love story

From upstairs in the lounge I can hear my lovely husband's voice droning on and on. He is stuck into a diatribe with our eldest about her next driving lesson. She is contradicting him, as teenage girls often do about everything and anything, and the more illogical she becomes, the more frustrated he gets. I pop down to the kitchen to intervene and note that he is at the 'waving his arms around like Animal from the Muppets' stage and is quite red in the face from trying to control his patience and not raise his voice. He can see a way of solving her problem for her and is so confused she won't just *agree* with him. He can fix it and he doesn't understand why she won't let him. The jibber-jabber continues and she is now red in the face from the effort of being so contrary for no real reason. No one is backing down and it feels like it could go on until Domesday. I shut it down by making everyone a cup of almost undrinkable tea – something for them to agree on.

This is the conundrum for many dads of teen daughters.

They often want to be the plumbers, the policemen, the teachers, the sorter-outers. And this isn't really what is needed at this point by their daughters, who want independence to be their own plumber or policeman. They usually want to prove they can do it themselves.

Dads sometimes find all this hard, as far as I can tell. They are perplexed, a bit worried and slightly scared. They can feel out of their depth with adolescent women-to-be and I often think my husband, like many I see of this generation of men, wants to be the hero, probably partly because it makes him feel good. But obviously in these moments it isn't about you and how you feel any more. Annoying as that can be. And he is an actual fixer: he is our practical DIY expert problem-solver; he is the calm one who makes everything OK, so these illogical arguments with teenage girls must be very frustrating for him.

Also, my husband has been the fun parent for so long; his default role makes him happy. His relaxed but supportive attitude (for he takes equal responsibility in every aspect of family life) has been amazing parenting for our four children. The yin and yang of us has worked well, but I have been much more involved in the less fun aspects of parenting, the daily specifics, if you like. It has meant I am the one to say when we have to leave something fun to be somewhere else on time, or the one to remember coats, snacks or vegetables as part of a healthy meal. To remind them about homework during the holidays, to tone them down as a foursome when I can see group hilarity turning to group bickering and then on into a massive falling-out.

He's worn the clown pants and basked in the glow of their adoration for his funny antics while I have been the fun sponge on many occasions. There are a million TikTok memes where the joke is dads telling teenagers, 'It is not up to me, is it? It's up to your mother,' when it comes to answering hard questions. Plus all the memes that say, 'When people ask to see the manager, it's like kids asking to talk to Mum.' This is often the default pattern of parenting in ordinary couples. It is not how all men are or how all dads are when it comes to teen girls, but many mums relay this pattern to me when I talk about it, so I am assuming it is fairly common behaviour.

This means that when it gets to the teenage years and the glow of dads starts to wear off, they might feel left out. They don't get the gaslighting treatment like mums do but perhaps they struggle to establish a new relationship with more adult themes as they witness the physical evolution of their baby girls into women, particularly the sexuality blooming in front of them. It may unsettle many men and means they have to re-establish their connections on a different footing.

Staying connected to their teen daughters, though, at this stage of childhood is vital, and research shows establishing a strong connection through adolescence with dads is one of the key factors in building a young girl's confidence. In Steve Biddulph's book *Raising Girls* he recommends 'dad dates' start early in a father/daughter relationship, and he says dads should be ready to be 'assistant mothers' for girls.

This was why I made my husband talk to our girls about their periods and demanded he commit to the conversation with me. Though that for sure was a slightly odd chat, it made him think about our daughters and what they were going through.

However, communicating with their daughters can be tricky for men; they aren't always the best listeners, as it isn't a skill I think many of our generation of men were primed to have. This is not to be confused with not caring, but active listening is a skill that takes practice. Many men are 'interrupters': they are used to stepping in when women talk and this perhaps makes it harder for them to listen to their daughters. And many men may be more instruction-driven; so they may be waiting to be told what to do rather than taking the initiative themselves, and I find they can recount anecdotes more easily than talk about feelings.

I notice my husband often counters a problem one of the girls is discussing with him by offering an experience of his own. This feels unhelpful for teen girls, as they may not care what you have been through; it won't help them. He had not noticed he was doing this until we pointed it out.

Over the teen years my husband has adapted to match the ebb and flow of our girls' evolution. He is now more used to listening as they relay something without trying to solve anything. But, most importantly, we have reached a place where we agree on the boundaries for our girls and, minor transgressions aside, we have muddled through. I have been lucky to have such a supportive partner on the parenting front.

Crucially, he is not a shouter: he rarely raises his voice. Lucie Hemmen, the US psychologist who wrote *The Teen Girl's Survival Guide*, says dads yelling often has a far bigger negative impact on girls than mums. Dads are often seen as protectors and if the yelling escalates it will have deep and long-lasting effect, unless Dad repairs the rift soon after the argument. It makes a world of difference.

What I think most daughters need is to have faith their fathers won't crumble during these more complex years as they evolve, that they won't back off, and that they will be alongside them for the journey into womanhood.

Here is a list of specifics for dads that could be helpful. It's based on experts' advice and the books focusing on dads and daughters.

1. Don't use nicknames for female sex organs – or anyone's sex organs, for that matter, even the dog's. It's just weird and implies that, as a man, you find something funny about them. And if you don't know the difference between a vulva and a vagina, look it up. So don't check out during puberty: it isn't just Mum's job. It is yours too.

2. It is not what you say so much, more what you do, so be

nice to Mum, to the other women around you. That can help set your daughter's expectations of partners in future. They watch and absorb all behaviour.

3. Avoid commenting on appearance as a metric of their achievements; stick to other things that are more useful in society today, but don't put pressure on them to succeed.

4. Be emotionally present: not just in the room, but interested in her world, her interests, her friends. Our daughter is mad about Formula 1 and now studying mechanical engineering at Bath University; that is easy for my husband to be interested in, but he has to be as interested in her magnificent nail art too, for his interest to feel genuine.

5. Let her speak; stop talking 'at' her. Learn to listen.

6. Let her fail and sort her stuff out herself; she is not made of china.

7. Don't show your shock at the fact she seems to have grown breasts overnight and you are not welcome in the bathroom when she is there any more.

8. Don't call her Princess. You know that is wrong, right?

23

If you see me, you don't know me

The enigma of teenage siblings and how to navigate volcanic bust-ups

My daughters are in the kitchen having breakfast one Saturday (it's 2 p.m.). They're looking at each other with shocked indignation, two sets of perfectly shaped eyebrows raised in caricature horror as they say in unison, 'But you can't go *there*.' Though London is vast, filled with acres of parks and heaths, it seems the urban sprawl is still not big enough for the both of them. The pair of them are headed separately to the same part of the heath to meet their friends; this means – drum roll, please – that there is a very real chance they will see each other outside of the house. This cannot happen, apparently.

The tension in the air is so fizzy I am gripped; it is like watching a camp, dramatic telenovela play out over our kitchen table.

The rules clearly state that if two siblings are outside of the house they must never acknowledge each other. Or even acknowledge each other's friends. I am not sure what happens if you do, but I think it is worse for the older one to be seen near the younger one. A fellow mum tells me her teenage twins go to extreme lengths to avoid being in the same place at the same time, once pretending they didn't know each other when they bumped into each other in town (they are identical twins).

Personally, I would make the rules the other way round, so that they avoid each other at home, because the nuclear flare-ups that occur over borrowed-without-permission (i.e. stolen) clothing are terrifying. Much worse than the bickering when they were little.

In fact, when they were small, mine shared a room. There were intermittent sibling fights, as you would expect, and I did once have to separate them with a Dustbuster to shock them into stopping their furious fracas. I thought they would grow out of the physical fighting, and envisaged a moody war of terse, sarcastic words as they hit adolescence, interspersed with great sisterly love, but this was not always the case, and I was quite shocked at how vicious teenage siblings can be. My teen daughters' rows could occasionally turn physical.

Other mums also related tales of fist fights, slapping, a younger sister pulled down the stairs by her ponytail, a daughter who had punched a wall and broken her finger, the teenager who'd given her sister a black eye. The fighting between siblings seems to escalate quite quickly. And there is no obvious cut-off to end a teenage-girl row. No one concedes when both of you have a giant sense of misplaced injustice and although, technically, one of you is right and the other is wrong, she won't admit it.

These Tom-and-Jerry-style outbursts take you by surprise as a parent and may make you feel a bigger failure than the days of early childhood, when you gave in over ketchup with everything or tried unsuccessfully to wrestle a writhing, howling toddler with one shoe on into a pushchair in front of your mother-in-law.

If you do witness these fights at home, it would seem you are not alone. It happens to us all sometimes and according to the experts I have interviewed it is not unusual. Obviously, what we're talking about here is run-of-the-mill bickering that occasionally gets out of hand. If physical violence is a regular occurrence, the context of the family dynamic is important. It may be there are more emotional issues at play and for that, you'll need to talk to a family therapist, or ask your GP to refer you.

But for the many mums who confess they've witnessed this kind of sibling rivalry or fighting now and again, there are some ways to deal with it – and that includes being OK with it, to a certain level. It's not unusual for siblings to row; it's how they learn to negotiate, to navigate the outside world. It gives them skills, teaches them how to interact with their peers, how to deal with different opinions, how to argue their point, to empathise and, occasionally, how to compromise. And while there may be a cultural view that siblings should end up as friends, that won't always be the case. Each child has a different personality with a different experience of your parenting from the one that came before or after them, and they all evolve at a different pace.

It is also worth remembering that in the heat of those horrible arguments you may not be able to solve the problem there and then. My husband will often step in to talk specifics with our girls when they row, to ask exactly who did what, quizzing the warring duo like a patient Poirot, but *mon dieu*, this is daft. No one is thinking straight, emotions are running too high and the argument might not be about what they say it is. I think it is best to stick to feelings not facts in such situations. There is often a build-up towards these feisty showdowns: grievances that have been brewing, previous misdemeanours that have been banked, awaiting revenge. So I like to wait a while and come back to it to discover if some ground rules (don't go into her room without asking, for example) can be set, or at least mentioned out loud, a few lines that cannot be crossed in future. This discussion may then lead to a more in-depth one about the previous grudges, a look at the backstory behind the fight, but I'm afraid it takes a while to resolve or help them make up.

Some mums tell me they set punishments for fights. The most outrageous punishment I heard of was the mum who makes her teenage girls sit on the sofa holding hands for two minutes if their fights turn physical. This is, of course, the worst. She yells, 'Is it time to hold hands now?' and they scuttle off instantly.

Tiredness, poor diet and external issues can affect the moods that lead to rows too, so sense-check all that before wading in. And in families undergoing change or crisis, rows could be escalating as part of the other tensions around them. So it is worth noting exactly what is going on across the whole family.

And there are some questions you can ask yourself if you are worried, if it gets physical too often, if it feels like bullying rather than rivalry, or if the rowing ruins family life. I can throw you a few lifelines to grab on to in the hurly-burly of these exhausting interactions between siblings (regardless of their gender, to be honest).

1. Are you giving your girls unhelpful labels, characterising them as certain personalities and saying things like, 'She always does XXX'? Is one of them 'the troublemaker' in your mind, or 'the good girl', or 'the mean one' or, worse, 'the favourite'? If these labels exist within the family your teens may either act as they describe or rebel against it, so drop the labels and don't let relatives use or make them labels either. Grandparents often do this, I notice.

2. Are you subconsciously or perhaps consciously scripting their relationship with each other for them? It's hard to be objective, but each daughter has a different relationship with you, and her relationship with her sister may be affected by your relationship with her sister. Are you expecting a relationship they don't want to have, trying to get them to conform to something that isn't realistic? It is possible your relationship with your own siblings is echoing

215

around in the way your teenagers get on too. Try not to make assumptions based on all sorts of previous experiences or expected outcomes.

3. Are you in denial about their growing up? They are not little any more. They might have got on like a house on fire when they were both wearing denim dungarees and watching *Fireman Sam* together, but now they're battling with forming their own identity, and anything or anyone who gets in the way of that may be loudly and rudely pushed aside.

4. Is it OK if you don't solve this, if they don't get along for a bit? Can you live with that, and perhaps put practical ground rules in place to keep them apart for a while? I marvelled at the mum who noticed the flashpoint for her girls' rows was the bathroom towels. One was always using 'the dry towel' and then leaving it on the floor rather than the radiator so daughter number two, who showered later, had to use a wet towel. It seemed to be the root cause of all rows about who was the favourite. The power play got out of hand and the girls were like terriers at the bathroom door, one once almost kicking it down. So mum bought two sets of towels in different colours for each girl; this made the towels their own responsibility. It cleared the air. Seems an obvious solution, but sometimes so much else is going on you cannot see a potential solution. It's worth taking a moment to give logical thinking a go, and not feel aggrieved you have had to spend extra cash on new towels because you seem to have raised two people who cannot put a towel on the radiator, despite no obvious physical disabilities.

As the day of our eldest's departure to university drew near, making us five, not six, at home, I wondered how our daughters' relationship would progress because 99 per cent of the time they muddle along happily, often enjoying each other's company.

Over the lockdown summer of 2020 I paid the eldest to look after our nine-year-old daughter for a few days while we worked. Off to the zoo they went, taking their thirteen-year-old brother with them. The three of them came back with four souvenir animal mugs. Diabolically ugly mugs that take up a lot of room in the cupboard and make me wince when I see them out. I assumed the eldest had bought one for each child, given there were four in total, but no, she had bought one for each of the younger siblings and two for herself. 'What about your sister?' I asked.

'She can borrow it,' she said, 'if she asks nicely.' Sibling rivalry burning strong, even at the end point of family life. Yet later that summer when my eldest had had her heart broken, I witnessed the ebb and flow of sisterly love with such sweet compassion it made me cry. Perhaps it's there, simmering under the surface, but only to be used in times of great need.

'Mum, What's Wrong With You?'
Conversations with Teens

Her: We are at table 147 in Wetherspoon's.

Me: What of it? I am on the sofa.

Her: You can send us drinks.

Me: I am not telepathic.

Her: On the app. You can send them to our table. Four pink gins with lemonade. [The drink of an adult and a child combined.]

Me: What's the magic word.

Her: Please. Oh my god, Mum. I'm eighteen, what's wrong with you?

24

The perfect storm

It's all the rage

Now you may feel this chapter doesn't apply to you because you are *not that old*. But this is hopefully one of the most helpful chapters, because it is about you, and if not the you of now, the you of tomorrow. Also it will explain some of the domestic dynamics you are or will be experiencing. So here we go. I'm fifty-two as I write and have accidentally become an expert on women in midlife through a podcast I co-host called *Postcards From Midlife*.

So listen up: there are at least thirty-eight symptoms of perimenopause and menopause. Most are caused by the gradual decline or fluctuation in hormones in a woman's body as she ages. For the majority of women, it happens from the age of about forty. Aside from the much-chronicled (and, annoyingly often, laughed-at) hot flushes and night sweats, you can also get sore joints, insomnia, depression, dizziness, tingling in the extremities, loss of libido, numbness, headaches and tinnitus. Tinnitus? I mean, who knew you could get menopause of the ears, for god's sake? There are also emotional or psychological symptoms, like anxiety and low mood, mood swings and panic attacks. But perhaps the most frustrating and surprising medically recognised symptom of the perimenopause is 'the rage'. God knows, the rage is bad when you hit midlife, but it is also very common. Almost every woman over forty will talk about the rage, or the 'mean reds', as Audrey Hepburn called them in *Breakfast at Tiffany's*. It's volcanic. I had my last child at forty-three and was still blissfully unaware of the rage, but when I hit forty-five, just before my eldest hit the teenage years, it kicked in, caused by the decline in my hormones.

In an interview in *The Times* the neuroscientist Lisa Mosconi described it thus: 'When you lose your oestrogen during menopause (as you age), your brain loses its super power, you really lose this incredible ally. It's like you have a team that's been working together for so long and all of a sudden your programme manager quits. Your energy levels are down, your immune system is down, your neurons stop growing.'

In short, you are on your own. This would make anyone cross.

When the rage hit me, it felt like the rabbit working the controls in my head after a thirty-year full-time career and four kids had finally slumped over. I had moments when I really felt I couldn't take any more until I started hormone replacement therapy. I had panic attacks, dizziness, crippling insomnia, night sweats. I was so exhausted that at one point I sat down in the lounge to catch my breath on a Saturday afternoon and woke up four hours later. This happened regularly as my hormone levels fluctuated. It was a surprise; it was infuriating.

My experience of perimenopause is not every woman's story, but the majority of women suffer some of the symptoms. Co-hosting the podcast opened the door on a huge community of women who told us how angry they felt in midlife. These powerful and moving stories of ordinary lives thrown this curve ball by the rage were over-whelming. They weren't just talking fury at late buses or lost keys

– they were talking clubbing their husbands to death with a spade for leaving the fridge door open by accident. Some would have been grateful for hot flushes, had that been one of their symptoms. Anyway, the rage is raw and uncontrollable, and women have told me absolutely mad stories about hurling hoovers out of windows, punching holes in walls and driving cars into lamp posts.

Obviously, what a perimenopausal, rage-filled woman needs to calm her nerves in that moment, just as the ship is becoming untethered from the dock and flung into a stormy sea, right in the middle of her demonic unravelling, is to live with a teenage girl. Or two, in my case.

Just as you come apart, she is coming together.

You want to feel normal again and she wants to find a normal that is right for her. It isn't as simple as the loss of your youth; for most midlife women it is not that that is making them cross. Most of us don't want to look younger – we just want to feel better.

It took me three attempts to get the right prescription for HRT to alleviate the symptoms, and within weeks my insomnia had gone, the anxiety subsided, my thinning hair (which had started to fall out in the shower due to lack of iron, caused by changes in hormones) grew back, and I was more myself again.

You may not be there yet – if you had your children earlier in life, say – but I think for many of Gen X women this perfect storm is predictably unpredictable. It means that just as you're squinting to read the instructions on bottles of shampoo for thinning hair, your teenage daughter is blossoming in front of your eyes, all bouncy hair and wrinkle-free smiles. A fresh, young woman-in-waiting, one filled to the brim with the hormones you're missing, full of energy and with the immune system of a Norse god (you've seen her bedroom). And you both have The Rage, which is rather unhelpful.

Frankly, the whole world should be giving you a break at this point, but there is one woman who won't, and that is the one you

221

gave birth to. It is an unfortunate quirk of timing on nature's part for this generation, many of whom had their children a little later than the previous one.

Before perimenopause you could just roll your eyes and twist the lid back on the milk, but now you don't do that because of the rage, and before you know it, you're a fireball. Of course you could be quietly patient about the Rice Krispies all over the floor every morning when you go into the kitchen, your best bread knife carelessly tossed into the bin by accident, your missing 'good mascara', the giant wine-glass stain on your expensive wooden table, because none of this is a big deal in the scheme of things, but when you are grappling what feels like vengeful, vicious grief, when you do the death maths and realise you are running out of time, you have NO PATIENCE, only lack-of-hormone-fuelled anger: it's the dominant emotion of midlife women. So these things make you a bit shouty (I am underplaying it with this description). Really, when they roll their eyes and say, 'What is wrong with you?' you should shout, 'Lack of oestrogen!'

Sometimes I think I hold on to the rage when I am rowing with one of my girls because staying furious with them is more comfortable and distracting than facing the other difficult emotion in the room during later teen years, which is the grief, mourning the end of their girlhood. Or fear – the fear of losing them.

You can and should take a moment to recognise the sadness and all these changes happening to you physically. It will pass and great things happen to midlife women, so there is no need to be an Eeyore; it's just a matter of getting the right support at the right stage and caring for yourself well. Not everyone is given HRT, so ask your doctor about alternatives, but do get a second opinion if you are offered antidepressants, as it seems to be the default setting of GPs, many of whom are still inexplicably reluctant to prescribe HRT in the UK, despite the guidelines on it. Anti-depressants may well be right for you but they don't have any of the preventative protection HRT provides against heart disease and osteoporosis.

The pressure of family life for what has been labelled the 'sandwich generation' (trapped between caring for kids and elderly relatives) can be tough. Just when you thought you'd be sipping cocktails and congratulating yourself on getting this far, you're actually on call twenty-four hours a day for sick parents, sad friends divorcing, other friends with more rage who do daft things, needy colleagues, late-in-life children, clingy husbands – all of them. It is a lot to take on alongside the festival of wrinkles between your eyebrows, which you always said would never bother you as you aged, but it turns out, do.

So even if you had a bulletproof self-esteem up until now, you may be momentarily shaken by midlife, and this isn't vanity; it is the depletion of hormones that affects you emotionally and physically.

And, annoyingly, the speed at which your teen girls seem to be growing up somehow hastens the speed at which you are getting old. Time is all stretchy for them, but it has suddenly gone rigid for you, like a ruler with your years on it. Once, when I asked the sixteen-year-old if she wanted to walk the dog with me, her dad and her nine-year-old sibling, she looked at me with confusion.

'Why would I want to go on a walk with a nine-year-old and two over-fifties?' she answered. This confused me. It took me ages to work out we were the over-fifties.

The moral of the story is take care of yourself so you can keep the rage under control. I marvel at this army of midlife warrior women being everything to everyone, just soldiering on, so many of us awake at 4 a.m. grappling with anxious thoughts but still getting up and walking through the day 'getting teenage done' as Boris would say if he had any inclination of how much harder mothering teenage girls can be than running a country or sorting Brexit.

While you face all this, you must also brace yourself for the willpower to be their most significant positive female role model. Are you up to the job? Wouldn't someone less angry, hot and bothered, more balanced and with perhaps a soupçon of patience be better at it? Maybe, maybe not, but this is a time in life when you may need to make some self-care adjustments.

The right hormones aside, you will probably need more peace; to carve out some time to yourself. Don't laugh, but I found yoga, something I had previously described as 'silly rolling around in Lululemon leggings', so disdainful of it was I. Annoyingly, everyone was right: yoga is good for you and helps you reset. I also found open-water swimming a chance to get away from everyone and be completely alone with like-minded midlife women. I cannot tell you how many midlifers I have met on the edge of lakes or beside the sea, swimming the rage away and ignoring texts about money for lunch from their teenagers. Also, it may be neither here nor there, but I started to drink a pint of water at 6.30 a.m. most days. Seems to help. And to drink less booze; this is like losing a superpower, but again, it seemed to help. Ditto dog walks with podcasts or audio books or music you love.

But find your way back to who you are with care and love; treat yourself well or it can all feel overwhelming. GPs may misunderstand you, even disbelieve you, when you turn up in the surgery talking of exhaustion and insomnia; many are not ready to effectively cure midlife women of their hormone deficiency quite yet, so be prepared, research the menopause and perimenopause and go in armed with the facts and save yourself time. You may not be able to cure your teenager's rage but you can reduce your own. Get help, ask for second opinions, become knowledgeable, because you deserve it.

You are not going mad, you are not alone (trust me I have listened to hundreds of stories from midlife women). Care for you and you can care for her. And watching you care for yourself is good for your daughter too.

'Mum, What's Wrong With You?'
Conversations with Teens

[11 p.m. on a weeknight. I am in bed]

Her: Mum, wake up.

Me: What?

Her: I cannot believe what has happened about Friday night. Mia didn't answer my Snapchat, and then Lidia rearranged her night with Jane, and then Eve said she would do something else, and now no one is around this Friday because I told them I was busy because you told me I had to be home, even though I got the wrong Friday and you meant next Friday and Friday is tomorrow and now I have nothing to do. Mum, wake up – what am I going to do?

Me: What?

Her: Why do you always arrange everything to happen on a Friday? What is wrong with you? Everything we have to do is on a Friday night. This is all your fault.

[Literally haven't arranged anything on a Friday night since 2002.]

25

Mothers are daughters too

I left home just after turning seventeen. I came from Cornwall to London to start my career as a journalist on a local paper. As I recall, I didn't give much thought to what my mother, then forty-five, may have felt when I left. I was just eager to start work. I had that blind confidence and arrogance of youth. I didn't contemplate failure – it just didn't cross my mind.

Luckily both my parents encouraged and supported this, especially my mum. Anything is possible, she told me. Looking back, I don't remember taking into account anyone's feelings as I left, again a typically teenage trait. Not my younger sister, aged fourteen, nor my dad, a former policeman, who drove me 200 miles up the A303 away from the quiet rural village I'd grown up in to deposit me at the office of the *Wimbledon News*, where I had managed to get on a journalism training scheme.

My earlier than usual departure no doubt caused a fracture in our small family unit. And as a mother of four myself, I wonder how it affected my relationship with my mum, who is in her eighties today.

We don't talk of it much, though, because Mum is from that tight-lipped post-war generation that just gets on with stuff. We're not big on exploring emotions and overthinking. No navel-gazing, as she'd call it.

My mum had me late for the time (twenty-eight) and she didn't work outside the home. She is a self-contained, well-read woman who in later generations would have had many more opportunities open to her than staying home with her family, which I suspect may not have been her first choice.

I had a normal childhood growing up in a bungalow in a small Cornish village and going to the local comprehensive, but I must have been an unusually independent, strong-willed and determined teenager to drop out of A levels and get a job at sixteen on my local Cornish paper. I wonder what it is like to mother a girl like that?

When my girls turned seventeen I would have found it tough if they'd wanted to leave home for another city. I would have resisted, advised caution, but I don't remember any resistance back then to my choices, just positive, can-do encouragement.

I don't see my parents often, given the distance and the busyness of all our lives. My sister lives close to them, though, and they are still in my childhood home. Everyone just gets on with their lives.

There are so many different versions of motherhood running through families as the maternal chain stretches back into the past, aren't there? Each influencing the next one in line. And there are so few boys in our family; it is a stream of daughters becoming mothers to more daughters.

My mum tells me granny was an orphan with several sisters, so what kind of mother was she, what kind of mothering did she receive and pass on, I wonder?

As my relationship with my mother is not a dominating force in my life, more a quiet rumble in the background of who I am, I am not always alert to patterns that have come with me from childhood. I did, however, explore some of my childhood in my mid-twenties. After the painful break-up of my first long relationship, I had two years of weekly therapy. I felt lonely and lost in my new city, despite a huge group of friends and a successful career. I needed an expert to untangle these confusing feelings, so I took a scientific approach and sought one out. I didn't enjoy therapy, but it was effective, practical and helpful. I was incredibly lucky that I found such an experienced therapist in the mid-1990s, when it was a rare thing in the UK. It soothed the bits of my soul that felt raw, helped reset my mind and explored some of the patterns of my childhood that were affecting my relationships at work and home. I hope it made me more self-aware, more forgiving and more understanding as a person. And, as I have aged, that mental journey has continued. I would recommend it highly if you can afford it, particularly when you become a mum of teen girls.

In the desperate times we can sometimes face during this bit of parenting, it may not be your teenager who needs the emotional guidance – it could be you. It might not be her behaviour causing the issues: it could be yours. I think it is useful to spend time to develop self-awareness, to see if your issues are affecting your mothering, to step outside of the cultural narrative around teen girls, which is often so negative, and think about the personal patterns that may be stopping you from enjoying your mothering and protect your daughter from repeating patterns that perhaps are unhelpful or negative.

In her book *How to Stay Sane*, the family psychotherapist Philippa Perry offers an exercise that I found extremely helpful as a mum – it's like a therapy session. It may work for anyone looking to have more self-awareness, or self-observation as she puts it, which leads to insight, which can lead to better relationships all round.

The exercise is called the Genogram. It is time-consuming and you have to really concentrate, so not one to do after arguing about messy rooms or looking for lost travel passes/headphones/keys.

You create a map of close relatives, a family tree. On the lines connecting each member you write adjectives to describe each person, not sentimental or nostalgic ones, but factual descriptions: words like 'conflicted', 'violent' or 'loving' perhaps, and then you answer a long list of questions detailed in the book. What you get is a picture of what has influenced you, and what will no doubt influence your parenting. It's a deep dive into the memory of family, a powerful picture of your emotional history, and it highlighted for me the threads of behaviour I would like to avoid during my years as a mother. It showed me the triggers that make me react in unhelpful ways around my wonderful teenage daughters; it reminded me that I should praise them more out loud, communicate better during the times when I felt nothing needed to be said. Like therapy, it softened my edges, loosened my emotions and enabled me to take a step back and observe them during those tense moments in our relationship rather than criticise them or call them out for what I deemed bad behaviour. It taught me to relax, which is a top mothering skill. It reminded me to replay the good times in my head, the days I knew I had been a great mum instead of dwelling on the days when I had misjudged my behaviour with my teens. We may let those good times become invisible so focused are we on getting stuff right all the time, or on our failures. It allowed me to 'feel with, not deal with' my children, as Philippa so eloquently writes.

There are so many varied routes to motherhood nowadays and I take great delight in learning new ways to parent from the mothers around me, who have all come to it via different paths. I know surrogate mums, adoptive mums, mums who were adopted themselves, very young mums, much more mature mums, religious mums, mums from culturally different communities from mine. So many women doing it in so many different ways. It pays to remain open to what other women say, perhaps be mindful of not being defensive about your own mothering and instead seek advice and absorb a different viewpoint. You don't have to always act on it; simply knowing all the different ways women mother is healthy. And it is good to be challenged on your own views occasionally, I think.

I found the idea of 'conscious mothering' helpful from family therapist Sil Reynolds' book *Mothering and Daughtering*. This means following your instincts about your daughter's very specific personality and adapting to her ever-changing needs, making no assumptions around her, relaxing your expectations of her. It's about concentrating on her properly when you are with her, observing her and reacting to how that moment feels, because each child is so very different, and no one self-help book will solve any problems you encounter. In fact, some advice that works for others in a similar situation may not work for you because of who your daughter is at that moment. Times of true togetherness, when you are there for her, sound so obvious, but we often forget to do this in the busyness of our days as a family.

Parenting an adolescent girl is like listening to a wind chime. They tinkle differently at different times; the chimes of a minute ago are subtly different from the ones you are hearing now, and you have to adapt to the speed of that change. What worked yesterday might not work as well today. Observe her closely and be thinking about her, rather than just managing her. There are times when it is absolutely right to say, 'I don't like it when you speak to me like that,' and times when, if you tune into your girl, it is best to ignore rudeness, and ask, 'Are you OK? Do you want a cup of tea, so we can talk about what is really going on?' even in the face of tremendous fury or poor behaviour.

The times I have confronted a tsunami of negativity from one of my teens with fury and my own outrage at their behaviour have never ended well. My default 'just get on with it and stop moaning' attitude has not been helpful, and I think caused a few needless eruptions. When I learned midway through the teen years to change the way I was with each of my daughters it was a light-bulb moment. While one was fine with 'just get on with it', the other really wasn't. My eldest has a completely different sense of humour from her younger sister and I didn't always take that into account. I had to match their personas with mine, be more attuned. I learned to pick my moments of interaction with them, lean into their personalities with the bits of mine that worked best. One of my daughters enjoys a loud debate, the other is less keen and in fact really hates noise, and, again, often I wasn't sensitive to these differences, I hadn't noticed enough about them. It was only when I did that our days were more harmonious.

In the early teens, I found I was always anticipating the girls' next move. I used to subconsciously presume feelings and emotions in my daughters because I had experienced them as a teenage girl myself, but of course their feelings are very different. Their experience of childhood is so different. You cannot possibly know what they are going through unless you take the time to observe each of them specifically, to sort of study them without demanding anything from them. And if you are doing this with a partner, their observations will be useful too.

And teenage girls are often grappling hard with the enormity of growing up into womanhood. If I were you, I'd watch the columnist and author Caitlin Moran's amazing talk for young women on YouTube. It defines that common thread of insecurity that runs under the surface of many teenage girls. It makes them so much easier to forgive and understand if you know how many doubts are swirling about inside them all day, every day, sapping their energy and sometimes removing the joy of life for them. Moran's four-minute monologue will remind you as a grown-up how it can feel to be a teenage girl, especially one going through 'the bad year', as she puts it, that year when your body is all wrong, your mind is a mess, school is a burden, and you feel unloved, whether you are or not. She asks teen girls to learn to mother themselves and that is perhaps one of the most hopeful things we can do for them: teach them to protect and care for themselves and each other.

26

This much I think I know

As I have said before, I am not a trained expert on parenting teenage girls. I am more of a trained observer, an imperfect human doing the best I can, like you I suspect, but I can offer you some guidance on this learning curve of letting go that I think will be helpful; friendly suggestions I have learned after interviewing actual experts and living with teenage girls (and their tribes) for the past five years. So, if you want a checklist, this is my 'do try this at home' collection of hopefully useful ideas to experiment with.

1. Side by side. Never face to face. Whatever the issue is, however big or small. Talk about it in the car, on a dog walk, at the park, on a bench. Try not to sit opposite each other. I like to go outside – Mother Nature is the best maternal influence of all.

2. Ask, don't tell. This is obvious, no? Tell a toddler; don't tell a teenager. Harder to do than it looks, of course, but make it your mantra. This requires you to listen well, the

hardest thing to do in the heat of the moment, but the most important of all your parenting skills, in my opinion.

3. Self-kindness. Learn to love and like yourself more. So important in so many ways. If you maybe don't like who you are, it will be a challenge commanding your teenagers – whose minds are emotional sponges, whose main reference or role model for being an adult woman is you – to like you. And later themselves. Make time to take care of yourself or you may not cope as well during these stressful years as a parent. And make time to lose yourself for a moment. By that I mean do something you enjoy so much it consumes you. I swim, slowly, outside in lakes; find your equivalent and it will help you put petrol in the patience tank, and patience is what you will mostly need. Plus, the summer they just vanish into their own worlds will be so much tougher if you don't have something to do in their absence.

4. Learn about active listening. Teenagers, perhaps more than any other group of humans, need to feel heard. They cannot bear interruption. Wait for them to finish their sentence, no matter how daft it may be. You aren't just waiting for them to come to the end of their tirade or mumbled explanation; you should endeavour to listen actively to what they are saying or asking. It's not just about letting them get it off their chest or replying, 'I really feel for you,' it is about being in the moment, giving them your attention. Try to concentrate fully, tune in, understand and respond based on exactly what has just been said. Take in their body language and tone. Observe them well. Try not to leap in with problem-solving techniques. It's harder than it looks, believe me, and I feel I don't always get it right, but it is a powerful tool when you do, because it makes your teen feel heard, which makes them feel safe and loved.

5. Read and feed. Rituals are the glue of a healthy family life in my opinion, the best way to maintain a connection as your child moves from pre-teen to tween to teen. They root a toddler or a teenager, make them feel safe as they start to separate. When they are small this mantra would be 'read to them', but as they grow, 'eat with them' could be your 'if you do one thing . . .' catchphrase. Once a week, eat dinner with them. We rely on a roast dinner to sometimes salvage our family's broken days; nothing is as comforting as grading roast potatoes based on their crispiness.

6. Happiness jars and slideshows. In the run-up to major family gatherings or milestone moments, tensions can be high. This is a technique that was recommended to me by family therapists who help families cope in crisis. Warning: there will be some teenage eye-rolling here, but it is worth persevering. Ask your offspring to write small notes about upbeat, positive things that have happened or they have witnessed over a specific time period. What has made them laugh and what have they seen that they would like to happen again. You put the jar in a place at home they can all see and then after maybe a month, open the notes and read them over a special meal. Weirdly, this worked for us in the office too. It's a little touchy-feely but does bring the notion of togetherness into the room, a connection to those who have been there with you over that time period. At home we did it before Christmas one year. If you have compliant adolescents who will also make a slideshow of family photos for the grandparents to watch (they don't mind pleasing grandparents), then this is a good bonding activity too. They can do it on their phones and you all send pictures that may help talk through a year as a family or a holiday as a family with those who don't live with

you. I remember doing this with my own grandparents when I was little. You are creating memories from memories, which tells the teens how important family life is, reminds them how far they have come. Milestones are super important for teenagers, as apparently most of our significant memories are created between the ages of fifteen and twenty-five, so use them for good.

7. Dandelion or orchid? Now, to be clear: I don't think you should label your children. So many books land on my desk declaring there is a neat box to put your child in with a set of rules to 'make them better'. Then you can blame something else for the problems you may have encountered without taking a harder look at their whole life or perhaps at what you are doing as a parent that is contributing to issues at home. Each teenager is unique, they change by the day and the set of influences on your child will be so different from anyone else's. So no to labels but yes to this book, which has defined two personality types. It really resonated with me and is one of the best I have read on parenting. *The Orchid and the Dandelion* by Dr Thomas Boyce is a beautiful story based on research and his work with families. It defines the two main characteristics of children as either sensitive orchids or the more resilient dandelions. The point is that the way you parent an orchid is crucial to their emotional and physical ability to thrive. It is different from parenting a dandelion. In the book Boyce retells the story of a mum of four boys who arrived at his practice saying 'these three are all right but there is something wrong with this one' about one of her sons.

'The same kind of parenting wasn't working for this young man,' Boyce writes. 'I believe there are no unbreakable children, but while some are able to deal with life's normal ups and downs just fine, some cannot cope. They [orchids] need a more intense form of parenting.' Biology and environment are at play with children who are born more shy or introverted, more fearful; these children are often hypersensitive to things like noise, taste, chaos around them. It's physiological for them, according to Boyce and other medical researchers. Boyce's book changed my approach to parenting my second child, whose personality is more orchid than dandelion. It doesn't mean she is more special than the others, or weaker – she is just a different type of person. Orchids need more routine, more structure, more compassion. They have big imaginations, which prey on their minds; they need to be overwhelmed with a more tactile, physical love, which they may be reluctant to accept; they need more play and less learning. They are essentially more sensitive individuals and this is as much to do with their biology, neurology and physiology as it is with the family they grow up in. Be mindful of it and read the book, which is a fascinating study of humans. It will help you know how you encourage each of your children to thrive. And it may explain some of your own neurology and psychology. This in turn affects your parenting.

8. Music changes everything. Make a family playlist: bear with me, because this one was recommended by a psychiatric nurse who specialises in healing families undergoing adolescent traumas. She has used it to great effect in family therapy sessions to change mood and lift spirits. Music really is important. A study in Arizona showed parents who listen to music with their teenagers have a closer relationships than parents who don't. Creating a playlist together is time-consuming but it has been scientifically shown to help improve teen resilience. Worth a try, no?

9. Don't assume the worst. A mantra for every tricky situation. Bad things do happen, but very often nothing is as bad as you imagine it to be. And we usually only ever hear about the extremes in the press, never the wonderful, ordinary everyday stories of mums and daughters getting it right. So don't panic and don't catastrophise. And also remember that we can do hard things, we can cope and our daughters are often more resilient than we give them credit for.

10. No helicoptering, no snowploughing. Don't leap in and try and solve their problems for them. Try the listen, nudge, coach approach, as advocated by coach Anita Cleare of the Positive Parenting Project. I spoke to Cleare, who has worked across many local authority children's services, for several pieces I was writing and she is a wise mum. Empathise with their problem, ask them to suggest a solution, and then chat through how that could work. You cannot step in each time and sort stuff out, or they don't learn how to cope with problems. Making mistakes means they learn something about life, and they can avoid the mistake later on. Failure is good for everyone. It's hard, because we are living in a world where the overwhelming parenting style of the last decade has been attachment parenting, which seems to linger unhelpfully, influencing some parents to move from attachment to babies and toddlers to helicoptering teenagers. I am reminded of the US parents who rang the college their teen was joining, to ask if it was possible to keep sauces away from main courses in the canteen, as their child didn't like sauce to be near her food. So yes, mums. Chill. Let your kids mess up.

11. Don't sweat the small stuff. So, there seems to be a theory among some parents that they are creating a perfect human:

one that does no wrong, one that needs to be moulded into a better version of the parents themselves. But teenagers are not bonsai trees. These parents may also believe adolescents learn from being punished, and the one thing I found to be absolutely true is that punishments mean little to them in the long term, and the threat of them is a poor deterrent, because teens live in the moment and you are in this for the long haul. You imagine they are thinking ahead, but really a lot of their life is Groundhog Day. We tried to work with consequences rather than punishments, as detailed in Ian Williamson's book *We Need to Talk*.

If our teen wants to come and go as she pleases without telling us where she is, or ignores curfews and the like, we set consequences. Mostly lack of cash and loss of the phone works. They like to monologue about how unfair all this is. I let them rant and rave about us controlling them and try to stay quiet after stating the consequence. But you can't do this with every transgression, every bit of what you view as bad behaviour.

You have to ignore some stuff, exasperating, irritating and infuriating as it is. I am not creating or moulding anything. I am merely observing, occasionally guiding, and still sometimes stopping mine accidentally getting run over.

In adolescence their behaviour may sometimes rip a giant hole in what was, up until that point, peaceful family life, but please pick your battles and stop seeing your teen's behaviour as some kind of reflection of your parenting, or your failure as a parent. Raising them is not your only job – it is one of your jobs. There are times when you will have to be curious rather than furious. But you do need boundaries: you do need to tell them what makes you uncomfortable and to be honest about that. You can still be the boss. The hierarchy at home is important and you should feel able to tell them what to do. Instinct should tell you when that is necessary. Don't be influenced by other parents and don't make your kids feel they are responsible for making you happy, either. In the same way you aren't there to maintain constant happiness or fulfilment for them, help them manage all those negative, disappointing, angry and less pleasant feelings they will experience as you set boundaries. That's what they want to learn from you – courage to face their own pain. Boundaries are also proof for them that you love and care for them, only a person that wants them to grow up safely would set boundaries they can lean on. And seek professional help if the problem you are dealing with overwhelms you; this isn't failing.

12. Try the ABC method for arguments if they get out of control. A is for accept the situation, followed by B for breath, which means stepping back, pausing before responding, or perhaps responding later, when everyone has calmed down, and C is for choice: you choose if you shout or not, you choose if you lose your temper or not, you choose what to do next yourself, what you want to feel.

13. Some days they may not like you. In the days of huge disagreements, accept that setting your consequences for worrying behaviour will make you unpopular. Accept there are going to be days when they just don't like being around you and you have to come to terms with that. But remember, it's not a crime for them not to do as they are told. And parenting is not a popularity contest. Don't be a best friend – ever.

14. Tomorrow is another day. You don't just get one chance

to be a good enough parent – you get every day to be an emotional anchor, to show compassion. When I interviewed Mercedes Samudio, author of *Shame-Proof Parenting*, she reminded me that we all mess up every day. We shout, we overreact, we make the wrong call, we punish when we should be forgiving. We can be as hurtful and cruel as they can. And I have spent a lot of time thinking I am useless as a parent, feeling shame, but Samudio presents the theory that it is a waste of energy to feel bad about it for a long time, because it is never too late to make things better. Never too late to repair the broken bonds, to say sorry, to love them. To connect again. Stop shaming yourself for your parenting and shaming them for their behaviour. We are all on a learning curve – don't take it all so personally, and forgive things, yourself included, to make it better the next day. And remember all the 'invisible parenting' you have done, the times when stuff went smoothly, a teen was soothed or helped by you, a moment you have taken for granted as you perhaps dwell on the more negative elements of your mum life.

15. The teenage conscience. Respect it. Your teenager has a conscience and it is very powerful. Sometimes it may not seem as though your teenager has a conscience, but all the psychologists will tell you: they do. They are almost never deliberately thoughtless or unkind or ungrateful. They are usually morally and psychologically driven to do the right thing, but may need help deciding what that is, given they are usually experiencing everything for the first time. You can try to trust them to make the right decision. During the lockdown days of 2020, experts told me that explaining to teenagers how they could put their older relatives at risk was a far more powerful deterrent to going out and taking

part in illegal gatherings than telling them they were at risk of catching the virus or being fined.

16. Teach your daughters to find their voices early on and especially to talk about money. In all my thirty-year career managing teams, I have rarely had a female prospective employee ask for a better pay deal during an interview, but men always ask. In her book *What Girls Need*, Marisa Porges, who worked in the Obama administration as a leading counterterrorism expert, explains how young girls and women need to find their voice to be self-advocates. It is so important in our society that women are not consistently talked over by men. The science and statistics around women being interrupted in meetings or any important or influential gathering is depressing, so we need to help our girls speak out, whether they are extroverts or introverts. We need to try to teach them to ask for what they want to thrive, and if they can conquer the money conversation, it will give them confidence to conquer other conversations, as it is the hardest one to crack. And I tell my girls never to start a conversation by apologising for what they are about to say. Needlessly saying sorry is a feminine trait we need to encourage our daughters to avoid.

17. Put your phone down. It is that simple. Don't be a distracted parent. You can't ask them to do what you can't do. Put it down for dinner, for family telly times, for trips, for visits to relatives. Just put it down when you are with them. And don't be too busy all the time. Make time to do nothing with them or even with yourself. Busyness is hard for them to break through.

18. You are Mum enough (or Dad or Stepmum). Don't compare yourself to others.

19. The ten-minute convo. Sometimes you can ask for a chat

with your prickly hedgehog daughter by telling her it will only take ten minutes. It is a hit-or-miss strategy, but it can help. Being heard is the best balm for any teenager; it is their ultimate goal. Giving a time limit to a conversation may make them more inclined to have it.

20. Are they doing it because you do it? Sometimes I look back on an event and realise the teenagers did what they did because that is what we do as parents. They were either mimicking us subconsciously or behaving in a way we had taught them to behave. All children absorb the way their parents behave and watching this play out can be uncomfortable. So be aware of it. Look at what is behind the behaviour. And it can be as basic as shouting: mine definitely end up shouting because I shout, I can see that, but there are often more subtle copycat behaviours. This is why language around teenagers is important too, as they subconsciously absorb your tone. Everything you say goes in even when you are commenting on a telly programme or arguing with the news on the radio. Be mindful of the words you use to critique things, yourself as a woman especially. And if you want a certain kind of behaviour, you may have to role model it yourself. This, my friends, is an uncomfortable truth I have learned to live with and deal with.

21. Teenage girls have secrets. It's healthy for them to have privacy; you cannot possibly know everything about your daughter, so make peace with that. They will exclude you as they define their new identity. It's healthy.

22. Slow down. If we structure our teens' days for them, or make sure they are always occupied, never staying in bed late or up too late, or we constantly want to see some evolution or learning in them, it may lead to us sort of

controlling them again like younger children. I think it is good to slow down. It is OK simply to sit with them. This feels like the best of the best as a parenting tip. I think it is good every now and again to reassess your daughter's pace of life, to observe her and ask if she is doing too much. Is life outside school as stressful as school, does she need you to help her slow it down? Orchid girls may find a fast-paced life affects them more, and they may need more downtime.

23. Do. Not. Freak. Out. I mentioned this in the chapter on love and sex. But it applies to most things. Maybe you can say it out loud before reacting to the more perilous situations they put themselves in?

24. Puberty and periods: find out as much as you can. Some girls may be so negatively affected by their periods their lives almost feel intolerable. Seek professional help via your GP.

25. Tell them out loud that you love them. I do it at least once a day.

26. It is OK for your daughter to be sad. As Philippa Perry writes, 'Feel with them, don't deal with them.' Trying to maintain a happy mindset all the time may feel like a huge pressure for some girls. Being there when they are sad and acknowledging they are down without trying to cure them of their sadness is a simple and effective way of helping them become more resilient.

27. It's all about identity. Life is all about your identity, refining one, changing one and in the case of a teenager, making one. I hadn't really taken into account how important this is before my girls hit their teenage years but it is the root of everything. It is an acute and profound developmental stage. This is what makes teenagers so amazing, so inspiring

and refreshing to be around. You are privileged to witness the beginning of their identity.

28. 'Let me think about that' . . . one of parenting's most useful phrases. Put it in your mum toolbox.

29. The worrying doesn't stop. It is never over. You are always a parent. You know that, right? And if you don't, 'what's wrong with you?'

27

Swimming in the river of love

It's 2020. Summer is over. New starts beckon. The time has come. My firstborn has to leave home. The thought of it is unbearable. A gentle blanket of soft gloom lies over the house. We're not quite ourselves. As the other three children head back to school, we all get a mild cold. This is no coincidence. We're emotionally run down. The stress of an unusual year has left us a little weary. The weird months of lockdown, job changes, abandoned exams, an eighteenth birthday, cancelled holidays and the teens saying goodbyes to school friends. Layers of unpredictable change we could not foresee on top of what we knew was looming. It has taken its toll on our family unit and now this: the final parting.

My husband, who copes with sadness by being oddly cheerful, wanders around the house like a middle-aged version of the upbeat snowman, Olaf, from *Frozen*. 'All good things,' he mutters under his breath.

I am exhausted and have to cancel almost every commitment. I cannot sleep and my midlife immune system has given in. It seems

I am not strong enough, despite years 'pushing on through' on the maternal front line.

Perhaps all this is overdramatic, because she isn't going far and we will no doubt see her again within weeks, but feeling all the feelings of goodbye seems to have a physical effect. Other women tell me they, too, are physically laid low the week before their little ones flee the nest. Sky, my eldest, seems, of course, oblivious to the detail of my hurt, but is herself clearly discombobulated. She worries about the dog and how much the annoying little terrier will miss her.

The two teen sisters are quietly kind to each other. And Sky drops her piles of unwanted clothes on her sister's bedroom floor. Suddenly everything that was fought over is given voluntarily.

I have set up camp in melancholy corner, where you will find me reading the Pam Ayres poem 'A September Song', about her son going to university – 'a ghastly leaden feeling like the ending of it all'.

Where we were once living daily family life in the Technicolor of childhood, this final week feels like we're trudging onwards in muted beige; we are fifty shades of dreary grey.

I walk Mabel, the youngest, to school in the mornings and when we stop to look for ladybirds on the wall, as is our family tradition, one that started with Sky all those years ago, we see none. I don't even know if it is ladybird season, but right now everything feels like a sign. It makes the heart ache just thinking about it. I see mums pushing buggies and wonder why I am suddenly in this stage of life; it feels like an experiment has occurred, a scene from *Dr Who* or a dream, and I can press a button or hold my nose and be transported back to where I should rightfully be. Pushing a double buggy, holding the small hand of the child walking alongside it and leaving a trail of raisins behind us as we go.

Sky's childhood seems to run in the background of our days, like hearing crockery clanking in the distance on summer evenings. Perhaps this is where we were happiest, but we just didn't know it then? The comforting smallness of little ones, busy pottering around in the evening sunshine before bedtime, life happening around us. I thought those moments would be endless, but now some kind of quickening has happened and landed me here, days before the dreaded drive to university.

'Shall we take brownies?' I ask.

'God, what is wrong with you? I am not nine, for god's sake, Lorraine.' She wants to take pink gin and she doesn't want to discuss mattress toppers or doorstops (so she can keep her room open on the first night and people can say hi). She thinks I am an idiot for wanting to label things and she tells me I have packed the bag of kitchen equipment bought in the sale from Sainsbury all wrong.

'I want to carry it on my shoulder, not from underneath. Why are you so impractical?' she humphs.

We chose one of the hottest days of the year to get all stuff on the uni list. The experience is about as far from the movies as you'd expect. Neither of us is happy about this state of affairs, and I take her to Wagamama for her favourite food, katsu curry, afterwards. I try to rekindle the memories of our family trips here, all the way back to the times one of them was in a highchair, which she, as the eldest, will remember. But she wants to look at Snapchat and is furious when I take a picture of her to send to the family WhatsApp.

She wants to take her comedy Christmas mug-in-a-teapot to halls with her. I got it for her when she was eight and I realised tea was the balm for her woes. I cannot say anything, because with our gloom and our sore throats and our lack of sleep we are rubbing each other up the wrong way. We all struggle to connect as the week trudges on and the planned Friday-night goodbye dinner is looming. Friends with older children who have already done the uni drop send me texts of support, but these simply emphasise the enormity of it all. They tell me 'she will come back, don't worry' and 'she will stay in touch – you just need to adjust', but I don't believe them. There is no comfort in any sentence beginning, 'Well, at least . . .' These friends can sit in the corner with Mr Candy/Olaf and think about what they have done.

Those some way off look at me curiously, wondering why I am so cataclysmically upset, such a dramallama, hinting at my martyrdom approach, secretly believing I am overthinking all this. I am not, trust me. You cannot protect yourself by pretending you won't feel this way in a few years. None of it seems real. I have gone radio silent on everyone and everything.

Of course, the days, months and years ahead will be exciting, hope-filled times for our daughters, but that first step into the big wide world alone is an epic challenge, terrifying – who is ever ready for it? It looks better from the outside than it feels on the inside. But who am I kidding? She is most definitely ready, excited and prepared to leave. She refused to go to a London university so she could definitively leave home; she is happy in herself about the departure, which is of course a wonderful thing to witness. She has survived us and is ready for the real world. What a triumph.

Life in the house continues around us. This is the week to be the champion of biting your tongue, to dig deep on the patience front. To ignore all the things we have previously discussed in this book. Definitely don't sweat the small stuff, or any of the stuff. Simply being is my best advice. I know mums cooking the favourite meals every night, or arranging big goodbye bashes or nightly Facetimes to relatives, but really, I think they want as little fuss as possible made, for it to feel as home as home can be, normal as always.

In his book *Raising Girls*, Steve Biddulph uses the phrase 'the river of love' to describe the support of all the people involved in helping raise your child, from grandparents to much-adored teachers and godparents. This is the time to let the river of love flow through your household. It's always there, so go with the flow.

But I almost explode when Mabel, then aged eight, tells me she wants to walk home from school alone now. After two decades of being a working mum, I can finally collect her more than once a week, now I am a full-time writer, and she doesn't want me to. Christ, the irony. I feel like a wet dog waiting to shake off the water, to feel lighter and bound off on a new adventure gleefully.

I wanted to be jumping around with joy, as if I had reached the end of a Tough Mudder. I want to be being congratulated on moulding such a capable and wonderful human, ready to be independent. There should be a ceremony to mark us all making it through alive and with all of our limbs attached and generally OK mental health. But there is, oddly, very little sense of achievement, because of the sadness (and the overthinking of the sadness).

Maybe it is just me, I think, until I go on Twitter, or Facebook, or Instagram or even the telly, and see all of my celeb Gen X contemporaries who have moved through the stages at the same time writing about their kids leaving home and talking about it on the news. Empty-nest syndrome isn't just a headline: it is a real thing. And 'tis the season. But it is what it is and thus we must move forward. Before I can do this, though, before I can gird any loins, I let the delicious memories of her childhood sweep over me. I remember her devotion to Sellotape (she loved it), her collection, aged six, of forty-seven plastic horses, her pile of 'interesting stones', which we would cart around with us on trips and spend much time preventing her baby sister eating, her neat, colour-coded homework charts, her love of *Bake Off*, her addiction to meringues, which lasted a whole winter and culminated in her eating one the size of our Airedale's enormous head in one sitting, her endless cups of tea. I remember her stoic and sensible attitude to life, her unreasonably small, dainty feet, her kindness to spiders and other small living things, all the sewing she did, the making, the gluing, the sticking. Her sheer sensibleness and ready laugh. Her wonderful and optimistic school reports, the way her DT teacher glowed every time she talked about her at parents' evening. My amazing, capable, caring, smart and spirited girl.

I find an old diary one of our nannies kept and in it she writes: 'Gracie told me to get my big bum out of the way today and Sky says she wants to be a car mechanic when she grows up'. Sky was six. Now she's eighteen and that's exactly what she is off to do. I cannot imagine anyone being as proud of their daughter as we are of ours, as proud of her studious and careful nature and her warm smile. She is the kind of woman you want by your side in a crisis, the one everyone relies on and the one you know will always be loyal and true. Everyone says their daughter is special and that's because they all are.

Motherhood feels like a rip tide at this point, dragging me back and back, away from the place I want to be. I can't fight it; I just have to swim across it and slowly back into the beach to do it all again with the other three. I think we should all meet at that bar at the end of the galaxy in *Star Wars* and toast the fact we made it through this extraordinary time.

This goodbye is a marker of such profound change it is hard to describe. Perhaps there are specific words for this feeling in Gaelic, or maybe Swedish. In the evenings this week we are watching a show called *The World's Toughest Race*, hosted by Bear Grylls. Finding shows all of us aged from nine to fifty-two can watch is hard, but this is an epic race across Fiji, which takes days to complete and isn't so much about the racing, more the human stories behind the racing. An ultrarunner in his late fifties who has dementia is racing with his son, and the love story between them chronicles fatherhood with gentle care. There is also a dad and his nineteen-year-old daughter. When asked why he is doing it, he says because he wants to 'hold his daughter's hand again'. It is incredibly moving; this man has taken on a monumental sporting challenge for which he trained for over a year for the chance to hold his adolescent daughter close again. 'When she became a teenager,' he explains, 'she stopped holding my hand. I couldn't help her any more but doing this means I can hold her hand to help her across rocks, through water, into forests. It's a privilege.'

So, you see, this leaving is bigger than just a rite of passage, because it feels as if such an enormous shift is occurring in the fabric of your life itself. Whether we choose it or not, we have to go through it. Again, I had not expected these monumental and profound feelings, and I think if you are heading this way, you should not underestimate the enormity of it or how it may affect your physical and mental health.

To help you face this in advance, here are some of my early empty-nest learnings.

1. You do not want to end up baby-talking the dog, so get a new hobby that gets you out of the house, not a new or another dog. Save that for later.

2. Stay current and involved in modern culture and life. Now that your personal youth consultant has left, make sure you do use social media and watch the latest shows everyone is talking about. You don't want your soon-to-be-adults talking about you like you talk about your parents when they attempt to use FaceTime. Not just yet, anyway. And you don't want the 'piles' to creep up on you. Almost everyone a generation ahead of us has piles of paper/books/odds and sods around the house and to me it feels like a significant sign of older age. Are we ready for that now? Of course not. Remember, your teen will return with fresh eyes, so no piles of doom just yet.

3. Allotted grief time stops the wallowing and wailing. Pick an hour to feel sad, to look at the photos, go into the empty bedroom and sit on the bed for a howl. Then get on with life.

4. What will you replace the time and thinking time with? Obviously this starts before they leave – as I have said, I found open-water swimming, but what's your wild swimming? Stay fit – it keeps you happy and endorphins are the best kind of drugs. Decrease the booze intake – it will make you feel happier, and increase the vegetables (infuriating but true). Add things into your life, though – don't do the extreme 'taking things out' thirty-day shred-type things. This is just distraction activity from what is the new normal for you. And it will frighten the teens left behind.

5. Start 'the list of lovely things', as I call it. This is the small stuff to look forward to. Ignore all the 'improve yourself' stuff, just put down lovely things to appreciate in the moment. I have also written a list of things I don't want to do any more. And I tell myself each morning there is untapped potential in my day for new discoveries. It's a bit Oprah, but maybe it is helpful.

6. So, who is who now? The new family dynamic gives everyone a new identity when one of you is absent for long periods. Child No. 2 is suddenly the oldest in the house, and in larger families perhaps the smallest one will feel the change in mood and activity the most. We talked about the times of the day we'd miss our eldest most and made sure we were there when we could be for the others, for example after school and early on Sunday evenings, when the house seemed busiest. We kept the connections. We kept up the family dinners; we didn't let our screen-time rules drop or lose the attention to detail with the others. We tried to be there and listen out for any needs not being met, consciously or subconsciously. And, of course, life carried on, as it does.

For her last family meal at home we made the kitchen into an Italian restaurant, complete with flags and red-and-white tablecloth. I cooked her favourite tea: spaghetti bolognese. The dog was allowed to sit on her lap for dinner for one last time and we all drank wine. I made her a huge cup of tea in her 'Class of 2020' school mug and then we went to bed and waited for the alarm to come. No one slept. All her clothes were packed, the trainers in the hall gone, the big puffy coat missing from our cupboard. Breakfast was a drab affair and the dog's sixth sense made her unbearable to be around as she darted about trying to find the imaginary villain that seemed to be haunting us all.

The siblings stayed close and even agreed to a final picture hugging each other. My husband went mute, focusing on packing a double bacon sandwich into some unyielding Tupperware for the three-hour drive. As we were about to head out, I was overcome with a nausea so powerful I thought I must have food poisoning and had to head to the loo.

'Oh my god, Mum,' she yelled. 'What is wrong with you?'

Such a psychosomatic reaction to this parting was a surprise. We headed off on the motorway, leaving the other three to fend for themselves, and No. 2, the new eldest, in charge. She texted as we were halfway there to say she was in Boots – could she dye the nine-year-old's hair pink?

We stopped at motorway services to buy brownies and an M & S Colin the Caterpillar cake for the student kitchen.

We arrived in good time, as my father would say, collected her pass, unloaded the car into her new home for the next year. It was all done in a comfortable silence under her no-touching rule. We headed to the Co-op to buy supplies, took some comedy pictures of fish sausages in a jar and wandered the campus watching all the families trailing behind their offspring. Those a bit ahead of us timewise were heading to cars with arms around each other and tissues in hand.

No speeches, no grand gestures. I left a card of goodbye in her kitchen-equipment bag alongside her new pasta sieve. I knew she'd find it there.

The hallways filled with music, all the doors held open. My daughter's bright-pink hair meant she was easily identified from the group chat, so people called her name as she walked past, which cheered me and her Dad up greatly. And then the moment came. In the late-afternoon sunshine of a September day we stood outside and she allowed us to hug her and kiss her. Then she turned her back and walked away. Our job was done. Just like that, in a fleeting moment, my angel of the morning had finally gone.

'Mum, What's Wrong With You?'
Conversations with Teens

Her: What are you doing now? I need the computer.

Me: I told you, I am finishing the final edit of my book about parenting teenage girls.

Her: Ha! You ain't qualified to write that, bossman.

Books, websites and resources for the mums (and dads) of teenage girls

Books

Pragya Agarwal

An academic, and mum to twin girls aged four and a grown-up daughter, Dr Agarwal has written a brilliant book for parents, *Wish We Knew What to Say: Talking with Children about Race*. She is a behavioural scientist, and her simple, fact-filled book will help you understand the issues better. She is an empathetic author and a new podcast of the same name accompanies the book.

Steve Biddulph

His books, particularly *Raising Boys* and *Raising Girls*, are game changers and have been bestsellers, clocking up millions of reads worldwide. They don't focus specifically on teens, though. But I also found his Facebook group helpful, and his articles in papers across the globe. Have a google and find the tips that are most useful to you, but be prepared to make changes after you have read his work, because he is on a crusade for us all to slow down and engage more with our families. https://en-gb.facebook.com/stevebiddulphraisingboys/

Sarah-Jayne Blakemore

Neuroscientist Sarah-Jayne Blakemore's book *Inventing Ourselves: The Secret Life of the Teenage Brain* and her TED Talks (all on YouTube) will help you understand what is going on with your daughter.

Anita Cleare

Parent coach Anita, founder of the Positive Parenting Project (anita-cleare.co.uk), a social enterprise, uses her personal and professional experience to develop strategies for children and teens. She is the author of *The Work/Parent Switch*, and I find her advice excellent for those small, niggly, day-to-day issues that require a step back and a moment of calm before you tackle them. She also has great advice for working parents who need strategies to improve connections with their children.

Jackie Clune

The actress, comedian, singer and mum of four captures much of what you may be feeling on a daily basis in her funny novel *I'm Just A Teenage Punchbag*. You'll like it, promise.

Malie Coyne

Love In, Love Out: A Compassionate Approach to Parenting Your Anxious Child is a book that reminds you, and helps you work out, how to look after yourself. I loved the empathetic nature of the advice from this psychotherapist.

Lisa Damour

The books, website and podcasts of family expert Lisa Damour, a US psychologist, are extremely specific and useful resources for parents of girls. *Untangled: Guiding Teenage Girls Through the Seven*

Transitions into Adulthood contains some expert advice based on her therapeutic work with parents, adolescents and schools. *Under Pressure: Confronting the Epidemic of Stress and Anxiety in Girls* is a reassuring read for worried parents. She also co-hosts a podcast called *Ask Lisa: The Psychology of Parenting*. She is a columnist on parenting for the *New York Times* and her website (https://www.drlisadamour. com/) has a selection of helpful videos.

Janey Downshire and Naella Grew

Their book *Teenagers Translated: A Parent's Survival Guide* came out of their business of the same name. They advise and coach parents, teens and schools, and are both qualified counsellors who run workshops.

Alicia Drummond

Alicia Drummond's Teen Tips (www.teentips.co.uk) is a reassuring subscription-based website. I have interviewed Alicia, a parent coach, psychotherapist and schools' mental health adviser, many times, and her advice is modern and relevant because she works with students and hears it all from the teenage girls' up-to-date point of view. Her book *Why Every Teenager Needs a Parrot: Tips for Parenting 21st Century Teenagers* will be useful for you too.

Jane Gilmour, Bettina Hohnen and Tara Murphy

The Incredible Teenage Brain, a good reference for the neurological changes happening in teenagers.

Kenya Hunt

Girl Gurl Grrrl: On Womanhood and Belonging in the Age of Black Girl Magic is a book by journalist Kenya Hunt, who is a friend of mine and with whom I worked for several years. It is a provocative, humorous and relatable read about what it means to be a Black woman and mother. It's a book from which I learned much about white privilege and unconscious bias. As a mum of daughters, you may find it helpful as well as entertaining.

Lisa Mosconi
Her book *The XX Brain: The Groundbreaking Science Empowering Women to Maximize Cognitive Health and Prevent Alzheimer's Disease* may help you get to the bottom of your changes as a woman in midlife.

Louise Newson
The book *Menopause: All You Need to Know in One Concise Manual* is the bible for women of forty-plus. Your perimenopause starts around then, and this book is a Haynes manual based on medical research by one of the country's leading experts. Dr Newson's website Newson Health (www.newsonhealth.co.uk) has a checklist for all women and can be used as a reference point for you to take to your NHS GP.

Peggy Orenstein
Girls & Sex: Navigating the Complicated New Landscape is one of the best modern-day books on what young women are going through as they define their identity. Go to Orenstein's website, www.peggy orenstein.com, for a curated edit of her informative articles on many subjects around teenage development. She is particularly good on the diversity of families and family life and is very easy to read.

Philippa Perry
The Book You Wish Your Parents Had Read (and Your Children Will be Glad That You Did) was a number one bestseller in the UK. It focuses on the beginning of your parenting journey, so it's not teen-orientated, but is a help, nonetheless. I also found her book *How to Stay Sane* to be useful for working out how your personality and own childhood may be affecting or influencing your parenting.

Brad M. Reedy
The Journey of the Heroic Parent: Your Child's Struggle & the Road Home. I saw Dr Reedy talk in London and found his idea that you need to sort 'you' out before you learn to support your teenagers useful and interesting. His work on addiction is thoughtful and may offer comfort.

Sil Reynolds
Mothering and Daughtering: Keeping Your Bond Strong Through the Teen Years. This is a book co-authored by Sil, a nurse practitioner and psychotherapist in the US, and her daughter Eliza. It takes a soft and warm approach to the relationship between a mum and daughter, and I found it heartwarming and practical. Their website and blog motheringanddaughtering.com has plenty of tutorials on parenting, with a focus on girls only.

Mandy Saligari
Therapist Saligari is an addiction and addictive processes expert; she founded the clinic Charter Harley Street, and is a former addict herself. She is a mum of three and has written *Proactive Parenting: Help your Child Conquer Self-Destructive Behaviours and Build Self-Esteem*, which may help those who are worried about this aspect of parenting teens.

Clover Stroud
Both Clover's books *The Wild Other* and *My Wild and Sleepless Nights* are about family and connections. She writes with such care about her teenage son in the latter; I found it a real help.

Rhyannon Styles
The New Girl: A Trans Girl's Tells It Like It Is. This book is a carefully written memoir by a friend of mine. It will help you as

a family if you are discussing transgender issues at home with your daughter.

Ian Williamson

His book *We Need to Talk: A Straight-Talking Guide to Raising Resilient Teens* is about communicating and connecting with your teenager. It's an easy-to-read book with sensible advice on parenting with boundaries in modern times.

Digital & Audio Resources

Fiona Pienaar

Fiona is a mental-health clinician of many years' experience and chief clinical officer of the charity Shout (https://givesusashout.org) and the organisation Mental Health Innovations. She has a new website which could prove helpful: Fionapienaar.com

Digital Mentality, www.digitalmentality.co.uk

I first met Emma Selby, who set up Digital Mentality, on a parenting panel. She is one of the UK's first NHS mental-health nurses who specialises in digital psychology or how this new digital world is affecting our mental health. The project she helped found connects the dots digitally and it might be useful if your workplace needs to help employees with good digital mental health.

Dinner: A Love Story

Fun recipes, a family blog and some great bonding activity on this US website, www.dinneralovestory.com. Jenny Rosenstrach has written some excellent cookbooks and, while it is very American in tone, I found it an entertaining and enjoyable blog. I am not sure how often it is updated, but it has many go-to family recipes for someone like me, who isn't a natural cook. The cocktails are good too!

MeeTwo

I know Suzi Godson personally and have been incredibly impressed with her award-winning work in the field of adolescent mental health. She was one of the founders of the teen app MeeTwo (www. meetwo.co.uk), which offers peer-to-peer advice for young people via a team of trained moderators and counsellors. It is a place a teen can get non-judgemental support and mental help. It is an emergency service and also collaborates on research with others offering child support in mental and physical well-being. Your teen could download the app, or you could buy *The MeeTwo Teenage Mental Help Handbook* from the website. It is also a directory of crisis services that can help you and your teen.

The Mix

Super-useful website (www.themix.org.uk) for under-twenty-fives. Good for parents on how to talk about sex, love, drugs, drink, vaping and smoking.

Net Aware

This useful website (www.net-aware.org.uk), produced by O_2 and the NSPCC, takes you through the basics of social-media platforms, plus popular apps and games. Knowledge is power here for mums, and this will explain things you may not want to ask your teenagers.

Postcards From Midlife

I co-host this podcast with Trish Halpin. We talk to women in midlife about all the issues that affect them. We also focus on parenting teens and how to navigate your midlife hormones so you manage that perfect storm of mothering and daughtering.

Sarah Dempster

There are many people much more qualified than I to recommend resources on eating or nutrition during the teenage years, but I wanted to highlight Sarah's website and podcast because she has such a no-nonsense positive attitude to the subject. These could be helpful for those of us muddling along as we feed and fuel our girls. The podcast is called *Eating Words* and her website is www.sarahdempster.co.uk

Shout 85258

I wrote about the launch of this charity textline: young people in crisis can text a team of trained counsellors and the aim of the responders is to take them from a 'hot' moment to a calm one. It may be worth your teen having the number, because texting is so much easier than talking about some subjects, and the team resounds with emotional and practical help You can text it too, if you need to.

What I Wish I Knew About University (WIWIKAU)

This Facebook group is a great resource for the parents of teens about to head to university, and is well moderated, so no extreme opinions. It is a group of informed parents who can help with practical advice on specific courses and UK universities. A great toolkit for those about to send their teens off. www.facebook.com/groups/488235648182391 and www.wiwikau.co.uk

Further Resources

The American site psychologytoday.com hosts many parenting experts for you to dip into, as does welldoing.org. If you want professional help and feel your daughter is in danger, you should contact your NHS GP first. On the general NHS website, there is also a list of charity apps that can help (https://www.nhs.uk/apps-library/). Finding a family therapist to help privately is a challenge, and word of mouth is usually the best way if you are not referred by your GP. But YoungMinds (youngminds.org.uk) is a good website, as is Papyrus (www.papyrus-uk.org), which works on suicide prevention, and the Samaritans (www.samaritans.org). Frank is the website best suited to help you with fears of drug use (www.talktofrank.com).

Reni Eddo-Lodge's multiple prize-winning and bestselling debut *Why I'm No Longer Talking to White People about Race* explores race relations in Britain today. She writes in an engaging, accessible way and her book is vital reading for teens and adults alike. The one season of her podcast is well worth checking out too: https://www.aboutracepodcast.com/

Anything psychotherapist Tanya Byron writes is helpful. One particular piece she wrote for *The Times* about mental health of young people during the pandemic provides many resources and she is an adviser to Kooth, a mental-health and well-being app (https://www.kooth.com). Here's the piece from *The Times*: https://www.thetimes.co.uk/article/what-to-do-if-your-child-is-not-coping-during-the-pandemic-qwx7b6hwx

Also check out the Mind Out (https://mindout.org.uk/) and Calm Harm (https://calmharm.co.uk) apps.

The website Family Man Movember, part of the Movember Charity, encourages dads to become better educated around parenting, as so few join forums or take part in parenting courses: https://familyman.movember.com/

The following resources around sexuality, gender, LGBTQ+ issues may prove useful:

https://sexpositivefamilies.com/book/, for sex-positive families, conversation starters and books

https://www.brook.org.uk/, a long-running educational organisation, Brook is full of sexual-health and well-being advice for young people and families

https://www.fumble.org.uk/category/sexuality-gender/, the sex education charity Fumble is staffed by young people for young people

https://www.outspokeneducation.com/ages-11-to-16, Outspoken Sex Ed runs events for schools and parents. The website is useful and clear to follow

https://www.theguardian.com/lifeandstyle/2020/jun/29/non-binary-four-teens-explain-gender-genderqueer-generation, this thread from the *Guardian* of first-person stories is helpful for parents discussing transgender issues

https://www.thetrevorproject.org/, charity the Trevor Project provides crisis intervention and suicide prevention for the LGBTQ+ community.

I also think it is worth downloading the podcast *This Much I Know* run by Chloe Combi, which features conversations with Gen Z teens about all aspects of their lives.

Notes

25 'According to the US neuroscientist': Frances Jensen, *The Teenage Brain: A neuroscientist's survival guide to raising adolescents and young adults* (London: HarperCollins, 2015)

26 'The 2017 *TIME* report': The Editors of *TIME*, 'The Science of Childhood: Inside the Minds of Our Younger Selves' (Time Inc.: 01 September 2017); Kessler RC, Berglund P, Demler O, Jin R, Merikangas KR, Walters EE (2005). Lifetime Prevalence and Age-of-Onset Distributions of DSM-IV Disorders in the National Comorbidity Survey Replication. Archives of General Psychiatry, 62 (6) pp. 593-602. doi:10.1001/archpsyc.62.6.593. Cited in this article: https://www.mentalhealth.org.uk/statistics/mental-health-statistics-children-and-young-people

29 'it's just their synapses': Sarah-Jayne Blakemore, *Inventing Ourselves: The Secret Life of the Teenage Brain* (London: Doubleday, 2018); https://www.ted.com/talks/sarah_jayne_blakemore_the_mysterious_workings_of_the_adolescent_brain

30 'This is the hormone': https://www.bbc.co.uk/science/humanbody/body/articles/lifecycle/teenagers/sleep.shtml#:~:text=One%20important%20change%20that%20occurs,produce%20the%20hormone%20at%201am

30 'Indeed, in some US schools': https://www.sciencedaily.com/releases/2018/12/181212140741.htm

39 'They call it brain fog': https://www.menopausedoctor.co.uk/menopause/menopausal-can-confused-dementia

49 'When we first hit the tweens': https://positivepsychology.com/attachment-theory/

49 'The US family therapist': Lisa Damour, *Untangled: Guiding Teenage Girls Through the Seven Transitions into Adulthood* (New York: Ballantine Books, 2016)

58 'The therapist Lisa Damour': https://www.theglobeandmail.com/life/parenting/drama-queens-whats-really-going-on-in-a-teenage-girls-head/article28549947/

63 'They have been dubbed': https://blog.gohenry.com/us/kids-and-tech/meet-the-cashless-natives/

65 'There is an excellent': Marisa Porges, *What Girls Need: How to Raise Bold, Courageous and Resilient Girls* (New York: Penguin Random House USA, 2020)

66 'The website Ditch the Label': https://www.ditchthelabel.org/

74 'Around 25 per cent': https://www.theguardian.com/food/2019/aug/28/vegan-food-becomes-uk-fastest-growing-takeaway

75 'When I spoke to the veteran': Interview with the author, 'Muffin Top Begone', *Postcards From Midlife*, 19 July 2020; https://podcast.app/muffin-top-begone-eating-habits-that-can-change-your-midlife-e107858803/

85 'Close the door': Lorraine Candy, 'How to Get Messy Teens to Tidy Their Rooms', *Sunday Times*, 30 September 2018; https://www.thetimes.co.uk/article/family-how-to-get-messy-teenagers-to-tidy-their-rooms-qk2s27kpz; and, Janey Downshire, *Teenagers Translated: A Parent's Survival Guide* (London: Ebury Press, 2014)

104 'worry less, and breathe more': Neal Thompson, *Kickflip Boys: A Memoir of Freedom, Rebellion, and the Chaos of Fatherhood* (New York: Ecco, 2018)

105 'The novelist Jackie Clune': Interview with the author, summer 2020

110 'I interviewed the US': Lorraine Candy, 'Is it OK for Your Teenagers to See You Tipsy?', *Sunday Times*, 14 January 2018

110 'Zoë Bailie at The Mix': https://www.themix.org.uk/

111 'However, the urge': https://ash.org.uk/wp-content/uploads/2019/06/ASH-Factsheet-Youth-E-cigarette-Use-2019.pdf

111 'It is too early': https://www.theguardian.com/society/blog/2019/dec/31/e-cigarettes-are-still-safer-than-smoking-scientists-find

114 'A survey published': https://www.verywellfamily.com/teen-girls-more-vulnerable-to-substance-abuse-67857; https://digital.nhs.uk/data-and-information/publications/statistical/smoking-drinking-and-drug-use-among-young-people-in-england/2018

117 'At one point': https://www.vice.com/en/article/ne4mvb/how-british-teens-got-hooked-on-xanax; https://www.vice.com/en/article/bjpn7q/what-you-said-about-your-xanax-use

119 'I had a light-bulb moment': Dr Brad Reedy, 'How to be a "Heroic" Parent', Prince of Wales Theatre, London, 09 October 2019; Brad Reedy, *The Journey of the Heroic Parent: Your Child's Struggle & The Road Home* (New York: Reagan Arts, 2015, 2016)

131 'In the UK now': https://www.bbc.co.uk/news/technology-51358192

135 'Screens are here to stay': Ben Machell, 'Children, smartphone addiction and the truth behind *Screened Out*', *The Times*, 30 May 2020; https://www.thetimes.co.uk/article/children-smartphone-addiction-and-the-truth-behind-screened-out-sb0gnhdvd

136 'When I interviewed the neuroscientist': Lorraine Candy, 'Why We Should Encourage Screen Time for Teenagers', *Sunday Times*, 31 May 2020; https://www.thetimes.co.uk/article/family-why-we-should-encourage-screen-time-for-teenagers-zxlw3lsm3

139 'I interviewed Suzi Godson': Lorraine Candy, 'Should You Share Pictures of Your Children on Social Media?', *Sunday Times*, 05 May 2019; https://www.thetimes.co.uk/article/family-should-you-share-pictures-of-your-children-on-social-media-0dslzjcjb

140 'A study by Professor': https://www.oii.ox.ac.uk/news/releases/study-finds-screen-time-even-before-bed-has-little-impact-on-teen-well-being/ https://www.oii.ox.ac.uk/news/releases/study-finds-screen-time-even-before-bed-has-little-impact-on-teen-well-being/

140 'Websites like YoungMinds': https://youngminds.org.uk/; https://www.net-aware.org.uk/

144 'Dr Bex Lewis': https://www.imom.com/; Lorraine Candy, 'Should you share pictures of your children on social media?', *Sunday Times*, 05 May 2019

147 'I think we partly': Ian Williamson, *We Need to Talk: A Straight-Talking Guide to Raising Resilient Teens* (London: Ebury Press, 2017)

154 'According to an Office': https://youngminds.org.uk/blog/worrying-rise-in-teen-suicides/

154 'And an NHS survey': https://digital.nhs.uk/data-and-information/publications/statistical/mental-health-of-children-and-young-people-in-england/2017/2017

156 'Over the past few years': https://giveusashout.org/

159 'This psychiatric nurse': https://www.thetimes.co.uk/article/anxiety-in-teenage-girls-have-we-got-it-all-wrong-v63nstxqm

161 'Clinical psychologist Dr Malie': Dr Malie Coyne, *Love in Love Out: A Compassionate Approach to Parenting Your Anxious Child* (London: Thorsons, 2020)

164 'The psychologist Lisa Damour': Lisa Damour, *Under Pressure: Confronting the Epidemic of Stress and Anxiety in Girls* (London: Atlantic, 2019)

165 'Mother-and-daughter writing duo': Sil Reynolds and Eliza Reynolds, *Mothering & Daughtering: Keeping Your Bond Strong through the Teenage Years* (Boulder, CO: Sounds True, 2013)

168 'I have found the mental': http://www.professortanyabyron.com/; https://www.thetimes.co.uk/article/what-to-do-if-your-child-is-not-coping-during-the-pandemic-qwx7b6hwx; https://www.rethink.org/

168 'And finally, I often': Glennon Doyle, *Untamed: Stop Pleasing, Start Loving* (London: Ebury Press, 2020)

172 'I turned to TV dramas': 'Women like Dr Karen Gurney', https://thehavelockclinic.com/meet-team/; https://www.youtube.com/user/hannahgirasol; https://www.bbc.co.uk/programmes/p066mgz9; https://soundcloud.com/user-863387665

172 'Sites like Brook': https://www.brook.org.uk/; https://bishtraining.com/; https://www.fumble.org.uk/category/sexuality-gender/; https://sexpositivefamilies.com/book/

180 'I interviewed the young cast': https://www.thetimes.co.uk/article/netflixs-sex-education-tackles-the-shocking-rise-of-sexual-assaults-on-public-transport-hdkr2q8gh

185 The American self-help: Brené Brown, 'Brené Brown on Empathy vs Sympathy', https://www.youtube.com/watch?v=KZBTYViDPlQ

190 'She had talked about': Lorraine Candy, 'How to Raise a Body-Confident Child, According to Honey Ross', *The Times*, 19 January 2020; https://www.thetimes.co.uk/article/how-to-raise-a-body-confident-child-according-to-honey-ross-bbqgqdd73

197 'It's called *Wish We Knew*': Pragya Agarwal, *Wish We Knew What to Say: Talking with Children about Race* (London: Dialogue Books, 2020)

198 'I bought the book': Valerie Schaefer, *The Care and Keeping of You: The Body Book for Younger Girls* (Middleton, WI: American Girl Publishing, 1998)

199 'Infuriatingly the taboos': 'One in Five Girls Bullied About Their Periods', *Guardian*, 28 May 2019; https://www.theguardian.com/society/2019/may/28/one-in-five-girls-and-young-women-bullied-about-their-periods-study

199 'I have spoken several': https://theharperclinic.com/

201 'Sites like HelloFlo': https://helloflo.com/about-us/; see also https://www.nhs.uk/conditions/periods and https://bettyeducation.com/

201 'One of my favourite sites': Maisie Hill, www.maisiehill.com and *Period Power: Harness Your Hormones and Get Your Cycle Working For You* (London: Green Tree, 2019). I also recommend Emma Barnett's *It's About Bloody Time: Period.* (London: HQ, HarperCollins, 2019)

201 'US gynaecologist Dr Jen': https://www.ted.com/talks/jen_gunter_why_can_t_we_talk_about_periods

202 ' I work with a charity': https://www.womeninsport.org/

204 'The Black Skin Directory': https://www.blackskindirectory.com/welcome-to-bsd

205 'Around 85 per cent of teens': https://www.gosh.nhs.uk/conditions-and-treatments/general-medical-conditions/acne

210 'Lucie Hemmen, the US psychologist': Lucie Hemmen, *The Teen Girl's Survival Guide: Ten Tips for Making Friends, Avoiding Drama, and Coping with Social Stress* (Oakland, CA: New Harbinger, 2015)

220 'Your energy levels': Damian Whitworth, 'Could the menopause trigger Alzheimer's?', *The Times*, 03 June 2020; https://www.thetimes.co.uk/article/could-the-menopause-trigger-alzheimers-this-scientist-says-yes-5kvxxdhhg

228 'In her book *How to Stay Sane*': Philippa Perry, *How to Stay Sane* (London: Pan Macmillan, 2012)

231 'If I were you': Caitlin Moran, 'A Letter to Teenage Girls', https://www.youtube.com/watch?v=EyDuG-gCX0k

236 'It really resonated': Thomas Boyce, *The Orchid and the Dandelion: Why Sensitive People Struggle and We Can All Thrive* (London: Bluebird, Macmillan, 2019)

238 'Try the listen, nudge': https://anitacleare.co.uk/

241 'When I interviewed Mercedes': Mercedes Samudio, *Shame-Proof Parenting* (Denver, CO: Paper Raven Books, 2017); https://shameproofparenting.com/

Acknowledgements

Thank you to the following for making this, my first book, possible.

The agent: Robert Caskie, my patient literary agent, who coaxed me into writing this book. He finally accomplished his mission with the use of cocktails (Punjabi sours). I am grateful for his empathy, which allows me to be my full ridiculous self on every phone call.

The editor: Mum of two grown-up daughters, Louise Haines of 4th Estate, with whom I bonded over the 'meanage' years. All journalists think book writing is easier than journalism. I now know the opposite is true, thanks to Louise's expertise. And also, the help of HarperCollins's Marigold Atkey, a wise woman indeed.

The cheerleaders: Couldn't have done it without the encouragement of these strong women. In no particular order: Nina Ahmad, Lisa Potter-Dixon, Dipa Shah, Victoria White, Gill Morgan, Kathy Lette, Trish Halpin, Cathy Brown, Davina McCall, Nadia Narain, Lyndsey

Reid, Claire Bowman, Laura Atkinson, Hannah Swerling, Meribeth Parker, Meg Mathews, Jane Cole and Suzi Godson.

The experts: A special thank you for the generosity of time and wisdom from these wonderful humans: Fiona Pienaar, Alicia Drummond, Lisa Damour, and writer and mum of five Clover Stroud, who kindly comforted me when I had a panic about privacy.

The virtual support crew: Thank you to the army of friends (fellow mums, mainly) that I have never met, those who sent supportive words over Instagram, Facebook and Twitter. I read all your messages; they were much appreciated. (heart emoji)

The family: My parents Anthony and Vivienne and my sister Barbara in Cornwall, and my Wiltshire in-laws, especially Grandma Pru, from whom I learned much about mothering kindly and unconditional love (plus the art of sending birthday cards).

And finally, the great love of all our lives, aka the World's Best Dad (he has the mug with a pocket for his biscuits), James Candy. We made it, Jimmy!